ENLARGED AMERICAN EDITION.

CELEBRATED PIANISTS

OF THE

PAST AND PRESENT.

A COLLECTION OF ONE HUNDRED AND THIRTY-
NINE BIOGRAPHIES, WITH PORTRAITS.

BY

A. EHRLICH.

PHILADELPHIA :

THEODORE PRESSER,

1708 CHESTNUT STREET.

INTRODUCTION TO THE AMERICAN EDITION.

It is the intention of the American edition of this work to present to its readers those pianists, resident in America, who are not in the original edition.

The difficulty of the task of selection in the case of living pianists who have won eminence—a class which is necessarily limited—may be readily understood. This difficulty has been increased by the fact that some to whom we have written have failed to respond. Some whose local reputation is great, have not as yet made an impression on national musical life sufficiently extended to be included.

The effort has been made, however, to present sketches of all whose widespread reputation renders their personality interesting to the musical public.

That mistakes of omission may have been made is possible, but when it is known that some objected to being included and others failed to respond to written requests, the censure of those interested, to be just, should be cautiously and not too hastily given.

In spite of shortcomings, we feel sure that this book brings information of interest and value to its readers. There have been larger works, covering more or less completely the subject of music and musicians, but none which confined themselves to a single class, collecting facts concerning it which may be quickly found and digested and used by the piano student and teacher in his every-day work.

We believe it to be a work which will augment the inspiration of every lover of the piano, by the knowledge it brings him of those who have achieved eminence in this particular phase of musical life.

A. L. MANCHESTER.

PREFACE.

IN causing my book of "Celebrated Pianists" to follow that of
"Celebrated Violinists", I am of necessity obliged to repeat what
I then asserted. Whoever looks at this book in its complete form
can hardly conceive what great difficulties have had to be surmounted
in its production. Although sufficient biographical notices of older
masters exist, it has in many cases been no easy task to obtain
reliable portraits of them. Still less easy has it been to find literary,
and artistic information respecting living artists. First-rate players are
like birds of passage, traversing land and ocean, and consequently,
opportunities of acquiring reliab'e accounts of their lives and portraits
of them, are infrequent. Personal accounts of them on the one hand,
and their portraits on the other, and in many cases even both, have
not been obtainable, so that at the last moment their names have had
to be omitted from the programme. For similar reasons the lives of
many artists have been scantilly described, rather than be omitted
altogether; while others by no means more entitled to consideration
have had more exhaustive accounts allotted to them, simply because the
biographical sources have been more abundant and easier of access.

In reality the art of compression had to be severely exercised to
avoid the possibility of running the work into volumes, which would
have been beyond the purpose of producing a handy book. For this
reason only the more noted historical masters: as, J. S. Bach, Mozart,
Beethoven, Chopin, Weber, Mendelssohn, Liszt, Field, Rubinstein,
Tausig, Brahms &c. could be dealt with in detail; but it is just in this
more extended description of the principal pillars of musical history,

that the progressive development of the art of piano playing in regard to composition as well as to technic, could be made clear and positive.

It was only by adopting the system of alphabetical arrangement that the insurmountable difficulties of artistic comparison could be avoided. A greater equality of excellence is more easily noticed among pianoforte players than with violinists. It is impossible to exactly guage the degree of excellence of one against the other. As regards technik younger virtuosi are very nearly equal. Still the discerning reader will observe that his attention has been directed as far as possible to the peculiarities of those described and their signification for the various periods of artistic progression. As also that the greatest possible care has been bestowed on the technical reproduction of their portraits.

Although it must be admitted that this book is to a certain extent incomplete, in consequence of the difficulties already mentioned, I trust it will be cordially welcomed by all friends of the pianoforte. For younger students of music it will afford instruction and supply fresh encouragement and stimulation to farther exertion.

A. EHRLICH.

CONTENTS.

VIII   CONTENTS.

EUGEN D'ALBERT.

I N consequence of the alphabetical order of the present work it is a remarkable co-incidence that the great number of musicians to be represented should commence with one of the youngest, who at the same time being one of the most renowned, has reached the height of modern pianoforte playing. Just as remarkable is it, that in his teachers and instructors the most advanced musical school is united with the most perfect knowledge of old pianoforte music, a circumstance, which has not been without influence upon his theoretical studies.

This young musician, born at Glasgow on the

10th April 1864 was the son of a French musician and a German lady. Receiving his first musical instruction from his father, he then entered the best existing school, in London, under Ernest Pauer, Pianoforte teacher at the Royal Academy of Music. He could already master to a certain extent the virtuoso style of playing when Hans Richter, who gave concerts every season in London, made his acquaintance, and took him to Vienna in the year 1880. At that time the first master of all modern pianoforte players—Franz Liszt, was still living, and rightly understanding what was still necessary for the perfection of d'Albert's talents, Hans Richter transferred him, in 1881, to Liszt's care to complete his studies. It is a peculiarity of the latter's life that just in his last years he took such a kind fatherly interest in those students who were successfully striving to advance in their career. This was the case with regard to d'Albert, for through Liszt's influence he made his appearance in the same year at concerts in Vienna, Berlin and Weimar with eminent success. He was appointed Pianist to the Grand-Duke of Weimar, and has far advanced in his career as a performer with increasing success, and at present exercises great and attractive influence at the best concerts.

As a composer d'Albert has published two concertos for the piano, a suite consisting of five parts, some lighter pieces, besides two overtures, (to Hölderlin's "Hyperion", and Hebbel's "Maria Magdalena") some songs, a string quartet and an opera.

Having been divorced from his wife, d'Albert married the distinguished pianist, Teresa Carenno in the year 1892, she having been twice married and divorced, her first husband being the violinist, E. Sauret.

JOHANN SEBASTIAN BACH.

Although this great musician was no celebrated pianist in the present sense of the word, yet there is no doubt that on account of his numerous musical works he must be acknowledged as one. Even to the present day his "wohltemperirtes Klavier" should form an incomparable work of instruction for all aspiring pianists. Of his other pieces for the piano many belong, as a never failing model, to the melodious, harmonious and technical material for the study of all really good pianoforte schools; they are also justly appreciated by the best teachers of modern times, as is proved by the present demand for revised

1 *

editions. A comprehensive characteristic of J. S. Bach's
position and importance in the musical life of all
times is impossible in this work. Bach's musical
genius like that of Goethe for poetry and literature,
rose magnificently; he combined the whole musical
creation of the past, as far as it was of importance,
and with wonderful power and foresight, he introduced a new style of musical science, which became a
precept for all important musicians succeeding him,
and especially for the composers of church music.
His works of this class are to the present day,
indispensable and have been excelled by no one
since his time; with their splendid harmony and sweet
melody they fill even the satiated ear with delight
and lead to devotion, springing as they do from deep
religious feeling. The whole secret of perseverance
in the work of those older masters, reduced as they
were to the humblest manner of life by circumstances
and the low position of art at that time is due to this
spirit of piety. The people possessed too little education to be able to appreciate Art rightly, and the
haughtiness of the great assigned with scarcely any
exception no higher rank to her best fosterers than
that of their dependents.

Thus J. S. Bach before whose immortal creations,
the great masters of later times, from Mozart and
Beethoven down to Wagner, bowed in veneration,
was nearly always in straitened circumstances, which
only renders his achievements so much the more astonishing.

He was born on the 21st March 1685 at Eisenach,
his father being Ambrosius Bach. From him he received his first musical instruction, which was continued by his elder brother, Johann Christopher, when
the orphaned boy in his tenth year was consigned to
his care. On attaining his fifteenth year he received
a free post at the School of St. Michael at Lüneburg,

whence he often wandered to Hamburg in order to hear Reinkens and Lübeck play the organ.

In 1703, he was appointed violinist in the private chapel of Prince Johann Ernst of Saxe-Weimar, but he soon after exchanged this post for that of organist in the town of Arnstadt in Gotha. From here he set out on a pedestrian tour, during his holidays in 1705, to Lübeck, to visit the celebrated organist Dietrich Buxtehude, and exceeding his term of leave he was very seriously threatened with dismissal. A year later, in 1707, he was appointed organist of the Church of St. Blasius at Mühlhausen in Thuringia, after having married a relative. But here he only remained a year, and then became court organist and chamber musician to the Duke of Weimar, in 1714.

His life took an important turn in 1717, when he became band master and director of chamber music to Prince Leopold of Anhalt in Köthen; in this position he was only occupied with orchestral and chamber music, and which he composed almost exclusively.

His wife died in 1720; in the next year he married the daughter of a musician, named Wülken. In the year 1723 he was elected Cantor at the Thomas School in Leipzig, and he retained this post until his death on the 28th July 1750, having become during the last years of his life almost totally blind. Six sons and four daughters survived him, five sons and five daughters having died earlier.

The number of his compositions is almost legion. For the piano he wrote pieces for two, four, six and eight hands in connection with one or more instruments or with orchestral accompaniment; Concertos, Adagios, Sonatas, Gigues, Gavottes, Sarabands, Fugues, Fantasies, Suites, Capriccios, Chaconnes, Rondos, Scherzi, Toccatos.

Up to the present time the Bach Society has published 40 yearly volumes of Cantatas, Oratorios,

Masses, Passion Music, Chamber Music, and pianoforte works, Magnificat and Sanctus, Odes, Works for the Organ, Orchestral works &c.

A comprehensive summary of J. S. Bach's Compositions, consisting of twelve pages, is to be found in the list of the Musical Publications of Breitkopf & Härtel. Leipzig.

KARL PHILIPP EMANUEL BACH.

THE father of the Saxon "Bachs" found in his second
son a good and worthy successor to his great
name, who throughout his whole life and by his
conduct strove to make amends for his elder brother Friedemann's frivolity. He preserved the valuable compositions inherited from his father, whereas Friedemann lost his share, and he alone of all
Sebastian Bach's sons distinguished himself as master
and composer for the piano, although he had not
originally been destined for the musical profession.

He was born on the 14th March 1714 at Weimar,
at the time that his father received the appointment
there, and in 1723 after the election of Johann Sebastian as Cantor at the Thomas School at Leipzig

he went with him, and was educated in that institution. He, like his brother, received a thorough musical education in his youth, although it was intended he should study law, which he began at the University of Leipzig. Besides this he had learned music engraving from his father and engraved his first work "Menuett für Klavier mit überschlagenen Händen" in the year 1731. He had scarcely removed to the University at Frankfort on the Oder for the continuation of his studies, when his love for music evinced itself very strongly; he formed a musical society for the performance of his own compositions, and practised the lighter style of pianoforte playing.

He went to Berlin in the year 1738, and to his father's annoyance devoted his time exclusively to music, although at first unsuccessfully. In the meantime the talented Crown Prince Friedrich was attracted by his playing and after succeeding to the throne appointed him as his harpist in 1740.

In this position it was his duty to accompany the King when playing the flute, and in his company Bach had hard work, the great monarch not being a strict musician as regards keeping time. During the King's wars he had much leisure and could compose at his ease, yet it happened in his case as also in that of other court musicians at that period, that on account of the King's difficulties the salaries were not punctually paid or frequently not at all. The King's musical efforts in his later years had to give way to serious political matters which engrossed his time, so that finally he devoted scarcely any attention to his old favourite Quantz, the flute player. Bach therefore resigned his post in 1767, retaining, through the influence of Friedrich's sister Princess Amalia, his title of bandmaster, and went to Hamburg as conductor of Church music in place of Telemann. Here he remained, honoured and esteemed by all until his death on the

14th September 1788. As a composer, especially of pianoforte music, Philipp Emanuel Bach achieved great distinction. On account of his having been the means of introducing an easier and more agreeable method in the performance of symphonies, Sonatas &c. he has been designated the "Father of Modern Instrumental Music" and the forerunner of the great classical masters, Haydn, Mozart and Beethoven. His work "Versuch über die wahre Art Klavier zu spielen" appearing between the years 1753—1762, explains the various styles of playing during the century in which he lived. The number of his compositions for the pianoforte is especially great, being 210 Solos, 250 Concert pieces, numerous Sonatas, Suites &c. Besides these he wrote 22 versions of the Passion Music, 2 Oratorios, and many Cantatas.

WALTER BACHE.

BOTH as virtuoso and teacher Bache was one of the most thorough pianists of modern times, but as a disciple of Franz Liszt he became especially celebrated. He was chiefly indebted to three of the best masters for his thorough musical education, namely, Moscheles, Plaidy and Liszt; the latter particularly being invaluable to him in the study of pianoforte playing.

Walter Bache was born at Birmingham, June, 19th 1842, in which town the organist Stimpson became his first music master. In the years 1858—1861 he entered the Conservatoire at Leipzig, where, besides Plaidy and Moscheles, Moritz Hauptmann and Ernst

Friedrich Richter conducted his studies. After finishing his course at Leipzig he went to Italy, visited
Milan and Florence, and finally Rome where Franz
Liszt, then Abbé, was residing. For three years, from
1862—1865, he was Liszt's pupil and followed in his
footsteps. As one of the warmest admirers of this
great master he left Rome and came to London.
Here he met with great success as teacher of the
pianoforte, pianist, and conductor. He gave a yearly
concert at which some great work of a living composer was performed. It was primarily Liszt's works
that he conducted, the Symphonic Poems, Legend
of St. Elizabeth and the Thirteenth Psalm; playing
himself the concertos in E-flat and A-Major.

By the introduction of more modern music he
has justly earned considerable reputation in England.

He was a true artist, with no other aim than
the furtherance of his art, an amiable unselfish character and his death, which took place March 26th
1888, was a real loss to musiced interests in London.

KARL HEINRICH BARTH.

PROCEEDING from a good school this musician has become one of our best pianoforte teachers and an excellent performer. He was born on the 12ᵗʰ July 1847, at Pillau in East Prussia; his father, a teacher, gave him his first instruction on the piano, which was continued from 1856—1862 by L. Steinmann at Potsdam. In the years 1862—1864 Hans v. Bülow was his teacher. Hans v. Bronsart and Tausig also had a share in his musical training.

In the year 1868 Barth was appointed pianoforte teacher at the Stern Conservatoire, and in 1871 he occupied a similar post at the Royal School for Music under Joachim's direction. His qualifications as pianist are proved by the fact of his having undertaken several concert-tours through Germany and England with Joachim and his wife. Barth, with the violinist de Ahna and the cellist Hausmann formed a trio which has gained a wide reputation. He was also Court Pianist to the Crown Prince Friedrich and his consort, and has received the title of "Professor".

LUDWIG VAN BEETHOVEN.*)

I⊤ does not necessarily follow that the greatest musician of the world should also be the greatest pianoforte player in order to merit the most important place in this work. Spohr, who met Beethoven, when the latter stood at the zenith of his fame, passed a very severe criticism upon his pianoforte playing, censuring it in every particular, but Spohr and Beethoven are opposed in many respects. Beethoven's power of composition occupied the first place, even impeded as he was by total deafness, being unable to hear his own playing, and in consequence of this defect combined with other causes suffering

*) From a portrait by A. v. Kloeber. By consent of the Publisher Carl Simon. Berlin.

from deep depression, even bitterness; whereas Spohr
it is true met with great success as a composer, yet
has always been regarded principally as a great violinist.*)

Nevertheless until the close of the last century
Beethoven was always considered an excellent pianist,
and especially attracted attention among true musical
connoiseurs by his manner of improvising, which
elicited the admiration of musical judges. He possessed this talent of improvisation in his 13th year after
having attained the facility of playing "Johann Sebastian Bach's wohltemperirtes Klavier." A review
of his early life may be of interest to his admirers.
His birthplace was Bonn, but there still remains considerable doubt with regard to the day of his birth,
although the 17th Dec. 1770 was that of his baptism.
He belonged to a family in which the study of music
had been cultivated through several generations. His
father was tenor-singer, and his grandfather bass-
singer and musical conductor in the Elector's chapel
at Cologne; the latter however was a more important
musician than the former, but he died before L. v.
Beethoven had attained his third year. It is generally
known from all biographies of the great tone-poet

---

*) The following is Spohr's utterance with regard to Beethoven:
"As Beethoven, when I met him, had already ceased performing in public
as well as in private circles, I had only one opportunity of hearing him
play. I happened to be at his house during the rehearsal of a new
Trio (D-Major). It was no enjoyment, for the piano was out of
tune, which troubled Beethoven little enough as he could hear nothing,
and on account his deafness few signs remained of his former much-
admired professional talent. When the expression "forte" occurred the
poor deaf man thumped to such a degree that the strings vibrated, and
when playing "piano" he played so softly that whole chords were lost,
so that if unable to glance at the notes all connection was at once lost.
Such a hard fate filled me with sadness. For every one it must be
the greatest misfortune to be deaf. How is it then possible for a musician to endure it without despair? From this moment Beethoven's
almost continual melancholy was no longer a riddle to me."

that the foolish and tyrannical harshness of his father deprived him of even the most innocent youthful pleasures. His intention of making a great musician of his son was praiseworthy enough, but he erred in his ideas of education; perhaps from nervous capriciousness, perhaps also because he felt bitterly his own musical incompetency, and his humble position; all that he could do was threatening, commanding, scolding, and punishing. Little Beethoven felt himself to be a youthful criminal to whom a daily amount of punishment must be administered; he worked hard, but in losing the harmless pleasures of childhood, he acquired a certain gloomy shyness, which clung to him and became a curse to him in after life.

His mother was the reverse of his father; her gentleness, and tender care fell like sunshine upon his hard life. Beethoven's want of self-reliance and carelessness in later years has most unjustly been attributed to his mother's indulgence and care of him, but her gentleness was only a natural out-come of motherly love at the injustice inflicted upon her unhappy boy. Unfortunately she died too early when Beethoven was about seventeen years of age.

The first instrument which the boy in his fifth year began to play was the violin. His father was his teacher, but as the child showed no talent for it, it became the cause of many a whipping. He made better progress on the piano, when in his eighth year the conductor Pfeiffer undertook his tuition. Beethoven's history was similar to that of little Paganini, he obtained technical proficiency at the cost of his own temperament. In his thirteenth year the Cologne Court Organist van der Eden began his instruction on the organ, and in the theory of harmony and composition; the organist Neefe also continued his studies on the organ.

Owing to the false method of education adopted

by his father to attain execution rapidly, the boy, scarcely thirteen years of age, produced six Sonatas for the Piano in 1783, performances which in riper years he rejected and only acknowledged those he had composed from 1795, onwards.

When fifteen years of age, he became assistant organist to the Elector Max Franz, to whom he had dedicated his first sonatas. With his patron, (the brother of the Emperor Joseph II.) Beethoven went to Vienna, and there made the acquaintance of a passionate lover of music, Count Waldstein, who was so attracted by his pianoforte playing, that he remained his enthusiastic admirer. He induced Beethoven to return to Vienna and become Haydn's pupil. After Beethoven, in 1792, had made the acquaintance of Joseph Haydn in Godesberg near Bonn on his return from England, the Count, a good pianoforte performer himself, wrote to him thus: Dear Beethoven! You are now on your way to Vienna to fulfil your long cherished desire. Mozart's genius is still mourning and lamenting the death of her pupil. This Genius found refuge with the inexhaustible Haydn but no occupation, and now seeks other company. May Mozart's spirit, by continual industry descend on you through Haydn! Your true friend Waldstein." Through Waldstein's influence, the struggling musician gained further patronage, namely that of Prince Lichnowski, Count Rasumowski and others, joined in the course of the next year by Count Brunswick, Baron Gleichenstein and St. von Breuning. Beethoven studied the finest works of Haendel and Haydn. The latter attempted to give him some help in the theory of composition but he is said to have been little adapted for a teacher.

Beethoven felt himself strongly drawn towards Schenk, the composer of the "Dorfbarbier" who corrected his work before it was submitted by him to

Haydn. When his teacher, for the second time, in 1795 set off for England, Albrechtsberger, took his place as teacher of counterpoint, while Salieri initiated him in the art of composing operas. Without doubt Beethoven recognized the necessity of adhering to a strict scholastic course in his study of music, for which purpose Jux's "Gradus ad Parnassum" was of considerable service to him; but in his works produced during this time he was neither influenced by Haydn nor Mozart but gave evidence of a style of his own which is especially noticeable in the three Sonatas for the Pianoforte, Op. 2. and excited both approbation and disapproval. It is a well-known fact, that throughout his whole life, Beethoven was never thoroughly understood and appreciated by his contemporaries, it being reserved for posterity to acknowledge the magnificence of his productions, and to render them their due. Haydn at this time was so biassed in his judgment, that he asserted Beethoven would meet with more success as a pianoforte player than as a composer. His misunderstanding of this growing genius strengthened the foundation already laid of Beethoven's embittered nature, the seeds of which, sown in his youth, became continually more noticeable.

Thayer in his unfinished biography of Beethoven makes the following remarks: Traits of self-consciousness and even arrogance, faults, which are certainly very common among talented young men who have met with success, and who are far less justified in possessing them than Beethoven was, are unquestionably to be recognized in him. The rather high tone too, which he at times assumed, was an excuse for Haydn's pleasantries. When Beethoven's visits to Haydn became rarer and only followed at longer intervals he used to ask other visitors: "What is our great Mogul doing?"— The same biographer adds another anecdote from Griesinger's memoirs. "When he (Griesinger) was attaché in Vienna he once met Beethoven in Prince Lobkowitz's house. At this time they were both young, and Beethoven, except for his pianoforte playing, was but little known. In conversation with another gentleman present, Beethoven remarked that he wished to free himself of all the responsibility attendant upon the disposal of his musical productions, and would like to meet with some person who would pay him a settled income for his life, in return for which the said person should hold the exclusive right of publishing all his compositions, and "I would not be idle" he added. "I believe Goethe does the same with Cotta, and if I am not mistaken Haendel's London publisher made a similar bargain with him." "My dear young man", replied the other "you must not complain, for you are neither a Goethe nor a Haendel, and it is not to be expected you ever will attain to such a height, the world will never again see such genius." Beethoven bit his lip and was silent. Lobkowitz sought to re-assure him, and in the conversation which ensued, said to him: "My dear Beethoven, the gentleman had no intention of hurting your feelings; most men cherish the firm opinion that the present generation are not capable of producing such great talents as those that are gone before." "So much the worse, Highness" returned Beethoven, "but I will not associate with people who have no faith and confidence in me because I am still unknown to the world in general."

Thus Beethoven even in his earlier years felt that he ranked high in his art.

During the first part of the time in Vienna which he devoted to composing, that is to say until the year 1800, he completed six pianoforte trios, and nine sonatas. The most influential paper then in circulation, the "Allgemeine Musikalische Zeitung" published in

2*

Leipzig, granted the composer the right to importance but blamed his "harmonious boldness" and "rhythmical extravagances". But all the opposition and admiration which the criticized composer received from his works moved him to no concession, which could be regarded as a deviation from his distinctive character as a musician; he refined his productions gradually, and, but for this one exception, has become an example of immovable constancy; the greater beauty of his later works evinced itself by a better style, and truly gigantic progress in the construction of his harmony, in figurative revision, rhythm, and wealth of ideas, so that in many respects he became an enigma not only to his contemporaries but also to posterity. In the first half, and indeed in the second half of our century, musicians and able conductors had trouble enough in getting Beethoven's works rightly appreciated. What has since been the case, in order to establish a universal musical idea (with Schumann and Wagner) was at all times evident with regard to Beethoven; many musicians neither would nor could penetrate the depths of his innovations, and the unlearned wearied themselves in the attempt. Thus, it was no wonder that the narrow-minded public at the beginning of the nineteenth century was not able to understand what he produced, and objected to placing him on a level with the musicians of the day, Haydn and Mozart, with their gems of harmony and melody and their simple style.

Nevertheless Beethoven withstood the struggle with rigid firmness; he had a strong and influential party, received good remuneration for his compositions—better than Mozart—, and without accepting any fixed post received annual salaries, 600 florins from Prince Lichnowski and 4000 from Archduke Rudolph and the Princes Lobkowitz and Kinski, but these he soon lost on account of the unsettled state of politics prevailing at that time and also perhaps on account of his uncouth manners. This personal roughness lay partially in his inclination to democracy, and also in his increasing deafness from the year 1800, which deprived his musical soul, o'erclouded as it was, of nearly every pleasure. It must also be mentioned that Beethoven's avaricious, inconsiderate and ungrateful relations,—his brothers and nephews, wearied his life out with their begging and intriguing, almost ruining him financially in spite of his good income, so that at times he was incapable of procuring the simplest necessities of life for his own wants. For household affairs he had neither time nor inclination, thus making it easy for others to plunder him. How far his disregard for exterior matters extended, his absentmindedness and forgetfulness, occasioned by the retired life he led, and his devotion to art, is shown by the following incident.— Beethoven dedicated his twelve Variations on Russian Dances to Lady Browne, and in return for this, as Franz Ries relates, Lord Browne presented him with a beautiful riding-horse. Beethoven rode it several times, and then forgot it, and what was still worse its food also. His servant began to lend the horse out for money and delivered no bill for its food in order not to recall the fact of its existence to him. Finally to Beethoven's great astonishment a very long one was presented to him when the horse and his neglect recurred to his memory. He even neglected his outward appearance in the morose solitude and secluded life in which he indulged, presenting the appearance of an artisan or peasant rather than that of a favoured musician attached to the most aristocratic and refined court. Spohr and other reliable authorities asserted openly that he possessed the roughest and most repulsive manners, yet evinced at times

traits of warmheartedness and sociability. The biographies which Ries, Schindler, Nohl, Ulibischeff,
Marx, Thayer, Breuning, Nottebohm, and Jahn have
written of him contain hundreds of interesting anecdotes, which show forth Beethoven's singularities and
which if repeated would enlarge this sketch to the
size of a book. Only one in reference to the manner
of his conducting will be given. Spohr tells us in
his autobiography that during the time of his appointment in Vienna, Beethoven was in very straight-
ened circumstances from which he was rescued
by the assistance of his friends. He had been persuaded to make several alterations in his opera
"Fidelio" which, upon its first representation during
the occupation of Vienna by the French met with a
very unfavourable reception. The overture in C.,
the jailer's song and Fidelio's beautiful Aria were
added, and in its new form it was received with great
applause in the Kärnthnerthor Theatre. "His friends
stook advantage of this favourable moment" relates
Spohr "to arrange a concert for him in the large
Redouten Saal, at which his newest productions were
to be performed. All possessing instrumental or vocal
talent were invited to take part in it and not one of
the great Viennese artistes was absent. I and my
orchestra were also present and I saw Beethoven
as conductor for the first time. Although I had heard
much of his manner of conducting, it surprised me
very much. His habit was to conduct the orchestra
with all sorts of strange bodily contortions. As often
as the expression "Sforzando" occurred he waved
his arms, which he had folded on his breast before,
in the most vehement manner, at "Piano" he bent
down and so much the lower the softer he wished the
passage played; when it deepened into "Crescendo"
he gradually rose, and when it increased to "Forte"
he sprang into an erect position . . . Seyfried, to

whom I expressed my astonishment at this strange
mode of conducting, told me of a tragic-comic incident
which took place at Beethoven's last concert in Vienna.
Beethoven was playing a new pianoforte concerto of
his own, but forgot at the first Tutti that he was playing solo, sprang from his seat and began to conduct
in his usual manner. At the first Sforzando he threw
his arms so far apart that he knocked down both the
candlesticks from the the piano. The audience
broke out into a laugh, and Beethoven was so angry
at this disturbance that he ordered the orchestra to
cease and begin anew. Seyfried, fearing that the
same mishap might again occur at the same passage,
directed two boys who sang in the chorus to stand
near Beethoven and hold the candlesticks. One of
them unsuspiciously stepped nearer and looked at
the notes, but when Beethoven came to the fatal Sforzando the boy received such a violent blow on his
mouth from Beethoven's right hand, that the poor child
in his fright let the candlestick fall to the ground.
The other boy, more cautious, had followed all
Beethoven's movements with anxious glances, and
was able to evade the blow by dexterously stooping
down. The audience had laughed before, but now it
burst out into fits of laughter, and Beethoven was in
such a rage, that with the first chords he struck he
broke half-a-dozen strings. All his friends' attempts
to restore quiet and order were for a moment
fruitless. The first Allegro of the Concerto was entirely lost. After this concert Beethoven would not
give another. This was the first time since he had
been persuaded to do so. The concert in the Redouten Saal was such a brilliant success that a second
with the same result was able to be given, from the
proceeds of which the composer was enabled to live
free of care for a long time.

With regard to Beethoven's political opinions the

circumstance connected with the Eroika symphony is proof enough; he is said to have written it in his enthusiastic moments, in honour of Napoleon, but afterwards threw aside his intention of dedicating it to his hero, when Napoleon, throwing off his disguise became an arrogant tyrant. He also refused a call to Cassel to the Court of the pleasure-loving Hieronymus of Westphalia in the year 1809, preferring to be independent in Vienna. What wonderful power of composition he evinced during this cheerless time, partly in his quiet hermitage at Mödling near Vienna, partly in his wanderings through fields and woods in the neighbourhood, producing many symphonies, the Missa Solemnis, numerous Sonatas and Quartets &c. suffering bodily as he did, and leading the life of a poor man. Yet what a depth of enthusiasm for the beautiful and sublime in art must have inspired him, surrounded as he was by so few animating external circumstances, which would not have left a man of ordinary capacity strength enough to perform the most common tasks, yet he was able to execute the greatest works for all time.

His favourite instrument had always been the piano, and the result of this preference was an unsuspected amplification of technical performance extending in all directions, and increasing with the greater importance of his compositions.

As the lyrical melodious style had been the ruling form until his time, it was Beethoven who introduced the dramatic, and in its train a wealth of character, execution, and effect which had never previously been attained. Through him the instrument gained a power and capacity of expression which led to an entirely new epoch of pianoforte playing.

In his biography with reference to the years 1796—1798 spent in Vienna, Thayer says: He was the most important pianoforte player of the metropolis. Karl Czerny, in "Cock's London Musical Miscellany" expressed the following opinion with regard to Beethoven's playing. "His capacity for improvising was most brilliant and astonishing; in whatever society he was, he understood the art of producing such an effect upon his listeners that frequently no eye was dry, and many burst into tears, for there was something most wonderful in his touch, besides the beauty and originality of his ideas and the ingenious manner in which he expressed them." Tomaschek who heard Beethoven in Prague, described him as "the giant of all pianoforte players", and says, when speaking of a crowded concert given by Beethoven in the Konvikt Saal: "I was most keenly touched by Beethoven's splendid playing, and especially by the bold execution of his fantasies, indeed—I was so deeply affected that for several days I never touched my piano, and only my ineradicable love for art and reasonable reflection enabled me to continue my pianoforte studies as before, and with increased industry." Tomaschek wrote this many years after Beethoven's death in 1844, and to other praises adds the following: "Had the first works of Beethoven which were published at that time, (in Prague) only appeared as classical compositions on account of their rhythm, harmony and counterpoint they would perhaps have discouraged me from the further prosecution of my studies, but thus, I was roused and firmly persuaded from Beethoven's works, that even the greatest genius must respect the marked signs of theoretical training, and redoubled my industry in order to reach that summit from which hallowed Art bestows the kiss of consecration upon those found worthy to receive it. Many people when speaking of Beethoven, involuntarily think at the same time of Mozart to the latter's disadvantage; but they forget that the works

of the former are composed with more knowledge
and grace than his later compositions and that these
advantages which still make a deep impression upon
the listeners are chiefly due to Mozart's clearly-defined
style. Beethoven left Prague and I felt the benefit
of having heard the productions of the greatest master of pianoforte playing."

In a little anecdote Thayer tells us what sad
prejudices prevailed about Beethoven during his
life-time, especially among musicians. Dolezalek
once brought a study of a Beethoven Quartet to
his teacher, Albrechtsberger, who had also been
Beethoven's teacher. "By whom is it?" asked Albrechtsberger. "Beethoven", answered Dolezalek. To this
the teacher in his wisdom replied: "Have nothing to
do with him, he has learnt nothing and will never
produce anything."

It can be easily imagined that such criticism
coming to Beethoven's knowledge would pain him
terribly, and that his increasing struggle with the
prejudices of narrow-minded and envious people made
him, (already rendered morose in his earlier years)
still more unsociable and embittered, without even
taking into consideration other hardships, his total
deafness, bad health, sudden cessation of all tender
affections and periods of pecuniary distress. It is
also certainly unjust to describe Beethoven as being
naturally rough and uncouth; a musician, capable of
expressing such tender and lofty musical ideas in so
touching and pathetic a manner, must of necessity
have possessed delicate feelings himself. A sad chain
of circumstances deprived him of almost every thing
that in human conception is capable of forming man's
happiness; he tried to struggle bravely against
misfortune, and in doing so became morose and
unsympathetic. The last years of the great musician's life,—now become a model for all posterity—

were troubled by painful illness. In addition to the heavy affliction of total deafness, he suffered from dropsy with which he had to contend, and on account of which he underwent an operation. The effects of a severe chill brought on by his habit of wandering over the moor in all sorts of weather and often bare-headed, hastened his death, which occurred on the 26th March 1827. He was deeply regretted by all who knew him personally, or had found delight in his productions. Unlike Mozart's wretched burial, his funeral obsequies were solemnized with all grandeur.

It has often been said in after years of eminent men, who during their, lives have been undervalued or have suffered from envy or rivalry: Ah! if he could return! Of Beethoven this saying constantly recurs: "If he were only amongst us now what triumphs he would achieve!" Indeed united Posterity has for a long time past been engaged in spirit, weaving wreaths of honour for him. Not only has Beethoven's music been appreciated by the upper and more exclusive classes in consequence of their deeper and more cultivated study, but it has forced its way to extended regions. Not confined to larger centres but in much smaller places have those powerful works the "Symphonies" formed the glory and pride of their local concerts.

Every intelligent director now finds himself at ease with those problems which in Beethoven's time were scarcely understood by the most proficient masters. The larger and lay Public accept the solution of those problems with taste and understanding, unwearied by their occasional length and enjoying them with enthusiasm. Players of instrumental parts as also singers have all striven to ensure the understanding and success of their performance, and in that success have been richly compensated for their trouble, whereas seventy or eighly years ago musicians hardly deigned to play those works at all, looking at them with scant courtesy. His violin concerto formerly never found in any program is now recognized as one of the most brilliant pieces for the most perfect players. His later quartets which even 40 years ago were looked upon as "music of the future" are now performed at all chamber-music gatherings and wherever good understanding for classical music exists.

He who can appreciate Beethoven honours himself by the act as he proves thereby what immense pregress the cultivation of and interest in genuine classical music has been made.

A still higher acknowledgment of Beethoven's greatness remains to be asserted. Not one of his successors has ever been able to shake the pillar of his glory. Even Richard Wagner never hesitated to acknowledge him as his master. And Beethoven remains that which he was in the second phase of his life: The Master of Masters.

The following are his compositions: For the Pianoforte only: 38 Sonatas, 242 Variatons, 54 smaller Pieces, a Sonata for two pianos, 3 Marches, 9 Variations; For the Piano together with other Instruments: 5 Concertos with orchestral accompaniments, 1 Concerto with violin and violincello, 1 Choral Fantasia, 1 Rondo with orchestra, 1 Rondo with violin, 16 Sonatas with violin, or violincello or horn, 11 Trios with the Violin, Clarionet and Violincello, 4 Quartets with the Violin, Viola and Violincello, 1 Quintet with the Oboe, Clarionet, Bassoon, and Horn: Orchestral Works: 9 Symphonies, "Die Schlacht bei Vittoria", "Die Geschöpfe des Prometheus", music to "Egmont", 1 Allegretto, March from Tarpeja, 1 Military March, 9 Overtures 1 Concerto, and 2 Romances for the Violin and Orchestra, 36 Dances:

Dramatic Music: the Opera "Fidelio", "The Ruins of Athens", Overture to "King Stephen", "The glorious moment", "Meerstille und Glückliche Fahrt"; Church Music: 2 Masses, "Christ on the Mount of Olives"; for Chorus and Orchestra: Aria and Scene "Ah perfido", 1 Trio, 1 "Song of sacrifice", 1 "Bundeslied", 1 "Funeral song": Chamber Music: 1 Septet, 2 Sextets, 3 Quintets, 2 Fugues, 16 Quartet, 5 String-trios; Wind Instruments: 1 Octet, 1 Septet, 1 Trio, 3 Duets, 1 Serenade, 1 Rondino; besides these: 65 Songs, (also canons) with Pianoforte Accompaniment, as well as about 200 English, Scotch, Irish and Welsh songs with piano, violin, and violincello accompaniment.

FRANZ BENDEL.

UNFORTUNATELY but little is known of this excellent pianist and composer for the pianoforte. He was born on the 23rd March 1833, some say in Bohemia, others at Schönlinde near Rumburg. Schönlinde is a small Bohemian market-town in the Rumburg district. The well-known Schubert dictionary newly revised by Emil Breslaur gives the same information, also stating that he received his first musical instruction in his native town from Proksch; according to this his native town must have been Schönlinde where Proksch was resident, but in reality it was the well-known school of Music of Joseph Proksch in Prague which still exists, and where Bendel studied. From Prague he went to Weimar to Franz Liszt, who completed his instruction. He then travelled through Germany, meeting with great success as a pianoforte performer; but no further particulars of time and places are known.

From the year 1862 he lived in Berlin, and for some years was teacher of the pianoforte at the New Kullak Academy of Music. He died on the 3rd July 1874.

Bendel was most active as a composer. The number of his compositions for the piano (light and descriptive pieces, Fantasias, Idyls &c.) is over one hundred. The most admired are the Fantasias on a theme from Gounod's "Faust and Margaret", Meyerbeer's "Afrikanerin" and on Bohemian National songs, (op. 8, 45 and 47). A Pianoforte Concerto, a Sonata for the Pianoforte and Violin, a Trio, several Masses and Symphonies, and various books of Songs are also among his compositions.

WILLIAM STERNDALE BENNET.

BENNET is indisputably one of the finest musicians England has ever produced. By many he is thought to be the founder of a special English school, but that is not the case. He has done very much for the culture of true art, and in this way has distinguished himself not only at home but in foreign countries. His musical style is very much akin to that of Mendelssohn, and it is often maintained, that he is an imitator, but this is doing him an injustice. On his first appearance as a pianoforte performer (playing his own Concerto in D-minor) at the Royal Academy of Music in London, of which he was a pupil, Mendelssohn was present and recognized his extraordinary capabilities. The latter was his friend and seven years his senior.

Bennett was born at Sheffield on the 13th April 1816. He belonged to a musical family. In his eighth year he became a chorister in King's College Chapel, Cambridge and in his tenth year, pupil at the Royal Academy, where he was taught by Holmes, Crotch, Potter and Lucas. In the year 1833, he passed his examination, and the Pianoforte Concerto composed and performed by him on this occasion was published at the expense of the Academy. In the year 1837, through the kindness of the pianoforte manufacturer, Broadwood, means of his own not being at hand, he went to Leipzig for a year in which town Mendelssohn had already taken part as Conductor in the Gewandhaus concerts for twelve months. Here he enlarged his artistic sphere, and Mendelssohn as well as R. Schumann took great interest in him.

In 1841 he went to Leipzig for the second time, and remained there another year. For several years he was actively engaged in England as a pianoforte performer and teacher, having many pupils and being in much requisition. In 1840, he founded the Bach Society in London, having as its aim the spread of Sebastian Bach's works by publication and performance. Thus, among other compositions, St. Matthew's Passion Music was performed for the first time in England. A proof of the high estimation in which he was held is the fact of his having been chosen conductor of the Philharmonic Society in London in 1856. Soon after this he received the degree of Doctor from the Cambridge University; in 1867, he was created Master of Arts, and in 1870, Honorary Doctor of the Oxford University. In the following year he was made a Knight by the Queen, but this distinction he only survived a few years, dying in London on the 1st Feb. 1875.

As a composer Bennett has written 4 Concertos, as well as a number of Sonatas, Caprices, and Rondos, 1 Symphony, 4 Overtures, 1 Oratorio, 1 Cantata, the music to "Ajax", 1 Cello Sonata, 1 Trio, and a number of Songs.

HENRY BERTINI.

THE Bertini brothers seem to have originated from a very musical Italian family, to which the conductor Guiseppe Bertini also belonged. The elder of the two brothers, Benoît Auguste, born at Lyons in 1780, received his tuition from Clementi in London, and made himself known in the year 1830, by a book which he wrote in English upon the "Phonological system for the acquirement of extreme facility on all instruments and in singing". His younger brother, Henri, born on the 28th October, 1798, in London, seems to have been quite dependent upon Benoît, for he was not only initiated into the art of music and instructed by him, but was taken to Paris and elsewhere when scarcely six years old. Unfortunately only few particulars of their lives are known.

Benoît, when a pianist, resided in London, where, as teacher his services were much in request. Henry lived in Paris, gave several concerts which must have proved successful, as some years later he was able to purchase an estate near Grenoble in the south of France, where he lived from the year 1859. His numerous Etudes distinguished for their especial technical utility, beautiful melody, and fine harmony were very generally used in schools and also brought him considerable sums. Buonamici published fifty of these études with introductory remarks and revised fingering.

Henri Bertini died at his country-seat on the 18st October. 1876.

JOHANNES BRAHMS.

THE greatest living master of composition in the present day, has also made himself a name as a pianist, and his compositions for the piano are chiefly master-pieces, which form a part of the peculiar charm of his musical nature.

Born on the 7th May 1833 in Hamburg, he received his first musical instruction from his father, (a double-bass player) and this was continued by Ed. Marxsen, a pupil of Seyfried and Bocklet. Fully trained and richly endowed with musical creative powers he started on concert-tours with the Hungarian violinist, Reményi, whose playing always showed a marked preference for everything Hungarian, and

this may perhaps have influenced Brahms' taste in
some measure. He then made Joseph Joachim's acquaintance, and being almost of the same age and
both inspired with enthusiasm, they set off on their
travels together. In the year 1853, they came to Düsseldorf, and here it was one of the last great deeds
of Robert Schumann before his fatal illness, to draw
attention to this young genius. He was astonished
at the young man's beautiful playing but still more
at the performance of his compositions, and with the
impartiality and foresight peculiar to his nature, he
declared in a decisive paragraph printed in the "New
Journal of Music" "New Paths", that in Johannes
Brahms a new Messiah had arisen from whom the
world might expect musical signs and wonders. "I
thought", wrote Schumann at that time "some one
would appear destined to give full expression of the
age in ideal form, not gradually, but like Minerva in
full panoply. He has now come, in his youth and
vigour, the Graces and Gods have been his guardians.
He is called Johannes Brahms, and comes from Hamburg where he has been quietly composing . . . in
appearance he bears all the signs of his high calling.
When at the piano, he unveiled wonders to us, we
seemed to be in enchanted regions. His playing was
like that of an orchestra, at one time pathetic, and
then again full of triumph. "Everything was there,
sonatas, hidden symphonies, songs;—full of poetic
feeling although without words, melody reigned
throughout; the pianoforte pieces were sometimes
wild, and then again wonderfully graceful,—all the
melodies of such a different character. Then it
seemed as if he united all into a waterfall, bearing
the peaceful rainbow over the dashing waves, and
surrounded on the shore by butterflies and accompanied by the songs of nightingales. His
companions hail his appearance in the world—

where, perchance wounds are awaiting him, but palms and laurels too—with joy."

Schumann's words proved true; a long time elapsed before Brahms was able to reap his palms and laurels. To begin with, he had a cold reception and met with no success with his Concerto in D-minor, which he performed at the Leipzig Gewandhaus. All the rare strength and perseverance which the young musician possessed were very necessary to him; for although this was apparent in his first compositions for the piano, ballads, and songs, yet he had to contend long against those still wandering in old accustomed paths, before gaining the day.

Brahms remained at Detmold for some time as Chorus Director and composed steadily; then he went to his birthplace and in the year 1862, to Vienna, in which city he had accepted the post of Director of the Singing Academy. Had the inhabitants of the Imperial city on the Danube then recognized his genius, he would most certainly have remained there, but as it was he left in 1864, and sought a permanency at various places: Hamburg, Zurich, Baden-Baden &c. In 1869 he re-visited Vienna, and then began for him an era of success. It was especially his "German Requiem" with its peculiar grandeur, which won the hearts of all listeners, and spread his fame in England.

When Herbeck was appointed Kapellmeister of the Royal Opera House in Vienna, he resigned the directorship of the concerts of the "Gesellschaft der Musik-Freunde", Brahms succeeded him and retained the position until 1874, when Herbeck in consequence of some difference vacated his post at the Court Opera House. Brahms never showed much inclination for the wearisome work which a conductorship involves, and never again sought a permanent post after Herbeck resumed his position as conductor in the

"Gesellschaft der Musik-Freunde". In order that he might be free and unfettered as a composer, he refused the most brilliant offers. After his retirement he lived at Heidelberg until 1878, and then selected, Vienna as his place of abode. In the previous year 1877, he received the title of Honorary Doctor of Music and Philosophy from the Cambridge University, and in 1881, the same title was conferred upon him by the University of Breslau.

Not without much toil, for the industry displayed in his great works must have been tremendous, but free and unaffected by any criticism a glorious success finally came to the master; all important concerts numbered his works on their programmes, and his compositions are now to be heard in many families where music is more than superficially studied.

In a biographical sketch prompted by a large portrait of Brahms, which appeared in the "Neue Blatt", the critical editor gave the following opinion of the great musician: "Brahms is the only living composer, to be recognized as individual among those creative musicians who follow in the Wagner, Mendelssohn or Schumann track. Not that he has kept free from the influence of other masters in thought and feeling; Brahms, however, possesses a peculiar mode of expression, distinctly his own; he is never loquacious in his music, on the contrary, generally serious and in earnest, putting his thoughts into pithy forms. Nothing sweet or sickly is to be found in his music; the construction of his greatest works displays a power of arrangement which perhaps has only been equalled by Beethoven; in most of them there is a shade of soft melancholy, at times they are even harsh. Brahms is frequently, like Rembrandt, a dark painter in his colours as well as ideas. For this reason many frivolous and superficial people have no love for him; and many musicians to whom

Brahms is a vexation because they get no applause when performing his compositions, assert that his music is colourless as a November sky or call it discordant and inharmonious. These are of course only mean, ill-natured speeches, and the fact that Brahms produces every year new compositions with which he delights and surprises his friends shows how little these unjust criticisms affect him."

Brahms is at present a long way from being popular in the sense that Mozart, Haydn, Beethoven or even Schumann are. His works are too difficult of execution, especially in point of rhythm, for that, for a composer can hardly be called really popular until the amateur plays his works and rhythm is always the amateur's stumbling block. But the same was said of Beethoven's and Schumann's works.

The day, however, is not far distant when Brahms will be understood and appreciated in all circles where there is a genuine love for really good music.

Brahms' compositions number more than one hundred. For the Piano: Solos, Duets, some with instrumental accompaniment, 1 Quintet, 3 Quartets, 4 Trios, 4 Duets, 4 Sonatas, Variations on one of Haydn's Themes, 8 Books of Hungarian Dances, Variations on a Schumann Theme, 2 Waltzes, Arrangements of his Symphonies No. 3 and 4; 4 Ballads, 4 Capriccios, 1 Chaconne in Bach's style for the left hand only, 1 Etude in Chopin's style, 1 Arrangement for performance in public of a Gavotte by Gluck 4 Intermezzos, 1 Presto from J. S. Bach in two arrangements, 2 Rhapsodies, 1 Rondo in C. M. von Weber's style, 1 Scherzo, 5 Studies, 2 Books of Variations on a Theme by Paganini, Variations on a Theme of his own and on a Hungarian Song, and one on a Theme of Haendel. Orchestral Music: 2 Serenades, 4 Symphonies, Variations on a Theme by Haydn, 2 Overtures. For Stringed Instruments: 1 Violin-

concerto, 2 Sextets, 2 Quintets, 3 Quartets, 1 Quintet
for the clarionet and stringed instruments, various
pieces for the Organ, and numerous sacred and secular songs with pianoforte and instrumental accompaniment.

LOUIS BRASSIN.

THE three brothers bearing this name have all distinguished themselves: Louis born on the 24th June at Aachen, Leopold at Strasburg, (Alsace) on the 28th May 1843, and Gerhard at Aachen on the 10th June 1844. The latter was a violinist, the two former were pianoforte players and teachers. The father of these three musicians was the well-known baritone Brassin, who for a long time was engaged at the town theatre at Leipzig, and whose performance was much admired both there and abroad. Thus with his own efficient knowledge of music he was admirably qualified to control the education of his sons. Leopold and Gerhard were teachers at the Musical Academy in Berne, and from 1857, the former was Pianist to the Duke of Saxe-Coburg-Gotha; he lived later on in St. Petersburg, and died in Constantinople in the year 1890. He has written several works for the Piano: Concertos for two pianos, with orchestral accompaniment, and other important pieces, overtures, string quartets, songs &c.

Louis was of more importance as a pianist and teacher. He gave many concerts in various countries, partly with his brother, the violinist, and filled in succession three good appointments as teacher: in 1866, as the successor of Hans v. Bülow at the Stern Conservatoire in Berlin, in 1869, at the Brussels Conservatoire and 1879, at the Conservatoire of St. Petersburg: thus he spent 18 years in tuition and during this long period trained many clever pupils for the piano.

He died in St. Petersburg on the 17th May 1884.

HANS BRONSART VON SCHELLENDORF.

BORN in Berlin, Feb. 11th, 1830, Hans von Bronsart
as pianist, composer and music director has made
a considerable name for himself. Belonging to a military family, his father being Lieutenant - General
Bronsart v. Schellendorf, and several of his nearest
relations holding high military posts, his inclination was
more in favour of the musical than the military profession. Coming to Danzig with his parents in his
early youth he began the study of music in his eighth
year, and made considerable progress on the piano,
so that in his eleventh year he was able to perform
Liszt's Transcription of Franz Schubert's "Lob der
Thränen".

  After having passed his examination at the

grammar school at Danzig at Easter 1845, he removed
to the Berlin University for the purpose of studying
philosophy; taking lessons at the same time from
Theodor Kullak and learning the theory of harmony
and counterpoint from Siegfried Dehn.

In 1854 he became Liszt's pupil in Weimar, and
after three years thorough study, he completed his
musical education. He then commenced his travels,
first going to Paris, where he gave two concerts in aid
of charities, and then performing in many German
towns and in St. Petersburg. Having in the meantime
attracted attention as a composer for the piano and orchestra, his appearance at Leipzig led to his appointment as conductor of the Euterpe concerts in the year
1860; when resident in this town he married Ingeborg
Starck (see next page.) in 1861. In the year 1865,
he succeeded Hans v. Bülow, as conductor of the
concerts given by the "Gesellschaft der Musik-Freunde"
at Berlin, but in 1867 he received a call to Hanover
as manager of the Royal Theatre, in which position he
brought forward good performers for the opera and
theatre. Later on he became manager at the Court
Theatre at Weimar, which position he still retains.

Of his compositions for the piano his Concerto in
F-sharp minor, "Aus der Jugendzeit", a Fantasia and
other pieces are widely known. Besides these works
he wrote an opera "Der Corsar", a Fantasia for violin
and organ, a "Spring Fantasia" for orchestra, a Cantata entitled "Christnacht", a Trio in G-minor, a Sextet
for stringed instruments and other pieces.

INGEBORG VON BRONSART.

INGEBORG, née Stark, the wife of the Court Theatre "Intendant" Bronsart v. Schellendorf, was born on the 24th August 1840, in St. Petersburg. Her first pianoforte teachers were Constantine Decker, and Nicolaus v. Martinoff an excellent amateur; later on Adolf Henselt continued her musical education and from the year 1858, Franz Liszt, who completed it.

She began composing at an early age; in her twelfth year she performed a composition of her own at St. Petersburg, which had been arranged with instrumental accompaniments by her teacher Decker.

When in St. Petersburg she published a number of studies, light pieces, Fugues, and Sonatas, the result of serious and careful study. When living in Weimar she published a Concerto, Sonatas, Fugues &c.

She appeared with much success as a pianist in various towns, including Leipzig, where she made Hans v. Bronsart's acquaintance and married him.

Ingeborg v. Bronsart has composed three operas, (one of them "Jery and Bäteli", has been performed many times), Songs, Romances for the violin and violincello with pianoforte accompaniment, a "Kaiser-marsch" &c.

IGNAZ BRÜLL.

ALTHOUGH Ignaz Brüll was for some years a performer on the pianoforte, yet he was soon induced to relinquish his career as a pianist owing to the success his compositions met with, in particular his opera "The Golden Cross", and from this period he devoted all his time and attention to composition.

Born on the 7th November 1846, at Prossnitz in Moravia, he accompanied his parents to Vienna in 1850, and as he displayed much inclination and talent for music at a very early age, he received instruction on the pianoforte and in theory from Epstein, Rufinatscha, and Desoff; he composed steadily and in the year 1861, his first important composition (a Concerto for the pianoforte and orchestra) was performed in Vienna, he himself taking part in it. Whilst travelling as a pianoforte performer an orchestral Serenade of his was performed at Stuttgart in 1864, and two other Concertos for the piano in Vienna, Berlin, Leipzig, and Breslau.

In 1872, he was appointed piano teacher at the Horack Music Institute in Vienna, and retained this post until 1878. He then gave up his time wholly to composition. His productions for one or two pianos alone or together with the violin, violincello, and orchestra are numerous; in addition he has composed a Violin Concerto, a Cello Sonata, a Trio, an overture to "Macbeth", a Ballet, a "Märchen aus der Champagne", Choruses and Songs; and besides the "Golden Cross" he wrote five other operas, "The Beggar of Samarkand", "Der Landfriede", "Bianca", "Queen Marietta", and "The stone Cross", but none of them were received with the same enthusiasm as the "Golden Cross".

DR. HANS VON BÜLOW.

As one of the cleverest musicians, authors, conductors and pioneers for true art Hans v. Bülow stands on an equality with the most eminent men of his time. He has achieved wonders for the elevation and spread of musical art, and even when the manner of his attack seems to have been misunderstood, it originated in his enthusiasm for all that is truly great and noble in music and its advancement in every day life. Almost unparalleled in its consistency, self-denial, and nobility is his furtherance of Wagner's music, and he is always full of eager generosity to forward into notice the works of important composers, whose productions have not met with a favourable

4*

reception from the public. To Wagner's name we need only add those of Brahms and Berlioz in order to rightly appreciate Bülow's efforts in this direction. By his brave championship, powerful writings, pianoforte playing and conductor's baton, Bülow has verified the words "Many foes, much honour"; spending his whole life in the service of music, he has only conquered after many a hard struggle.

Hans Guido v. Bülow was born at Dresden, Jan. 8th 1830. In his childhood he displayed little talent or inclination for music. It was a lady, Fräulein Schmiedel, who gave him his first pianoforte instruction, for she possessed more energy and perseverance than many a man, and never rested until she had instilled the boy with a love of music. Later on, Friedrich Wieck, Litolff, Eberwein, and Moritz Hauptmann became his teachers.

In consequence of his father's removal to Stuttgart in 1846, Hans v. Bülow entered the grammar school in that city; in 1848, he removed to the University at Leipzig for the purpose of studying law, but left there for the Berlin University in 1850. In the last mentioned city he commenced literary work, writing for the "Evening Post", and adopted the ideas of the prevailing political movement which had been especially fostered in him by Wagner's treatise "Art and the Revolution".

After having visited Richard Wagner in his exile at Zurich in the year 1850, who gave him ready advice concerning his future career, and practical instruction in the art of conducting at the town theatre at Zurich, Wagner recommended him to Liszt at Weimar, who undertook his tuition in pianoforte playing in 1851. In the following year, he appeared for the first time as a performer at a Musical Festival at Ballenstedt conducted by Liszt and in 1853, and 1855, he went on concert-tours through Germany to Vienna.

The result of his appearance as a pianoforte player in Berlin was his appointment at the Stern Conservatoire to the post rendered vacant by Kullak's resignation in 1855. In 1857, he married Liszt's daughter Cosima, and in 1858, was appointed Pianist at the Prussian Court. In recognition of his services on behalf of music and literary work, the Jena University, in 1863, conferred upon him the title of doctor of Philosophy. In the year 1864, he visited Russia as a pianist and director of concerts, and in 1865, went to Munich as Pianist to the King of Bavaria, in which city his method of conducting Wagner's musical drama "Tristan and Isolde" gained him a high reputation.

Political motives being probably the cause of his departure from Munich in the year 1866, he went to Basle in Switzerland, but soon after received the royal appointment of conductor and director of the Academy of Music at Munich, which necessitated his return to that city.

He now devoted much time and energy to Wagner's operas, as well as to the Academy. Being divorced from his wife in 1869, who afterwards became the wife of Richard Wagner, he resigned his appointments and went to Florence, where he remained three years and devoted himself to introducing German music into Italy. In 1872, began the new era of his European concert-tours which procured for him the reputation of being one of the most important conductors of the age. He gave concerts in America in 1875, and in England in 1876.

In 1877, he was made conductor at the opera house in Hanover, where he remained until 1880, and then received the post of manager of music (Intendant) at the Meiningen Court. At the concert-tours which he undertook with the orchestra and by consent of the Duke, he showed in a practical form how a good orchestra, by strictly obeying an efficient leader, is capable of penetrating the depths of classical master-pieces, and of doing them full justice. The fact of his resigning this post in 1885, in consequence of some difference, was less of a loss to him, than to the Institute which he had brought into repute. From this period, by conducting large orchestras, Philharmonic Societies in St. Petersburg, Berlin and Hamburg, he has brilliantly revealed his capacities as a conductor, and accomplished wonders both as a conductor and pianist.

His memory is marvellous; playing and conducting without the aid of notes, and through him the art of conducting in this manner has become the fashion; although he has never had a rival, for the repertoire which he retains is the most extensive; he masters it so completely that under his guidance the greatest and longest works are accurately performed even to the smallest detail. Meanwhile, without for a moment doubting Herr v. Bülow's talents as a conductor, especially in what concerns an exact and precise performance, yet I must not omit mentioning that his peculiar individual conception of many classical master-pieces is open to criticism. Whether a conductor is justified in supplying his own conception of the work instead of that established by tradition remains a question which other critics may decide. The result may be a success, and any deviation can easily be tolerated when such a perfect musician as Dr. v. Bülow is concerned. Yet unfortunately many others, with inferior talents for conducting have arisen as imitators, who believe themselves equally justified by the example of their great predecessor in introducing all sorts of peculiarities into the works of the great classical masters. Thus, it happens that now-a-days one hears performances of the works of Beethoven, Mozart, Haydn, Mendelssohn and Schumann, which most certainly do

not coincide with the intentions of these great men,
and which altogether give a false idea of the compositions. Hurrying or slackening Tempi, Accellerandos,
Rallentandos, and even pauses are introduced; all this
does violence to the spirit of the works. Every conductor of a small theatrical orchestra think himself
entitled to use his judgment in the performance of
"Fidelio" or any opera by Mozart, and to give his
reading of this or that part instead of doing their
utmost to express the composer's intention.

The same disagreeable tendency prevails among
painters and authors as well as musicians, and the
only motive is to get their productions noticed at any
price. The public must be roused, and as this cannot
always be accomplished by fair means on account of
the lack of fine appreciation of real art, imaginary
connoiseurs set themselves up, who unfortunately em-
ploy foul ones.

Thus Herr v. Bülow cannot escape the charge
of having encouraged this quite unjustifiable musical
mania by his capriciousness in conducting.

As a pianist he has always proved himself to be
a faithful and enthusiastic exponent of classical music,
thus, by his performance of the five-last Sonatas by
Beethoven, he has made the public acquainted with
them, as well as procuring recognition for new compositions.

His indefatigable, unflinching perseverance corres-
ponds with the extent and depth of his musical knowledge. In America he gave 139 concerts during one
single visit over there. He does not allow such mean
attacks, as those lately prepared for him at two Philharmonic Concerts in Berlin, to daunt him from devoting himself entirely to the noble art of music with
his entire soul.

Hans v. Bülow has published a number of pieces
for the piano besides having made himself a name by

his editing of Beethoven's Sonatas (beginning at op. 53) also that of Cramer's Studies. He has also arranged a series of works by Wagner and Berlioz in a masterly manner, besides composing an overture to Shakespeare's "Julius Cesar", a ballad "The Singer's Curse" by Uhland, "Nirwana", Songs &c.

TERESA CARENNO.

ALL critics of the present day agree in putting Teresa Carenno at the head of modern pianists. Her playing is unequalled, her technical knowledge is perfect, and she captivates even those who make it a rule to admire nothing. In fact her whole performance is great and phenomenal. At the same time, her greatest admirers admit that it is not all perfection, although her playing is impassioned and full of power, yet it lacks tenderness and her touch is often hard. But it is well known that on her first appearance in Germany she excited great enthusiasm by her artistic peculiarities, and her expressive playing. In 1889, she appeared in Berlin, and gave a concert in the Sing Academy; Hans v. Bülow hearing her on this occasion described her as "the most interesting pianoforte player of the present age". With regard to the strength of her playing she is only to be compared with Sophie Menter, who, in the overcoming of technical difficulties, for instance in the performance of Liszt's and Rubinstein's concertos, excels even male performers. It is said of these two pianists that they are the only ones, who, in spite of the restrictions laid by nature upon their sex, have been able to overcome tremendous pianoforte difficulties.

Teresa Carenno's southern temperament may have decided her artistic tendency. Born at Caracas in the Republic of Venezuela on the 22nd December 1853, her father being a Minister of Finance she displayed musical talent as a child and according to reliable authorities received pianoforte instruction in New York from Moritz Gottschalk who died in 1869.

It is also asserted that she was sent to Paris for further study, and was taught by H. Matthias, one of Chopin's pupils. She then returned to America and celebrated many triumphs in large American cities. It was in America too that she made the acquaintance of the violinist Sauret, whose wife she became. They went on concert-tours to large American cities, meeting with a hearty reception every where. After several years had elapsed they were divorced, and Madame Sauret married again. Being divorced from her second husband the married the pianist d'Albert, whose compositions she now frequently plays in German towns, her powerful performance often proving the means of furthering their success.

In Leipzig the artiste appeared for the first time on the 29th March 1890, and met with decided success,

Since then she has been enthusiastically received in all the large musical towns of Germany. Quite recently she performed her husband's newest composition, (a piano Concerto in E) at a Philharmonic Concert in Berlin.

E. CHOPIN

FREDERIC CHOPIN.

W E can only repeat of Chopin what has already often
been asserted; he was a genius of rare originality, a musical poet, who neither imitated the styles
and ideas of others, nor troubled himself about them,
but formed his own thoughts, made experiments and
evolved works from the abundance of his own ideas
and feelings. His compositions at times give evidence
of a gay humour, but still oftener they are serious
and often melancholy. The performance of them

is nearly always technically difficult, and to ensure their success, good taste and musical knowledge are requisite on the part of the performer, whether the composition selected be a dance, variation, nocturne, prelude or étude, but then, if well played, success is certain.

A connoiseur once expressed his opinion upon the especial style of Chopin's music. "Poland impresses it with sorrow; France with animation and grace; Germany with depth." Chopin in his youth when studying at the Conservatoire at Warsaw was taxed by many with taking a course of his own. One of his teachers, Elsner, would then reply to the charge "Let him alone! He does not follow the beaten track, becauses he possesses unusual musical abilities. He does not adhere strictly to the old method but instead of it follows one of his own, and in his works he will display an originality, unknown up to the present time."

Elsner was right. Chopin introduced a new style in essential matters, and especially in technical work, which was recommended by Liszt, who also adopted it, as well as many other musicians. He treated the piano as a living being always seeking new peculiarities and charms. Thus for instance he had a preference for extended chords, and as, on account of the natural formation of his hands he was unable to master them, he procured artificial means by constructing an apparatus which forced the fingers apart and which he even wore when asleep. According to the opinion of all his musical contemporaries he was a first-rate pianist, always original, and inexhaustible in the application of all sorts of contrivances for the improvement of instruments.

Frederic Chopin was of French and Polish origin, his father Nicholas, born at Nancy, was an enthusiastic adherent of Stanislaus Leszczynsky, who had inherited the dukedoms of Lorraine and Bar. The sympathy which was shown for the descendant of the Polish throne by the inhabitants of Lorraine, was conferred by his friends and countrymen on Poland, the home of the exiled. Nicholas Chopin removed thence and accepted a tutorship in Warsaw in the year 1787. He afterwards held three posts in succession at academies in Warsaw; he then established a boarding school for boys, and married a Polish lady named Krzyzanowska in 1806. Chopin was born on the 1st March 1810, at Zelazowa Wola, near Warsaw. His home was one of grace and refinement, which was of great importance in deciding the boy's character. He was a gentle, nervous child on whom music had a strange effect. He received good pianoforte instruction and made rapid progress. Like Mozart, for whom in later years he cherished the deepest veneration, he displayed considerable capacity for composing even in his early years, and was considered a prodigy by those who heard him, yet he, unlike Mozart, did not play for money and was taken on no tours.

When Frédéric was ten years of age the singer Catalani came to Warsaw; she was delighted with the boy's playing and as a souvenir presented him with a watch, bearing the following inscription: „Madame Catalani à Frédéric Chopin, agé de dix ans."

Early as Chopin began composing, he did not limit himself to the practising and performance of new or complete compositions, but loved to improvise his own fancies, for hours together; especially liking to do this in the dusk, thus being able to live entirely in a world composed of his own thoughts, but from this cause his nature received touches of melancholy.

The following is a marked incident in his life. In 1825, when Chopin was fifteen years of age the

Czar Alexander came to Warsaw and wished to hear a newly invented instrument performed, the Aeol-melodicon— probably our harmonium, and Chopin being considered the most competent pupil of the Lyceum, was chosen to perform on it. The Czar was so pleased with his playing, that, full of admiration for Chopin's wonderful talent, he presented him with a costly diamond ring.

According to some authorities Chopin left Warsaw and Poland in 1828, but what seems more reliable is that he left it in 1831, driven away by the outbreak of the Polish revolution; his gentle quiet nature being averse to all violence. He went on tours as a pianist and met with success everywhere, especially at Vienna and Leipzig. It was in the latter town that his playing, especially the performance of his Variations on a Theme from "Don Juan" (op. 2), so charmed young Schumann.

Chopin then went to Paris, which became his permanent abode. He met with a warm reception both as a pianist and composer; a number of eminent men, Meyerbeer, Berlioz, Liszt, Ernst, Balzac, Heinrich Heine &c. honoured him with their friendship and sympathy. The best circles welcomed him, he became the fashion, and in this case at least the fashion showed good taste.

Madame Dudevant (Georges Sand) was one of his most enthusiastic admirers, and when in the year 1838, Chopin showed symtoms of disease of the chest she persuaded him to accompany her to the island of Majorca for the benefit of his health. After an apparent improvement they returned to Paris; but as he remained in weak health, this pleasure-loving woman left him.

Only the most perfect regularity and absence of all exhausting pleasures kept Chopin alive. In the spring of the year, 1849, however, carrying out his own wish and that of his friends, he travelled to England for the purpose of giving a few concerts. His journey seems to have absorbed his little remaining strength, and he died in the same year, on the 17th October, being interred beside Cherubini and Bellini amid the strains of Mozart's "Requiem".

Chopin's compositions comprise 2 Concertos in E- and F-minor, 3 Sonatas, 4 Ballads, 4 Fantasies, 12 Polanaises, 52 Mazurkas, 13 Walzes, 3 Ecossaisses, 1 Krakowiak, 1 Bolero, 1 Tarantella, 1 Barcarole, 1 Berceuse, 25 Preludes, 19 Nocturnos, 5 Rondos, 4 Scherzi, 4 Variations, 1 Funeral March, 1 Concert Allegro, 27 Concert Studies, 1 Trio, 1 Rondo for four hands, 2 Sonatas for the piano and cello, and 16 Polish Songs.

MUZIO CLEMENTI.

As a pianist, teacher and composer for his own instrument Clementi has become very celebrated. As a pianist he rivalled Mozart and he taught Cramer, Field, Moscheles, and Kalkbrenner. His position in the history of music is characterized but not exhausted with this assertion; it was said of him that with his "Gradus ad Parnassum" he laid the foundation of modern pianoforte playing.

An older competent and critic makes the following comparison with regard to him. He says: "As Viotti is the father of modern violin-playing, so is Clementi to be regarded as the father of modern piano playing. Cherubini and Clementi are considered to be Beethoven's predecessors, Cherubini in a greater and Clementi in a lesser degree. Beethoven always thought highly of him. He is the first composer of ability as regards the Sonata, the fundamental form of which remains the same to the present day."

Born at Rome in the year 1752, (day unknown) Clementi received instruction in pianoforte playing from the organist Buroni, and in thorough bass, counterpoint and singing from Carpani and Santarelli. From the year 1761, he played the organ in public, and in his fourteenth year he excited so much enthusiasm in Rome by his playing and composing that a rich Englishman, named Beckford or Bedford persuaded his father to let him take the boy to England, where his patron had him instructed in music, especially in piano playing. As a performer he made considerable sensation in London society. Pupils thronged to him and he became conductor at the Italian Opera House in London, but in 1781, he made a long concert-tour on the continent. At Vienna in competition with Mozart he played for a wager before the Emperor Joseph II., in which contest Clementi came off victor. He seems to have gone to Paris some years later, in 1785. Then he remained many years in London entering into partnership with the firm of Longman & Broderip, music publishers and pianoforte manufacturers, and this firm failing some time later, he formed a similar partnership with Collard, under whose name the business still flourishes.

In the meantime he composed for the piano and gave lessons, and particularly to Johann Baptist Cramer, and some years later to John Field. With the latter he went on a tour, visiting Paris, Vienna, and St. Petersburg in 1802, and wherever they went they met with an enthusiastic reception owing to their masterly performances. As Field remained in St. Petersburg, Clementi continued his tour with Karl Traugott Zeuner. In Berlin, L. Berger, Moscheles and Kalkbrenner were his pupils, the two latter only for a time. Klengel also had the benefit of his instruction in Dresden. He was married in Berlin but lost his wife a short time afterwards, and travelled with Berger and Klengel to St. Petersburg, where he seems to have remained some time, for it is said he did not return by Vienna and Italy to London until the year 1810. He was married for the second time in 1811, and from this period only left England once (in the winter of 1820—1821) when he visited Leipzig. He died on the 10th March 1832, at his country seat at Evesham, near London, leaving a very large fortune.

Besides his important work of instruction "Gradus ad Parnassum" he wrote 60 Sonatas for the piano, and 66 Sonatas for the piano, partly with violin accompaniment and partly with cello and flute accompaniment; a Duet and some Caprices, and characteristic pieces &c. for the piano; he published an anthology of the pianoforte works of classical composers, besides leaving some posthumus Symphonies and Overtures.

FRANÇOIS COUPERIN.

IN the 17th and 18th centuries the Couperins were a
brilliant race of musicians living in France, who
were especially distinguished as organists and composers. François excelled them all, and has therefore
acquired the designation "le grand"; he also seems
to have been the only one who has made a name
as a pianist.

He was born in Paris on the 10th November 1668.
His father was Charles Couperin, organist at the
church of St. Gervais, but he died in 1669, whereupon
his friend and successor Thomelin became the boy's

tutor and teacher. Some years later the Couperins again came to the front as organists at St. Gervais; first Charles' brother and then François in the year 1698. Three years later the latter became dulcimer player and organist of the Royal Chapel to Louis xiv. who was the reigning sovereign. In this position he astonished and delighted the court by the beauty of his playing, and especially with the performance of his own compositions.

After François' death in 1733, one of his daughters Marguerite Antoinette was appointed harpsichord player to the King, a second daughter Marianne who was a nun, was organist at the Abbey of Montbuisson.

As a composer and author Couperin opened out a new era for pianoforte playing, which is proved by the fact that Sebastian Bach in many respects took him as a model,—for instance in the treatment of French styles of Dance Music, and that Johannes Brahms has published Couperin's pianoforte works in a revised form in Chrysander's "Denkmälern der Tonkunst". In 1713, 1716, 1722 and 1730, Couperin published four Books, "Pièces de clavecin", in the third of which there are four concertos; in 1717, "L'art de toucher le clavecin", in 1724, "Les goûts réunis" with some more concertos and a Trio "Apothéose de Corelli". In addition to these, "Apothéose de l'incomparable Lully"; "Leçons des tenebres" and "Trios pour deux dessus de violon, basse d'archet et basse chiffrée".

JOHANN BAPTIST CRAMER.

CRAMER like his teacher Clementi won a brilliant reputation both as a pianist and composer for the pianoforte.

It is true that in the present day many of his compositions are considered out of date, but the second part of his "Grosse Pianoforte Schule" the "Schule der Fingerfertigkeit" consisting of 100 daily studies, and the fifth part, 84 Etudes (59 of which have been published in a revised form by Hans v. Bülow) are still in use as a means of instruction.

J. B. Cramer was born at Mannheim on the 24th February 1771. His father Wilhelm Cramer was a violinist, and the latter being called to London as Royal Bandmaster in 1772, Johann Baptist Cramer spent his youth in the English metropolis, and received musical instruction from Johann Schröter and Clementi; yet he studied theory almost entirely without the help of a teacher. His models were Händel, Bach, Scarlatti, Haydn and Mozart.

As early as 1788, he began his concert-tours as a pianist, meeting with great success everywhere. London was his place of residence.

Thayer in his excellent biography of Beethoven, asserts that Cramer went on a tour to the continent in 1799, in order to hear the finest pianoforte players. "He renewed his acquaintance with Haydn in Vienna, whose especial favourite he had been in London and at once entered into close friendship with Beethoven. Cramer excelled Beethoven in the perfect neatness and correctness of his performance; Beethoven assured him that he preferred his touch to that of any other player. His technical ability was wonderful; yet he was still more admired on account of his fine taste, feeling and expression; but Beethoven excelled him in power and energy, especially in improvisation. They were both perfect in their own peculiar styles, were of infinite help to each other, and in later years met with full appreciation of their mutual capabilities. Ries gives Beethoven's opinion as follows: Among pianists, he only distinguished one as an excellent performer, and that was John Cramer. All others were of small account to him." On the other hand Cramer a long time afterwards expressed his opinion, that no one could assert that he had ever heard improvising who had not heard Beethoven.

Beethoven too was equally just with regard to Mozart's genius. At an Augarten Concert in Vienna Beethoven was with Cramer, and they were listening to a performance of Mozart's pianoforte concerto in C-minor. Beethoven suddenly stood still and attracting his companion's attention to the exceedingly simple

yet beautiful melody which came in towards the
end of the piece exclaimed: "Cramer, Cramer, we
shall never attain to that!"   And when the movement
was repeated and increased in motion Beethoven kept
time to it, moving his body to and fro, and displayed
his enthusiasm and enjoyment of the music in every
possible way.

Cramer brought Beethoven's Trios, Opus 1 back
to London with him, and once after having played
them he exclaimed "That is the man, who will console
us for the loss of Mozart!" And once in conversation
with Potter he exclaimed in enthusiastic exaggeration.
"If Beethoven were to upset his inkstand on to a piece
of music paper, you would still admire it!"

He spent some time in Paris, in 1832, and in
1845.   In the year 1828, he and Addison opened a
music business in London; mostly for the sale of
classical works, under the name of Cramer & Co., which
he conducted until 1842, and which is still flourishing.
He died on the 16th April 1858 in London.

Besides the Studies already mentioned he wrote
7 pianoforte concertos, 105 Sonatas, 1 Quartet, 1 Quintet, several variations and Rondos &c.   Adolf Henselt
has arranged a selection of his best works, with the
addition of a second piano.

An older musical biographer when speaking of
the value of his compositions says: "Cramer did not
attain to Clementi; 40—50 of his Sonatas are good
and about a dozen of them are beautiful."

KARL CZERNY.

FOR more than thirty years this excellent exponent of pianoforte playing was the most important and successful teacher in Vienna, and still has great influence on less advanced students by the use of his masterly and unequalled Etudes.

As he himself had the benefit of the best instruction, so as teacher he taught a number of important musicians, Liszt, Döhler, Thalberg, Jaell, Frau v. Belleville-Oury and others, who owed their success in later years to the good foundation laid by him.

He was born in Vienna on the 21st February 1791; his father, the pianist Wenzel Czerny, was his teacher, and instructed him most carefully and impartially with regard to his future, not merely as a pianist. Then for some time no less a genius than Beethoven was his teacher. With such genuine and good instruction he made rapid progress, so that before attaining his fifteenth year he felt himself fully qualified for the office of teacher, and pupils belonging to the best society in Vienna thronged to him. Beethoven's friend and supporter, Prince Lichnowski was also Czerny's protector and patron. His reputation spread by his visits to Leipzig, Paris and London, and pupils from all parts came to him for instruction.

In 1805 he published his first composition (20 Variations) but nothing more until the year 1818, in the latter year when he got to know of the firm 'Cappi & Diabelli", he published a Rondo brillant as a duet, and from this time publishers vied with each other for his works.

Czerny then published a series of studies entirely for educational purposes; Schule der Geläufigkeit op. 299, Schule des Legato and Staccato op. 335, Daily Studies op. 337, Schule der Verzierungen op. 355, Schule des Virtuosen op. 365, Schule der linken Hand op. 399, Schule des Fugenspiels op. 400, Schule der Fingerfertigkeit op. 740. The Toccata in C op. 92 also serves the same purpose.

Altogether this productive musician wrote about 1000 works, among which are to be found Masses, Offertories, and other church music, as well as orchestral compositions, chamber Music and numerous arrangements. He never married and left a princely fortune.

EDWARD DANNREUTHER.

P OSSESSING unusual talent and ability for music,
and being well instructed, Dannreuther obtained
considerable reputation and in a certain direction
has been of much service to the composers of the
present day. He has done very much in England
for the furtherance and spread of Wagner's music,
which had met with little appreciation up to that time.
In many English newspapers he wrote in favour not
only of Wagner's works but also of those of other
modern composers. He is the author of "Richard
Wagner, his tendencies and theories" (London,
Augener & Co.) and translated Wagner's treatise

"Zukunftsmusik" (The music of the Future) and his "Beethoven" into English.

Edward Dannreuther was born at Strassburg in Alsatia on the 4th November 1845. He accompanied his parents to America in his childhood and received his first pianoforte instruction in Cincinnati, from H. L. Ritter. Being highly talented and making rapid progress, his parents sent him to the Conservatoire at Leipzig, where Moscheles and Plaidy became his pianoforte teachers and Richter instructed him in the art of composition. In 1863, he went to London, to commence work there. He now became a zealous promoter of Wagner's music, advancing it in every possible way; in 1872, he was the originator of a London Wagner Society, and conducted the concerts in connection with the society.

In the following year he formed a Choral Society, which he trained so efficiently that it was soon able to take part in performances of difficult modern music. He played at the Crystal Palace performing in the first place works by Liszt, Tschaikowski, Grieg, Scharwenka &c., for the purpose of getting them acknowledged and appreciated by the English public. He also arranged concerts for the performance of chamber-Music with the same intention. These musical evenings took place every fortnight during the winter in his own house and were kept up for years.

FANNY DAVIES.

MISS Fanny Davies, now one of the most eminent pianists, is distinguished both for her thoroughly musical and literary education. Long before it was decided for her to study as a pianiste, she had pursued the study of music with genuine earnestness at home, participating constantly in quartet parties and other musical gatherings.

Born, June 27th 1867, in the island of Guernsey, her parents being of English origin, she went to Birmingham in her childhood and speaks of this place as her native town. Her aunt Miss Woodhill, a lady well known in the educational world, gave her music lessons, and when scarcely three years old the child was able to play little duets by ear with her. When five years old, Miss Welchman became her teacher for the pianoforte, and in her seventh year she played

in public for the first time at a charity bazaar at the
Birmingham Town Hall. She performed Beethoven's
Sonata with the Funeral March, without octaves, her
hands being too small to stretch them. Her parents'
friends called her a prodigy.

In 1882, she went to Leipzig to study at the
Conservatoire where Reinecke, Oscar Paul, and Jadas-
sohn gave her lessons; but she only remained there
a year, going to Frankfurt-on-Main to study with Frau
Clara Schumann. For two years she had the benefit
of her instruction, Bernard Scholz teaching her composition at the same time.

In 1885, she returned to England after com-
pleting her studies and played, first at the Crystal
Palace, and afterwards with great success at the
Monday and Saturday Popular Concerts at St. James'
Hall; where since then she has often performed with
Professor Joachim, Lady Hallé &c.

In 1888, Miss Davies appeared for the first time
in the Gewandhaus at Leipzig, and then made a tour
through Germany. In the same year she played at
the Musical Festival at Birmingham, and in Rome, at
the "Orchestrale", and several times before Queen
Margherita. In Oct. 1882, she had the honour of
playing before Queen Victoria at Balmoral.

LOUIS DIEMER.

LOUIS Diemer, born on the 14th Feb. 1845, in Paris, was a pupil of the conservatoire there and is now professor and teacher at that institute. With his colleague, Francis Planté, he enjoys the reputation of being one of the best Parisian artistes. He is master of considerable technical difficulties, his playing is thoroughly correct and smooth, every melody and embellisment, as Professor Hanslick expresses it "seems to stand out clearly" which means to say that he is not a musician who will take the world by storm, but modern and tastefully cultivated.

His style of playing, also the works he chose, are thus described by Ed. Hanslick, who wrote about Diemer's appearance lately in Vienna. "The musician in question played at a Philharmonic concert, and then at one of his own in the Bösendorfer Saal, which was well attended and the building echoed with applause. In a long series of solo pieces, beginning with Beethoven's C-minor variations, and ending with a Liszt Rhapsody, Diemer displayed his most attractive talents. For such works as Chopin's Ballad in F of course a more impassioned rendering seems desirable, but a few pieces by the older French composers soon transferred him into his own element. The exquisite old Gallic grace of Couperin, Daquin, and Rameau cannot be rendered in a more delicate or graceful manner than by Mons. Diemer. His transcription of the Overture to the Magic Flute performed so gracefully and smoothly created a great sensation. The Variations for two pianos by Robert Fischhof also met with a good reception, and performed by two such excellent pianists as Diemer and Fischhof the work was heard to its best advantage, and had a brilliant effect. Thus there were composers of the most opposite schools: Beethoven, Liszt, Chopin, Couperin, Rameau, Mozart, Fischhof, whose works were interpreted in the most elegant, correct, and finished style."

Diemer has made a name by his transcriptions, as well as by his own compositions for piano, and in conjunction with Alard and Frankhomme he published Haydn's, Mozart's and Beethoven's piano works with fingering and marks of expression.

ANTON DOOR.

THE dangers of a professional life often prevent parents from cherishing the idea of such a career for their children, even if they show marked ability for it. Such was the case with Anton Door's father, a celebrated doctor, who entertained no great hopes of success for his son in adopting a musical career. Anton Door was born in Vienna, June 20th 1833, and at an early age, when receiving instruction at home, gave promise of unusual musical ability. The youthful prodigy performed in public for the first time in his ninth year, and with such success that he was finally permitted to follow the bent of his own inclinations after being well-grounded in science; and even if there is any truth in the assertion that he gave concerts of his own when fourteen years of age, it is certain that after doing so, he received for several years musical instruction from Czerny and Sechter, as a preparation for his professional life.

In his nineteenth year Door began to travel and met Peter Pixis at Baden-Baden, who took a great interest in him. He travelled through Italy with Ludwig Strauss; then turning his face northward he remained for some time at Königsberg. When there the danish musician Kellermann, invited him to visit Copenhagen, which he did and then travelled through Denmark, Norway, and Sweden, remaining a year in Stockholm, where he was appointed a Member of the Royal Academy of Music. He then passed on to Helsingfors, Finland, finally arriving at St. Petersburg. Here he met A. Rubinstein, Henselt, Dreyschock, and others from whom he received encouragement and help. Count Wielhorsky, a passionate lover of music became his patron; through his influence he was appointed Professor at the Royal Institute of Music at Moscow after the resignation of Joseph Rubinstein. He remained there until the Conservatoire was built when he left the Institute for the new School of Music. He spent his holidays in making many successful professional tours through Scandinavia, Germany and Austria which led in 1869 to his appointment as professor of the pianoforte class at the Vienna Conservatoire.

ALEXANDER DREYSCHOCK.

BORN on the 15th October 1818, at Zack or Zachotin in Bohemia, Alexander gave promise of musical talent when a child; he learned diligently and in his 8th year had acquired considerable proficiency. He lost his father when very young and his mother must have been of a simple nature, for after her son went to Prague in his thirteenth year (whether in her company or not, is unknown) it is said she believed he was devoting his time to the study of medicine whereas he was receiving musical instruction from Tomaczek.

6*

When twenty years of age Alexander was so proficient as a pianist, that he was qualified to undertake his first professional tour in Dec. 1838. He travelled through a number of towns in northern and central Germany. In the years 1840—1842 he extended his concert-tours, visiting Russia, Belgium, Holland, France (Paris), and London, meeting everywhere with a good reception.

It was in Paris that Cramer heard him in his latter days and exclaimed "The man has no left hand, they are both right hands". Dreyschock was, as an experienced critic says, "the hero of octaves, sixths, and thirds, his playing being the non plus ultra of mechanical skill, especially in the performance of classical compositions; although it is said that his execution lacked warmth.

In 1846 he visited several Austrian towns his musical genius being fully acknowledged both by audience and critics. In Vienna he was appointed imperial pianist.

It is said that he went to Weimar and Cassel to visit Liszt and Spohr in 1858. Spohr at that time was already ill and infirm, and as he says in his letters "usually very downhearted on account of my failing powers" he had given up his last pupils. This visit of Dreyschock's is not mentioned in Spohr's own writings.

A few years later, in 1862, (after having ceased his professional tours) at Anton Rubinstein's suggestion Dreyschock was appointed professor of the pianoforte at the newly erected Conservatoire of Music at St. Petersburg, and at the same time Director of the school of music for the operatic stage. He held this double post for six years only and was always ailing, the Russian climate apparently not agreeing with his delicate health. He was often obliged to ask for leave of absence to recruit his strength in the south.

He died of consumption at Venice on the 1st April 1869.

Many of his numerous pianoforte compositions are fascinating and brilliant, but possess no depth; his variations upon the British National Hymn "God save the Queen" are well known. His Opera "Florette oder die erste Liebe Heinrich's IV." was a dead failure.

JOHANN LADISLAUS DUSSEK.

JOHANN L. Dussek's life as a musician was most interesting and stirring. He was of great distinction in his day, and a number of his compositions are still highly appreciated.

He was born on the 9th February 1761, at Tschaslau in Bohemia. In early youth he became a chorister; he was destined for a literary career and was brought up in the Jesuit Colleges at Iglau and Kuttenberg. At this time he was so far advanced in music that he was able to play the organ. He then

removed to the University of Prague to study theo-
logy. When there, he determined to become a monk,
but his influential patron and his love for art seem
to have prevented him from carrying out his intention. He left the University with the title of "Bachelor
of music". Under Count Männer's patronage he devoted his time to the study of music and through the
Count's influence he was appointed organist at Mecheln,
and after leaving this post he accepted a similar one
at Bergen op Zoom.

In 1782, he went to Amsterdam, where he established
his reputation as a pianist and composer; for twelve
months he was tutor to the sons of the Stattholder
William V. of Orange at the Hague.

He left there in consequence of the war in the
Netherlands, and travelled to Hamburg where Philipp
Emanuel Bach received him warmly and encouraged
him to continue his pianoforte studies. Afterwards
he made his appearance as pianist in several cities,
especially in Berlin and St. Petersburg. He accompanied Prince Radziwill to Litthauen where he remained for two years. He went to Paris in 1876,
where he played before the ill-fated Queen, Marie
Antoinette; from there he went to Italy returning
again to Paris, but left in consequence of the revolution, going to London, where he established himself
in a music business with his father-in-law by name
Corri. But the times were bad, and the firm became
bankrupt. In 1800, Dussek went to Hamburg, where
he formed a romantic attachment to a lady there, remaining with her for two years.

After visiting his home in 1802, he travelled to
Magdeburg and visited the musical Prince Louis
Ferdinand, who retained him as his pianist until the
tie was severed by the death of the unhappy Prince.
His "Elegie harmonique" witten on the death of the
Prince forms one of the most beautiful and pathetic

works for the pianoforte. A Prince of Isenburg then took an interest in Dussek, whereupon he became conductor in the chapel of Prince Tallyrand at Paris in 1808. The prince esteemed him highly and left him much leisure time for composing. He died on the 20th March 1812, at St. Germain-en-Laye near Paris.

Dussek understood the art of eliciting rich, full melody from the piano, and wherever he went his style of playing met with great appreciation. For the piano he has composed 12 Concertos, 1 Double Concerto, 53 Sonatas for 2 hands, 9 Duets, 10 Trios, 1 Quartet, 1 Quintet as well as numerous minor pieces; a valuable book of instruction for the piano which appeared in three editions (English, French, and German) and 80 Sonatas for the violin.

HEINRICH EHRLICH.

ALTHOUGH Ehrlich some years ago exchanged the career of a musician for that of literature and has made a name as a very clever writer, yet before this period he was a virtuoso and teacher of no mean repute.

Born at Vienna in 1822, he became the pupil of men of note,—Thalberg, Bocklet, and Henselt; Sechter instructing him in the art of composition.

He made long tours and then became Pianist to King George V. at Hanover where he remained several years. In the year 1858, he removed to Berlin, and played at various concerts with much success. He was considered an excellent player of

Beethoven's compositions. From the years 1864 to 1872, he was teacher of the pianoforte at the Stern Conservatoire; in 1886, he was appointed teacher for the second time at this institute of music. Mannstädt, Marsop, Nagel, Spiro, F. Dreyschock and others are mentioned as his pupils.

His compositions for the piano include 12 Etudes, Variations and 1 Concerto in the Hungarian style. He also published Tausig's Etudes, and was the author of a treatise "How to practise the piano".

ALBERT EIBENSCHÜTZ.

ACCORDING to all critics this pianist is distinguished for his brilliant execution, soft precise touch, (as charming when playing "Forte" as "Piano") rhythmical precision and grace in his performance; but his speciality was grace and beauty of expression, combined with richness of tone. All his visits to Leipzig, Dresden, Hanover, Brunswick, Magdeburg, Darmstadt and Cologne have proved very successful.

Albert Eibenschütz was born in Berlin in 1857. His father, a native of Hungary was an opera singer, and his mother an Italian, née Marochetti, was a concert singer. Thus in his childhood he had the advantage of good elementary musical instruction. In consequence of his parents' life being an unsettled one, he was chiefly brought up at Frankfort by his grandmother, a singer formerly in Russia. He had an excellent teacher in Professor Sachs.

In 1874, he went to the Conservatoire at Leipzig where Professors Reinecke and Paul were his teachers. After two years spent in study he left the conservatoire with this certificate, "one of the best and most distinguished pupils".

From the years 1876—1880, he lived at Charkow, as a pianoforte performer and teacher, then he was appointed to teach at the Leipzig Conservatoire. He exchanged this position in 1883, for a similar one at the Cologne Conservatoire. When applying for the position he played Brahms' Concerto in Bflat. His concert tours commenced from the year 1887.

In 1891, he became Director of the choral society for mixed voices at Mülheim on the Rhine, and has recently undertaken the conductorship of the Cologne "Liederkranz" (a choir for male voices consisting of 200 members) he has however not given up his position as teacher at the Conservatoire.

ILONA EIBENSCHÜTZ.

ABOUT twelve years ago this youthful prodigy, who was born at Budapest on the 8th May 1872, appeared for the first time as a pianoforte performer and having received the best instruction is now justly admired as a pianiste. She was first taught music by her brother Albert when four and a half years old, somewhat later by Carl Marek, and from her sixth year by Hans Schmitt at the Vienna Conservatoire.

In 1878 she played for the first time in public in Vienna and created a sensation. Being further educated until she attained the age of twelve, she spent three or four months of every year in Austrian, German, French, Danish, Swedish, Norwegian and Russian towns playing at concerts. As a matter of course, numbers of people took great interest in this wonderful child, who although so young in years could perform difficult music with unusual proficiency. She played before the Queen in Copenhagen, and before the Czar and Czarina at Gatschina, in Vienna before the Emperor and in Pesth before Liszt. When in Vienna, she received an Imperial stipend for four years.

With increasing years she keenly realised her lack of musical education. Fortunately for her she secured the interest of the best teacher, Clara Schumann at Frankfort-on-the-Main, and for nearly five years she had the advantage of her instruction, an aristocratic Frankfort family defraying the expenses of her studies. In November 1889 Clara Schumann described her in the certificate handed to her as "a highly gifted, clever artiste".

She then re-commenced her concert-tours, and whereever she appeared all those who had heard her as a child noticed with glad surprise the great improvement in her performance, the result of several years additional hard work. She now played the compositions of Bach, Mozart, Beethoven, Scarlatti, Schumann, Chopin, Liszt, Brahms &c. with technical perfection and intelligence.

For the last four years she has taken part ten or twelve times every season at the Monday Popular Concerts in London, with Joseph Joachim, and for the last two years she has performed with equal success at Leipzig, Cologne, Vienna. Now in 1893 she purposes going to America.

ANNETTE ESSIPOFF.

AMONG living pianoforte players Annette Essipoff occupies one of the most prominent positions. Classical musicians such as Bach, Mozart, and Beethoven, and the modern composers Hummel, Chopin, Schumann, Mendelssohn and Liszt find in her an excellent exponent of their works.

She was born on the 1st February 1851, at St. Petersburg and was the daughter of a functionary (a court counsellor). She inherited her father's love of music, and he gave her her first musical instruction; then Wielopolski the pianoforte teacher of the French boarding-school where she was educated became her

master. In her fourteenth year she went to the
Conservatoire at St. Petersburg for further cultivation, and was taught by Professor Leschetitzky.
Having a rich and full voice she was advised by
Anton Rubinstein to devote herself to singing, whereas
Leschetitzky persuaded her to adhere to the career
which she had already chosen and for which she was
preparing, and she followed his advice. Leschetitzky
devoted all posssible care to her and corrected her
style of playing which was rather too unrestrained.
In her childhood she had the habit of playing impromptu all kinds of music which she had once heard
or tried. Not being allowed to do so openly at the
Conservatoire she did it secretly in her teacher's absence, proud of the applause of her companions. Professor Leschetitzky once passing the class room and
hearing music listened, and heard with astonishment
Liszt's Rhapsodies and other technically difficult pieces
being played wildly in the room.

He opened the door, and surrounded by a circle
of attentive listeners he espied Annette sitting at the
piano playing. Very angrily he put an end to this
practice once for all, and forced Annette to adhere
to very strict rules, which proved a great hardship to
her. But at last his firmness and her energy and
self-conquest gained the victory. She passed her
examination brilliantly and from this time, 1872, travelled far and wide playing at many places with
great success.

Professor Leschetitzky kept her continually in
sight and took the greatest interest in her, and in
1880, she became his wife. They took up their residence in Vienna.

JOHN FIELD.

JOHN Field was as original in art as in his ordinary
every day life, displaying a mixture of geniality,
hearty good-humour, and excentricity which is seldom
to be met with. The following remarks of Franz Liszt
uttered with regard to his performance and artistic
qualities may not be out of place here. "He forms
one of those particular types of the old school which
are only to be met with in certain periods of art;
when, having become acquainted with their resources,

they have not so far exhausted them as to be
tempted to extend their province further, and to
reveal themselves more freely; whereby they have
singed their wings more than once by attempting to
get rid of their fetters."

Being Clementi's favourite pupil, the great master
imparted to him the secret of the most beautiful execution which that epoch could boast of, and bestowed a species of poetry upon it which has caused him
to be regarded as an inimitable master of natural
grace, melancholy naïveté, freedom and simplicity.
Liszst in his edition of Field's Nocturnes says in the
preface: "Field's Nocturnes always seem new among
so much that has become old-fashioned; thirty-six
years have gone by since they were first published
and yet a balmy and delightful freshness still pervades
them. No such rare originality can be met with elsewhere. Since Field's time no one has been capable
of expressing himself in such a touching and heart-felt
manner, it affects the listener in many ways, now like
a tender glance and then like the gentle rocking of
a boat or the swaying of a hammock; we almost
hear gentle kisses dying away in a soft whisper. No
one but Field ever conceived such marvellous harmonies akin to the Aeolian harp such halfbreathed
sighs floating and fading away in the air. What inexhaustible richness and variety exist throughout
these Nocturnes; the composer's imagination was full
of beauty".

Field's Nocturnes were also Chopin's models, and
more than anything else helped to establish Field's
fame; but the same remark may be equally applied
to his Caprices, Variations, and Rondos.

He was born at Dublin, July 16th 1782. His father
played the violin, his grandfather was an organist;
in later years he relates that his own childhood was
quite a sad one,—both his father and grandfather

having in the roughest manner spurred him on in
pianoforte playing; so that in fact, on one occasion he
ran away from home in despair, not returning until
compelled to do so by dire distress. His father then
took him to Clementi who certainly taught him until
his 22nd year, but through all these years in London
as well as at St. Petersburg, made use of him in his
music-shop as a salesman, making him show off the
beauties of the various instruments to the intending
purchasers by his playing. This fact is also mentioned
by Spohr in his diary. Writing among other
things of Clementi's stay in St. Petersburg, he says;
"Clementi often invited me to have a game of billiards
after dinner. In the evening I sometimes accompanied
him to his large pianoforte-warehouse, where Field
had to play for hours in order to exhibit the instruments to their best advantage. I still have a vivid
remembrance of the pale, overgrown youth, whom I
never saw again. When Field who had grown out
of his clothes sat down before the piano, his long
arms stretched over the keyboard, so that his sleeves
appeared far too short, and his whole figure looked
awkward and English; but as soon as his beautiful
playing began, all was forgotten in listening. Unfortunately I could only express my sympathy and
gratitude to him by a mute clasp of his hand, as,
with the exception of his native tongue he could
speak no other. Many anecdotes were related even
at that time of the rich Clementi's meanness and
avarice, which in later years when I met him in
London, had greatly increased. Thus, on all sides
it was reported that Field was kept very close by
his teacher, and was forced to purchase the advantage of his instruction by much denial and self-
sacrifice. I witnessed a proof of Clementi's real
Italian nearness, when one day I found teacher and
pupil with turned-up sleeves before a wash-tub

7*

busily engaged in washing stockings and other articles of attire."

From this we can easily believe that Field's younger days were very devoid of sunshine, and it would appear as if Clementi's behaviour towards him increased in some measure Field's habitual shyness and misanthropy. He remained a long time in St. Petersburg with his master, not returning to England till 1832, and exciting the same enthusiasm in London as he had done in the Russian capital. He then made concert-tours through Belgium, France, and Italy. In Naples he suffered severely from a nervous disease, and when convalescent travelled with a Russian family to Moscow, where he died on the 11th January, 1837.

In his unexampled perseverance in practising he resembled Paganini, never resting until he had conquered the greatest technical difficulties by repeating the passage hundreds of times. It was no rare occurrence for him to play a specially difficult piece two hundred times in succession, sitting stiff and motionless the whole time, merely moving his long pointed fingers. He laid a coin on the back of his right hand which, by steadying it, while playing, prevented its falling. Another peculiarity of his was to place a box full of counters before him, and with every repetition he would extract a counter, not ceasing his exercise until the box was empty. His playing was always gentle and soothing, without brilliancy; but with increasing years it became powerless and apathetic on account of his nervousness which increased to an infirmity. He grew old early in life, and was always very shy and embarrassed. All applause displeased and disturbed him, and he was even known to leave off playing suddenly if it became too loud, but his performance gained in life and beauty when silence reigned.

His seuse of humour never forsook him. In Moscow, when on account of the use of strong tobacco and the habit of drinking punch, his health was quite broken up, he was asked by his hospitable hostess who had taken compassion upon him on his return from Italy, whether he were a Fatalist or Calvinist he replied "Neither, a pianist!"

He paid but little attention to his appearance, his usual covering being an enormous bear-skin even when playing in public, but when he drew the sweetest tones from his instrument, all this was entirely forgotten in listening to him.

His compositions consist of 30 Nocturnes, 7 Concertos, 4 Sonatas, 1 Quintet, many Variations, Rondos, both solos and duets, Capriccios, Divertissements &c.

ROBERT FISCHHOF.

LIKE his uncle Joseph Fischhof, who was teacher at the Vienna Conservatoire from the year 1833, and was an excellent pianist, Robert Fischhof received his musical education in Vienna, and his successful studies have enabled him to surround his name with fresh interest. He was born in Vienna in the year 1857, not 1858, as we are told in more modern biographies, and was taught the pianoforte at the Conservatoire in Vienna by Professor A. Door, and composition by R. Fuchs, Krenn and Bruckner.

After completing his course at the Conservatoire,

he continued his study of the pianoforte with Franz Liszt. In his seventeenth year he appeared for the first time in public, and from that time travelled almost uninterruptedly for several years, playing in numerous Concerts in Europe under the direction of celebrated musicians, such as Abt, Dessoff, Reinecke, Hiller, Gade, Svendsen; he performed in the Leipzig Gewandhaus in 1883. He had also the honour of playing several times at European courts in Prussia, Austria, Denmark, and Sweden.

In 1884, he was appointed Professor of the finishing class at the Vienna Conservatoire, and still holds this position. In latter years as a pianist he has only performed his own compositions publicly, among other pieces his pianoforte concerto two years ago in Paris, and last year in the Philharmonic Hall in Berlin. Compositions of his have been published in Vienna, Berlin and Paris.

ROBERT FREUND.

ALTHOUGH Robert Freund completed his musical education about fifteen years ago, he did not appear in large German towns like Berlin, Leipzig &c. as a pianist until the year 1890, but he did not adhere to this restless career. Taught by the most important pianists, Moscheles, Liszt, Tausig, he has become, as critics also acknowledge "a master of his instrument" and unites to his artistic knowledge the most careful execution, a lovely touch, and great expression and intelligence in his performance; he has never troubled himself about external effects, but conscious of his aim, devotes himself to the spreading of classical and modern music, confining himself to narrower spheres, having been able to display his capabilities as a solo player of the first order several times in the Berlin Singakademie, and in the Leipzig Liszt Society.

Robert Freund was born at Budapest in 1852. His first pianoforte teacher was J. Huber. When 13 years old he went to the Conservatoire at Leipzig, where Moscheles and Coccius gave him instruction on the pianoforte, and Richter and Papperitz in theory. After completing five years of study there, he worked for another twelve months with Karl Tausig, in Berlin; to whom according to his own assertion he is "mostly indebted". From the years 1870—1872 during the winter months he was fortunate enough to have the advantage of Liszt's teaching in Budapest.

Through an influential friend of his, Weber, in Switzerland, he received the post of pianoforte teacher in a rich manufacturer's family in Wesserling (Alsatia) from 1872—1874; then he was appointed teacher of the piano at the School of Music at Zurich, founded in 1876, which position he still retains. He has educated a number of clever pupils, and takes part in the orchestral concerts as well as in the concerts of chamber-music at Zurich with considerable success, playing with great intelligence the works of classical as well as of more modern composers, Schumann, Liszt, Brahms, Saint-Saëns, Huber, Chopin, Grieg. He has composed and published Preludes, 1 Notturne, 2 Impromptus and Songs.

ARTHUR FRIEDHEIM.

STRUGGLING against all kinds of obstacles and fighting against innumerable difficulties, Friedheim has attained an important position in the profession.

In the beginning of his career in 1884, he achieved a triumph in Liszt's presence at the Blüthner Saal at Leipzig. Later on when he met the great pianist again in Pesth Liszt condemned his playing, but at last was forced to acknowledge it, and tried to assist the young and persevering musician, who merited the praise accorded him by his critics, his performance being described as distinguished by an extraordinarily well-developed execution, a wonderful touch, great exactitude, rare power and truth of expression.

Born in St. Petersburg on the 26th October 1859, Friedheim lost his father when very young and with his mother was assisted by wealthy relations who provided for his education. He began his musical studies in his eighth year, and in the following year he appeared in public, playing Field's Concerto in A-flat, in his tenth year he played Karl Maria von Weber's Concertstück, and was termed a musical genius. But in the meantime he had to pass his examination at the Academy. From this period (1877) he devoted his time exclusively to music, but his relatives suddenly losing their fortune he was harassed by pecuniary difficulties. He commenced his concert-tours, and went to Pesth where he was unkindly received by Liszt. He then accepted appointments as conductor to small provincial travelling companies. In 1880, when in Weimar he was again introduced to Liszt by the Councillor Gille from Jena, who criticized him rather more favourably, but it was only after much further aimless wandering, that he was allowed to play before the Court at Weimar in Liszt's presence. From this time the latter kept Friedheim with him, accompanied him on his journeys, and at last with Liszt's recommendation went to Paris, but being a German he was entirely ignored. In 1882, he was induced by an agent to go to London, but he never even succeeded in giving a trial of his musical powers there.

With much trouble and in great distress he returned to Paris, where Saint-Saëns recommended him to a rich man who assisted him in so far that he was enabled to give a concert. But the French again soon got rid of this hated German, and full of disappointment he was obliged to leave Paris in 1883.

Some years later he went to Vienna, where Liszt was then staying. He recommended him warmly to Bösendorfer and at last Friedheim was successful, and his concerts met with applause. He then travelled to North Germany and established his reputation as one of the best pianoforte players of the present age in Berlin, and in Leipzig where he conducted a series of concerts in the Crystal Palace with the Weimar orchestra. He has now been in New York for some time and seems to have taken up his residence there.

ARABELLA GODDARD.

THIS artiste is not only considered one of the most important English pianists, but she is also looked upon altogether as one of the best performers; and having played in nearly every country she has made a world-wide reputation. She was born at St. Servans, near St. Malo in France, on the 12th January, 1838, received instruction in Paris from Kalkbrenner and in London from Thalberg, and Mrs. Anderson, and in 1850, performed for the first time in public in the latter city in Her Majesty's Theatre, playing at a concert got up by the composer Balfe. Then on Thalberg's recommendation she received lessons from J. W. Davison, who gave her a special insight into the works of the great classical masters and contributed to the depth and evenness of her playing. She married him in 1860; and was left a widow in 1885.

In the London musical world Arabella Goddard made a name by introducing classical works; for instance she was the first to play Beethoven's Sonata in B-flat op. 106 in London with brilliant success. In England she has always been a very great favourite, and as a pianist for a long time performed at the famous Monday Popular Concerts, which in England means a-first rate position among pianists.

From the years 1873—1876 she made a voyage round the world, giving numerous concerts in America, the East Indies and Australia.

LOUIS MORITZ GOTTSCHALK.

BORN on the 8th May 1829, at New Orleans, (America) Gottschalk, when a boy, came to Paris to be educated as a pianoforte player. Camille Marie Stamaty who taught Saint-Saëns among others is said to have been his teacher there, yet Chopin and Hallé are also mentioned as his teachers. In the year 1845, (according to other reports not until 1847) he appeared as a concert-performer for the first time in Paris, and showed decided talent, which enabled him to undertake long and successful journeys through France, Switzerland and Spain. In 1853, he returned to America, and for several years in succession gave concerts in the Eastern States. In 1865, he travelled to San Francisco, and from there to South America where he remained several years, and met with great success by the execution of his own somewhat sentimental compositions on the Spanish National melody.

As success in the other hemisphere depends very much upon making a brilliant effect Gottschalk met with great approval, as his technical abilities were great and his execution marvellous. He was also a good drawing-room performer and understood the art of pleasing even connoiseurs of music.

During a long residence in Rio de Janeiro he fell ill, and died in the year 1869.

EDWARD HAGERUP GRIEG.

Educated in Germany and by German teachers in an entirely German musical style, Grieg belongs to that race of hardy Scandinavians, who, (like Björnson in literature), try in a somewhat original and exceptional manner to bring their northern character to bear upon art. They are of opinion that Norway is important enough to claim a national speciality and in the same way in which they make their mark in politics by their obstinacy and cool Northern tenacity, labouring in absolute independence, they also claim to have originated a new school of their own in literature and art. The question is, whether such a universal art as music can be forced into narrow limits, without its becoming one-sided and losing its value; and with special regard to this so-called northern school it is very doubtful if it will prove a lasting one. All peculiarities are commonly short-lived. The continual monotony of the north, which, is very apparent in the "Peer Gynt" Suite, often savours of bad taste and soon becomes intolerable to the listener.

Grieg was born at Bergen in Norway, on the 15th June 1843. His mother was a pianist, and from her he received his first musical instruction. Later on in the year 1858, at Ole Bull's instigation he was sent to the Leipzig Conservatoire where Moscheles, Reinecke, Hauptmann, Richter and Wenzel, taught him each in his own particular branch of study. It was rather a concession to his country than an urgent necessity which caused him, after the completion of his thorough education to go to Niels W. Gade, in Copenhagen, for further study. During this time he made the acquaintance of a young Norwegian composer, Rikard Nordraak, whose influence he acknowledges in the following words: "It was as if the scales fell from my eyes; from him I first learnt the music of the northern people and got to know my own nature. We abjured the effeminate Scandinavianism of Gade and Mendelssohn, and enthusiastically founded a new Northern school which still exists." Nordraak did not adhere long to this new school, as he died shortly after making Grieg's acquaintance.

In the year 1867, the latter established a Musical Union in Christiania, for the special propagation of the "northen school", such as Björnson also attempted with regard to the drama but apparently without success. In addition to this he composed diligently and performed his own works. Twice in 1865, and

Celbr. Pianists.   8

1870, he was in Germany and Italy. He met Liszt in Rome, but the southern and northern natures were not in sympathy with each other. He was repeatedly in Leipzig, and in the year 1879 performed his pianoforte concerto, op. 16 in the Gewandhaus.

From the year 1880, he took up his abode at Bergen, frequently paying visits to England and Germany, and on such occasions was often heard as a pianist, generally playing his own works.

He has composed a great deal for the piano, which has been published under the Opus numbers, 1, 3, 6, 9, 11, 12, 14, 15, 16, 17, 19, 24, 28, 29, 35, 37, 38; the most important are the two suites arranged for the piano from the music to Ibsen's Drama "Peer Gynt", a pianoforte concerto in A-minor, symphonic pieces, Norwegian dances, Valses-Caprices, and Elegiac-Melodies. He also composed Sonatas for the piano and violin; Sonatas for the violoncello; 1 String-Quartet (one of his best works, although very little played), orchestral works, cantatas, songs &c.

ALFRED GRÜNFELD.

A Pianist in the highest sense of the word, Grünfeld belongs to those masters of the instrument, who, versed in all styles and with equally great technical proficiency and mental penetration are able to perform Beethoven, Mozart, Schubert, Chopin, Liszt, Schumann, Mendelssohn and Brahms.

Therefore the programmes of his numerous concerts form a kind of Genesis of pianoforte music. For instance, at one of his most recent concerts given in Vienna, which took place in the spacious hall of the Musical Society, the following pieces were announced in his programme; Mendelssohn's Prelude and Fugue in C-minor, Beethoven's Rondo in G, Leschetitzky's "Siciliana all' Antica", Schubert's Impromptu in G, Dvořáks "Plauderei" from op. 85, Grieg's Ballad in the form of Variations on a Norwegian

Melody, Schumann's Etudes Symphoniques, Chopin's "Nocturno" in E, and Waltz in E-minor, Schubert-Liszt's "Lebewohl", Lamberg's "valse expressive", Gotthard's "Sarabande" and his own compositions, a Hungarian Rhapsody and "Tanzarabeske"; these pieces were all played in succession.

Edward Hanslick made the following remarks in reference to Grünfeld. "He is a musician beyond criticism; in public and in private one of the best known members of Vienna Society, and the greatest favourite with all musical people. By his brilliant playing as well as his sweet expression and gay humour, he understands to perfection the art of charming his listeners in Vienna."

Alfred Grünfeld is a German Bohemian, and was born at Prague on the 4th July, 1852. He received his first musical education at the Prague Conservatory, where Hoyer gave him instruction on the piano. Then he became Th. Kullak's pupil in Berlin. At an early age he began to travel and soon attracted the sympathy and attention of all pianoforte lovers and also that of the critics. Some years ago he gave a great number of concerts in America with the greatest success. After performing at a court-concert in Berlin he received the title of Pianist to the Emperor. He had his fixed residence in Vienna, and was appointed Imperial Pianist in that city, and in that capacity he frequently takes part in concerts at the court. The Emperor Franz Joseph esteems him highly, continually praising his "wonderful piano".

Grünfeld has also made himself of repute as a composer for the piano, having written several effective pieces.

SIR CHARLES HALLÉ.

A German called "Karl Halle" was born at Hagen in Westphalia, on the 11th April 1819, but as he afterwards settled at Paris and gained a reputation there both as pianoforte performer and teacher, he changed his name by adding a French termination to it. His father was a conductor, and gave him good instruction in music, which was carried on in the year 1835, by the old organist Johann Christian Heinrich Rinck at Darmstadt. A year later the young musician went to Paris, where he was in touch with prominent men like Cherubini, Kalkbrenner, Berton, Chopin and Liszt, which was of infinite advantage to him as a pianist. He was soon busily occupied particularly

as a favourite pianoforte teacher. Together with
Alard and Franchomme he originated Chamber-Music
Soirées in the small room of the Paris Conservatoire,
which were much patronized by the musical public.

In the year 1848, Hallé removed to London
where in May of the same year he excited much
interest at a Covent Garden Concert by the performance of Beethoven's concerto in E flat, which obtained him a great number of pupils.

In 1850 he went to Manchester to undertake the
conductorship of the "Gentlemen's Concerts". In this
city under the title of "Charles Hallé's Orchestra" he
organized a Society of his own, which from its excellent character heightened the reputation of its
founder. With this orchestra he arranged many
subscription concerts which were very well attended.

Yet he did not on this account relinquish his
musical duties in London, but gave Piano Recitals
in St. James' Hall every season, at which both classical
and modern compositions were performed. He also
took part in the Monday Popular Concerts for many
years, and is considered an excellent Beethoven performer, or rather a conscientious exponent of his
works. Hallé's perseverance was of great advantage
to him in making him popular in England, a country
where the above quality is highly esteemed, and this
may be the cause of his receiving such high praise
as a player of Beethoven's productions. For 30 years
the public in England listened to Hallé's rendering
of Beethoven, and were satisfied to acquire their
knowledge of this great composer through his playing.

In 1890—1801, he went on a tour to Australia
with his wife, the excellent violinist Madame Neruda
(Lady Hallé), which proved both artistically and
financially, a great success.

STEPHEN HELLER.

ROBERT Schumann, whose keen perception and high sense of art has opened up a path to many men of excellent talents, considered Heller at the beginning of his career to be "a great and imaginative musician", and in the "Neue Zeitschrift für Musik" declared, when discussing his Etude, opus 11, that they contained enough clever ideas to supply a number of Parisian composers for a long time. Indeed the time soon came when his celebrity as a pianoforte player was less esteemed than his talents as a composer. As the latter he has gained a high position and is accounted a real musical genius.

His numerous pianoforte compositions are celebrated for their originality, grace and elegance. With his harmony he occupies a higher position than

Chopin, and his brilliancy and strength of thought are superior to Mendelssohn, but much inferior to Schumann.

Heller was born on the 15th May 1814. Displaying at an early age both inclination and talent for music, his father, who lived at Pesth sent him to Vienna, where Anton Halm became his teacher. In the year 1827, he appeared in public in Vienna and in 1829, his father accompanied him on his first tour to Hamburg; but he appears to have reckoned too much on his son's physical powers; the boy was taken ill on his return journey at Augsburg, where he was nursed and remained until his twenty-fourth year, when he left for Paris. Like Hallé he met many musical celebrities there and established a good reputation as concert-performer and pianoforte-teacher. He composed very many works, but for some considerable time was not able to meet with success with his compositions, as they in many respects deviated from the uniform rules of composition. R. Schumann, by his critical reference with regard to Heller's works has done much to make them known.

The number of his compositons amounts to 150; but many are often included under one title; for instance, opus 150, contains 20 preludes. His works include Sonatas, Sonatinas, Nocturnos, Ballads, Caprices, Scherzos, Etudes, Tarantelles, Valses, Country Dances, Mazurkas, "Blumen-, Frucht- und Dornenstücke", "Wanderstücke", "Kinderscenen" &c.

ADOLF VON HENSELT.

THE great support which Henselt in his youth received from King Ludwig of Bavaria, was in
every respect well-earned and deserved; Henselt
was born on the 12th of May, 1814. After the instruction which he received from Frau von Fladt at
Munich, and which succeeded that of Hummel at
Weimar, he developed into one of the most important
pianists, who followed the bent of his own ideas. In
fact he tried like Franz Liszt to play in a peculiar
manner by extending his hands as widely as possible,
and by dint of continual finger-exercises has attained
to great technical proficiency. One of the most reliable

critics of his time when speaking of him, says: "Henselt certainly received lessons from Hummel, but can scarcely be recognized as his pupil, for his style of playing was entirely different, being a combination of Hummel and Liszt. With steady hands and a powerful movement of his fingers he executed that which Liszt produced with his wrists and the use of the pedals. As Mendelssohn also informs us, his power consisted in his capacity to stretch long chords, for which purpose he continually practised arpeggios, playing them prestissimo." For an hour each day he practised these extensions invented by himself, which are scarcely worth mentioning, depending as they do upon an abnormal form of the hand. Nevertheless compositions of Liszt and Chopin were rendered by him in a splendid style. Schumann, Lenz and other competent judges reckon him among the most celebrated performers.

After he had left Weimar for Vienna, and had benefitted by Sechter's instruction in theory for several years, he began his concert-tours which gained him great reputation everywhere; in 1836, he was in Berlin, 1837, in Breslau, and in 1838, in St. Petersburg. In the last-mentioned city he found full scope for his great talent and attractive personality. After the first concert all the succeeding ones were besieged by the best society. He was appointed pianist to the Empress, and pianoforte teacher to the Imperial princes. Possessing an accomplished wife, a native of Silesia, he was still better liked at the strict and formal court of the Emperor Nicholas, and the superintendance of the musical instruction at the high school for girls in the Russian empire was entrusted to him, and as a special distinction he received the Wladimir Order of nobility, and the title "councillor of state".

An older biographer writing about Henselt and his style of playing, says: "his wonderful Legato which he strove to cultivate by means of continued study, his mastery of broad, full-toned chords which gives an orchestral impression to his performance, as well as his poetical, delicate and yet fresh and powerful manner of playing have raised him to great eminence as a pianist. In his compositions he holds himself aloof from everything that is ordinary, displaying a grace, naturalness and delicacy of expression emanating from the depths of his purely German nature. He never could quite overcome his shyness when appearing in public; only a small number of friends, acquaintances and relations heard him perform when in Germany."

This is also confirmed by Gerhard von Amyntor, a comrade of his son in Breslau, in an excellent essay on Henselt in the "Neue Blatt", in which he relates that Henselt when on a visit to his son was recognized in a public garden, and the military band performing there gave him an ovation which he managed to evade by escaping through a back-door with his two companions.

He died on the 10th October 1889, at his little country-seat at Warmbrunn.

Of his compositions, the pianoforte Concerto in F-minor, the Concert-Etudes op. 2 and 5, some drawing-room pieces, and paraphrases as well as a Trio are well-known. He has also published Weber's pianoforte works, and revised a selection of Cramer's Etudes.

HENRI HERZ.

Henri Herz no longer belongs to the more celebrated pianists and composers for the pianoforte
of modern times, but in the prime of his life was of
importance and more popular than most of his profession, especially in Paris. His rather easy and
superficial compositions are principally written and
intended for amateurs, and these pieces helped to form
a new style by the more careful treatment of technical work; the numerous Variations, Rondos, Fantasies, Divertissements &c. which he has written are
very effective and have become widely known.

Henri Herz was born at Vienna on the 4th January

1806; in his childhood his father removed to Coblenz, where he taught him the piano; the organist Hünten was also his teacher. He appeared in public when eight years old, and in the same year began composing, but without having acquired the necessary groundwork. His father was then wise enough to send him to Paris, where he succeeded in getting this lad of ten years old admitted into the Conservatoire where his elder brother Jacob Simon had also been taught. The boy was put into the pianoforte class under Pradher, and soon made such progress that he received the first prize at the Conservatoire. Dourlen taught him harmony and composition; in 1818, he published two easy pretty pieces "Air tyrolien varié" and "Rondo alla Cosacca" which met with a large demand. From that time he soon became popular as a composer and by his numerous concerts. It is said that he was greatly influenced by Moscheles. In the year 1831, he accompanied Lafond on a concert-tour in Germany, and in 1834, he went to England, where he excited much enthusiasm, thus being induced often to visit this country.

In 1846—1847 and 1849—1850, he travelled in all parts of America. In 1851, he wrote an account of these tours which were financially very profitable. As Professor of the pianoforte at the Paris Conservatoire, he obtained a great reputation by his sound instruction; as a pianist and composer he was completely put into the shade by better musicians, Chopin, Liszt, Steffen Heller &c. He has become known throughout the world as the originator of a very important pianoforte factory, in the large hall of which he gave many brilliant performances. but at first he lost money by this speculation. His journey round the world supplied him with fresh means; he then began pianoforte construction on his own account

and met with success. At the Exhibition in 1855,
his instruments which were equal to those of Pleyel
and Erard, received the first prize.

KARL HEYMANN.

KARL Heymann is well known as a thorough virtuoso, especially as he travelled with the violinist Wilhelmj on his tours.

He was born on the 6th October 1853, at Amsterdam, where his parents (German) were then residing. He received his musical training at the Cologne Conservatoire, which was still under the directorship of Ferdinand Hiller. He then went to Berlin, where one of the most thorough teachers of theory in modern times, Friedrich Kiel, instructed him in thorough-bass and composition. Unfortunately the teaching of this excellent school was put an end to by a lingering illness; the few compositions of his known are, a pianoforte Concerto, "Elfenspiel" and a Masquerade show a certain amount of promise.

In 1878, he was appointed pianoforte teacher at the Hoch Conservatoire at Frankfort-on-the-Main, but on account of the illness already mentioned he had to resign his post, and to give up his tours as a virtuoso.

FERDINAND HILLER.

THE reputation of this musician has in the first place become widely spread by his conductorship of the Gürzenich concerts, and the Rhenish Musical Festivals. Yet he has also been of influence as a pianist, (particularly as an exponent of Beethoven,) and composer, and by his association with the great men of the time has left his mark upon the history of music and modern musical life. There is scarcely one important musician of the last sixty years whom Hiller has not met at some time or other; Cherubini, Rossini, Meyerbeer, Mendelssohn, Schumann, Liszt, Chopin, Berlioz, Spohr, Hauptmann, Brahms, Bruch and others knew him intimately. Spohr in his

biography says that in the year 1857, when arriving at
Cologne on his journey to the Netherlands, Hiller gave
a brilliant dinner-party in his (Spohr's) honour, and
with great bravour performed one of his new compositions, a very difficult sonata for the pianoforte.
He also made Max Bruch acquainted with Spohr and
other notabilities; he has done a great deal for many
other young struggling musicians and composers, and
obtained recognition for many of them.

He was born on the 24th October 1811, at
Frankfort-on-the-Main, where one of the cleverest
teachers, Aloys Schmitt undertook his musical tuition;
Karl Vollweiler also instructing him. In 1825, he
was sent to Hummel at Weimar for further improvement. Two years later he went to Vienna, probably
with Siegfried Dehn, (born 1799) his senior by many
years; and here he is also said to have been introduced
to Beethoven, but as the great musician died on the
26th March 1827, this must be a mistake or else the
visit took place during Beethoven's last severe illness;
this can be of no moment with regard to music, as
Beethoven was scarcely accessible at this time.

The years 1828—1835, Hiller spent in Paris
giving concerts, and playing with the violinist
François Baillot at well-attended soirées; at this time
the latter was already fifty-seven years of age. For
several years Hiller was piano-teacher at Alexandre
Choron's "Conservatoire de musique, classique et
religieuse", finding an excellent opportunity there of
acquiring a more intimate knowledge of classical
masters. The July Revolution put an end to the
celebrated Choron institute. This was of little pecuniary consequence to Hiller as he belonged to a
very wealthy family, and had large means at his
disposal, being in no need of paid appointments.

The death of his father caused his return home
to Frankfort; here he undertook the conductorship

of the Cecilia Society succeeding Johann Nepomuk Schelble who had originated it. He then travelled to Italy and in 1839 at Milan, attempted the representation of his opera "Romilda" at the Scala; but the work met with cold reception, (which was also the fate of all his six operas). In 1840, he went to Leipzig, where he became very intimate with Mendelssohn, through whose influence his oratorio "The Destruction of Jerusalem" was performed at the Gewandhaus. He spent the following year in Rome, where he studied old church music.

In the winter 1843—1844, Mendelssohn procured him the conductorship of the Gewandhaus Concerts. In 1847, he became conductor at Dusseldorf; in 1850 he received a similar appointment at Cologne, also the task of organizing the conservatoire at the head of which he was then placed. At the same time he became Director of the Concert Society and Choir, two institutions which worked in conjunction with the Gürzenich concerts and the Renish Musical Festivals.

Hiller retained these influential positions until the 1st October 1884, and a short time after that died at Cologne on the 11th May 1885.

As a composer Hiller adhered somewhat to the styles of Schumann and Mendelssohn; he has produced over 200 works; among them, for the pianoforte 1 Concerto in F sharp minor, numerous Sonatas, Suites, Etudes, a number of books containing shorter compositions, both elegant and melodious. 1 Operette arranged as a Duet without words, 1 Suite 'in Canone' for the piano an violin; 3 Symphonies, several Overtures, Violin and Cello Sonatas, 3 Trios, 10 Quartets, 2 Oratorios, several Cantatas, Ballads for Solo, Chorus and Orchestra, Psalms, Anthems, Vocal Quartets and Songs &c.

Hiller was also a very productive musical author. His works are "Die Music und das Publikum",

9*

"Beethoven", "Mendelssohn - Bartholdy", "Aus dem Tonleben unserer Zeit", "Wie hören wir Music?", "Briefe und Erinnerungen", "Musikalisches und Persönliches" &c. He also gave lectures on the history of music in various towns, with illustrations on the piano.

The university of Bonn conferred the title of Doctor upon him.

JOHANN NEPOMUK HUMMEL.

IN his childhood Hummel's father took him on concert-tours for a long time, but he afterwards underwent further study and became one of the most celebrated performers on the pianoforte, of his time; in some measure he was the means of originating a new era, his playing and compositions forming a transition from the classical masters to modern professionalism.

He was born on the 14ᵗʰ November 1778, at Pressburg. After having benefitted by musical instruction at home, he was taken to Mozart at Vienna, who took great interest in him, and taught him for two years. From 1788—1795, he was obliged to go on tours to make money; he was then wise enough to go to Vienna for further cultivation, Albrechtsberger,

Salieri and Haydn becoming his teachers. When
Father Haydn on account of age and growing infirmity gave up the post of conductor to Prince
Esterhazy, the vacancy was offered to Hummel in
the year 1804, and he retained it until 1811. Then
for several years he remained in Vienna without
any fixed appointment, but gave lessons and composed; in 1816, he left the latter city for Stuttgart,
being appointed conductor there, but here the condition of music was at a very low ebb,—musicians
being treated more like servants, and on this account
Hummel resigned the post in 1820, and accepted a
similar one at the Grand Ducal Court at Weimar.
During the time spent at this court he often obtained
long leaves of absence which he used for the purpose
of making concert tours, visiting St. Petersburg,
Berlin, Leipzig, London &c., and attracted much
attention everywhere. His playing was brilliant, but is
said to have lacked warmth and passion. Exaggerated
admirers of his performance, especially Beethoven's
enemies, falsely asserted he was equal to the latter.
He played as he wrote. In Weimar he was much
sought after and highly esteemed by talented young
men, who since then have also become celebrated,
and was the recipient of more distinctions than many
of his artistic contemporaries. In some biographical
sketches referring to other matters, mention is also
made of Liszt's having received instruction from
Hummel in Weimar, but that the latter charged a
Louisd'or per lesson which was considered too high
a price. The years 1818—1821, are given as the
date of this scheme, but this is very doubtful,
as Liszt's father who alone was the moving agent in
the matter placed his son with Czerny in Vienna;
and even in 1823—1824, considered the boy, then
scarcely twelve-years old, superior to both Hummel
and Moscheles. Adam Liszt speaks of Hummel's

avarice in a letter which he wrote to Czerny from Paris on the 14th August 1825, in which he says: "Hummel when in Paris may have expected more remuneration than he actually realised; at first he asked too much, having an imperfect knowledge of the French people, and put too high a price on his services. For one Soirée he asked 30 Louisd'ors, but unfortunately no one was inclined to give such terms, finally he would have been glad enough of 10 or 5, but no one offered so much."

In the latter years of his life Hummel suffered much from ill-health which necessitated his frequent resort to watering places. He died on the 17th October 1837, at Weimar. His wife was an opera-singer, Elisabeth Röckl.

He composed 124 works, mostly for the piano, everything very conventional, and carefully worked out. Among them are 7 Concertos, 5 Solo pianoforte Sonatas and 3 Sonatas as Duets, 1 Fantasia for pianoforte with orchestra, 6 pianoforte Trios, Rondos, Caprices, Fantasies, Variations, Etudes, 1 pianoforte Quintett, 1 Sinfonie concertante for piano and violin, 1 Serenade for piano, guitar, clarionet, and Fagot, 3 String-quartets, the celebrated Septet, 1 Overture, 5 Masses, 1 Graduale, 1 Offertory 4 Operas, cantatas and Ballets &c.

ALFRED JAELL.

JAELL came into repute as a virtuoso in consequence of a number of tours which he began as a so-called prodigy, but he has been eclipsed by pianoforte performers (of deeper artistic temperament) of more modern times.

Alone, and also accompanied by his wife (née Trautmann) a clever pianist, and since the year 1854 with Carlotta Patti, he has repeatedly visited Germany, but excited less enthusiasm there than in Italy and France.

Born on the 5th March 1832, at Triest, he was destined in his childhood to become a violinist, but in his sixth year he began the piano and made rapid progress. From 1843 he was taken on concert-tours through Italy and the South of France, and with great success. In 1845, he went to Brussels, completed his studies, and visited Holland. Two years later he appeared for the first time in Paris, and his clever and elegant playing met with brilliant success. The Parisians have always been real friends and admirers of his.

After the outbreak of the revolution in February 1848, he started on a long concert-tour to America, where he met with a good reception and remained several years. He then visited Germany, Poland, and Russia. He also received the distinction of being appointed Pianist to the Hanoverian Court. Then he spent some time in Leipzig. In 1860 he was constantly travelling in France and Holland, 1864, to 1865 with Carlotta Pattti, re-appearing in Germany and visiting Vienna.

His success in Italy was still more brilliant. The French welcomed him anew and most enthusiastically when in 1870 he showed his sympathy for them, but in a manner which had little in common with art. His death took place on the 27th Febry. 1882.

As a composer he has produced Drawing-room pieces, Fantasies, and Transcriptions full of brilliancy, but lacking in depth. His wife is also the composer of several works: a concerto in D, a pianoforte quartet, 1 book of dances etc.

RAFAEL JOSEFFY.

BORN in 1852, at Pressburg Joseffy was taught in the best manner conceivable at the Leipzig Conservatoire, where Karl Reinecke, acknowledged as one of the most excellent teachers of the pianoforte as well as of composition, superintended his studies, and he is mentioned as being one of Reinecke's best pupils.

He then went to Berlin, and following in the footsteps of Karl Tausig, and under his guidance he soon became a virtuoso capable of mastering the most difficult technical work, able to vie with the best pianoforte performers of his time. He was a great favourite on the continent, and understood the art of converting the favour he met with into money by turning his footsteps towards America— the gold country of all virtuosos. New York remains his residence, in which city he takes part in important concerts with great success and is also active as a teacher.

He has composed some pieces for the piano which are distinguished for their smoothness, fullness of tone, and facility of execution.

FRIEDRICH WILHELM MICHAEL KALKBRENNER.

THE date of birth of this virtuoso is not known for certain, but he was born in the year 1784, when his parents were on their way to Berlin, and in those days when travelling could only be accomplished by easy stages the registration of baptisms was not so strictly enforced as at present. His father Christian, was an important musician occupying the post of conductor at the Prussian Court, which he afterwards vacated and removed to Paris, being engaged there at the Grand Opera, and dying in 1806. Young

Kalkbrenner received his first instruction in Paris from Adam at the Conservatoire, and from Catel in theory. In 1803, his father sent him to Vienna to study the German school, but he did not return to Paris until the death of his father made the homeward journey necessary. He appeared in that city with great success as a pianist, and a number of pupils thronged to him.

He lived in London from the year 1814—1823 where in 1818 he joined Logier, the inventor of the practical, but not very valuable "Chiroplast" (a machine for the hand when playing) and shared the profits of the patent. In 1823, he made a tour through Germany with the harpist Dizier, and again settled in Paris in 1824. The wife of the pianoforte manufacturer Pleyel had been his pupil and in consequence of this, he was made partner in that celebrated firm.

It is said to have been Kalkbrenner who offered Chopin his services as teacher, and Chopin in a letter which he wrote about him certainly said, that Henri Herz as a performer could not compare with him, yet he seems to have also been of Mendelssohn's opinion, that personally he could learn nothing from him. A somewhat severe musical contemporary describes him as having been very vain, and that he made use of doubtful means to establish his reputation. Once in 1834, he visited Professor Marx in Berlin and complained that the good old art of improvising had nearly gone out of fashion, for with the exception of Hummel, he, as he asserted was the only musician who still practised it. Whereupon he seated himself at the piano and played for a quarter of an hour all sorts of pieces pell-mell, in order to give a good impression of himself in thus improvising. Another day Marx received some new works from Paris, and among them was one of Kalkbrenner's compositions: Effusio Musica—and in it the supposed impromptu stood note for note as he had played it.

Until a short time before his death, which resulted from cholera, and took place on the 10th June 1849, at Enghien, Kalkbrenner was engaged in literary work. His last book was on the theory of harmony "Traité d'harmonie du pianist" (1849); a Pianoforte School "Méthode pour aprendre le pianoforte à l'aide du guide - mains" (under which title the famous "Chiroplast" is meant). His aim was to promote the best possible finger proficiency without the use of the arm. He wrote special pieces for the left hand only, the Sonata op. 42. He has published numerous pianoforte compositions in an easy, light style: Fantasies, Caprices, Variations &c. and besides these several other larger and more important works, Concertos, Rondos, Sonatas, Trios, Quartets, Quintets, 1 Sextet, 1 Septet &c.

HENRI KETTEN.

Born on the 25th March 1848, at Baja in Hungary, Henri Ketten showed inclination, and talent for music in his home circle and was well taught at the Paris Conservatoire, afterwards performing in Paris with great success as a pianoforte player. He then commenced his tours and won from all connoisseurs the reputation of being an excellent and highly gifted virtuoso. He had scarcely attained his thirty-fifth birthday when he died on the 1st April 1893. He composed several effective drawing-room pieces, a Sonata for the piano and clarionet, an Orchestral March, and various songs.

THEODOR KIRCHNER.

ALTHOUGH Kirchner is considered a very clever pianoforte player he has won a still more important name as a composer for the piano. He is unrivalled in the peculiar effectiveness and sweet tone of his smaller productions which are also widely known.

He was born on the 10th December 1824, at Neukirchen near Chemnitz, and his was the first name inserted in the list of pupils attending the Leipzig Conservatoire in 1834. Having completed his studies he commenced giving lessons; in 1862, he became an organist at Winterthur in Switzerland, and lived there for about ten years as teacher of music and director of societies. He went to Meiningen in 1872, where he spent a year composing industriously, and from 1873 until 1785, was Director of a music-school at Würzburg. He then lived for several years in Leipzig, and was finally appointed teacher of the piano at the Dresden Conservatoire.

Among his numerous compositions for the piano, are two books of Preludes, Album Leaves, 5 Books of Sketches, 5 Books of Fantasies, "Neue Davidsbündler-Dances", Legends, 5 Books with pianoforte pieces taken from his own songs, 2 Books of Aquarelles, 2 Books "Still und bewegt", 2 Books of "Nachtbilder", 2 Books of Caprices, 4 Books of studies and pieces, 2 Books of Walzes, Playthings, 12 Etudes, "Rural Stories", 2 Books of Mazurkas, 4 Polonaises, 30 Children's Dances, Humoresques, 2 Books New Album Leaves, 3 Books, New Pianoforte Book, 60 New Preludes, a Trio, a quartet for Strings &c. He has also composed songs with pianoforte accompaniment, and has re-arranged many songs of other composers (Brahms, Jensen &c.) for the piano.

CLOTILDE KLEEBERG.

THIS virtuoso was born at Paris, (not at Mayence as is often asserted) on the 27th June 1866. Her father was a German, a native of Mayence, but at the time of her birth was established in Paris. At an early age Clotilde showed signs of musical talent which since then has been cultivated to perfection. She received instruction at the Paris Conservatoire, first from Madame Retig and then from Madame Massart. In her eleventh year she won the first medal of the Conservatoire awarded her for her industry, and among competing pupils gained the highest honours in the examination. Her clever execution, and poetic playing attracted so much attention, that Pasdeloup and Lamoureux gave her an opportunity of playing in public.

When she was twelve years old, she played among other pieces Beethoven's C-minor Concerto as well as some of Chopin's compositions at the "Concerts populaires" all of which were received with the greatest enthusiasm. She studied with still greater diligence, and in her seventeenth year ventured to appear in London, where she soon made a great name. She did not entertain the idea of performing in her native country until she felt quite at home in England, and had become a favourite London pianiste. She appeared for the first time in German towns in 1887, as a fully experienced artiste, playing with great brilliancy and showing thorough knowledge of classical as well as of modern pianoforte music. She played Bach, Mozart, Beethoven, Chopin, Mendelssohn and Schumann with equal intelligence. She won the hearts of her listeners more by her tender grace and poetical refinement than by her brilliancy. Bearing some resemblance to Clara Schumann, her playing reveals the charm of womanly grace and loveliness, and these are the special characteristics which ensure her a high position among modern pianists.

ANTON VON KONTSKI.

TWO members of the large musical family of the Kontski's are of especial repute, the celebrated violinist Appolinary, and the pianoforte virtuoso Anton. The style of playing and numerous compositions of the latter are more distinguished for brilliant outward effect than for any special depth of thought. His "Reveil du Lion" in which there is varied expression, from the most delicate passages to the greatest brilliancy, is known throughout the world, although the term Caprice would be more correct as the true characteristic of this composition.

Born on the 27th October 1817, at Cracow, he,

with his brothers and sisters received musical instruction at home, after which he started on concert-tours; he was in Paris in the year 1851; 1852—1853 in Berlin where he was appointed Court pianist; and in 1854, he was in St. Petersburg. He continued his travelling until the year 1867, when he settled in London as a teacher. His work of instruction "L'Indispensable du Pianiste" is of much value. His pianoforte compositions comprise Fantasies, various other pieces and Etudes.

MARY KREBS-BRENNING.

WITH regard to this excellent pianiste we may
be permitted to make use of the well-known
humurous definition of a matter in itself of great
importance, namely that she was especially lucky
in the choice of her parents. Her father, Karl
Miedke, who received from his adopted father an
o_rera singer, the name of Krebs, was indebted to
him for the good preparation for the musical profession, was a very capable theorist, director, composer and pianist, who married the popular singer
Aloysia Michalesi when occupying the post of conductor at Dresden. Thus both her parents were

devoted heart and soul to music, and were able to give their child (born on the 5th December 1851) a good musical education. Mary's mother in particular is said to have been her instructress in the elements of pianoforte playing, which she began when very young thus preparing the child for further study which was superintended by her father.

When she was nine years old, her father let her perform for the first time at a performance given by the Dresden Concert Society, which was followed by her appearance at concerts in the neighbourhood, and in October 1863, a concert was arranged for her at Dresden, at which she played with the Royal Orchestra. In the same year she was heard at a Euterpe concert at Leipzig, and afterwards at Hamburg, Bremen and at a Court Concert at Dresden, where her performances were crowned with applause and success.

The twelve-year old artiste, (for we can truly give her this title considering what her repertoire was at that time) had to fulfil an English concert engagement in the same year; she was engaged by Mr. Gye the director of the Italian Opera at Covent Garden to play for four years consecutively, at a series of concerts beginning in the month of May. She performed in 170 of these concerts, playing Beethoven, Weber, Mendelssohn &c. overcoming easily all technical difficulties, and playing with great expression and intelligence. Her stay in England proved such a success both artistically and financially, that she has always returned there at regular intervals.

In her thirteenth year King John of Saxony, conferred upon her the title of Royal Pianiste. Accompanying Adelina Patti she visited Italy, performing in Trieste, Venice, Bologna, Florence, Genoa; she then passed on to the south of France making a stay at Cannes, Arles, Avignon, Nimes, Cette, and Montpelier &c. afterwards taking part in concerts at Paris.

She played at Prague and in several Dutch, Belgian and Russians towns—Riga, Mitau, Wenden, Wolmar, Dorpat, St. Petersburg, Moscow, and Warsaw.

In the years 1870—1871, she made a trip through the United States, being in Chicago at the time of the great fire. She returned to Germany twenty-two months later rich in "gold and honours".

In 1872, she joined an "Ullman concert-tour" and spent several weeks in visiting German towns.

In 1887, she married Theodor Brenning, a merchant, but did not relinquish her artistic career.

One of the most important of her numerous concerts was given on the 18th February 1892, in the Gewerbesaal at Dresden, when she, accompanied by Rubinstein, played Schumann's Variations for two pianos, op. 46; the audience being delighted with the performance of two such celebrated musicians.

THEODOR KULLAK.

PROFESSOR Th. Kullak was one of the greatest pianoforte players and teachers of the present day.
He has done much for the furtherance of modern
technical training of many important musicians, such
as Scharwenka, Erika Lie, Alma Holländer, Grünfeld,
Hans Bischoff, Heinrich Hoffmann, Franz Kullak &c.
He was born on the 12th September 1818, at
Krotoschin, and became a pupil of A. Aythe in Posen,
where in his eighth year, his playing secured the
interest of the artistic Prince Anton Radziwill. Through
his influence Kullak was permitted to take part in a
Berlin Court Concert in his eleventh year, and appeared

with Henriette Sontag. The King usually very moderate in his opinion, was delighted with the boy's playing and presented him with 30 Friedrichd'or. After a stay of six weeks he travelled to Breslau, where his playing was received with great applause. Then through the kindness of Prince Radziwill he was educated at the school at Züllichau. From his thirteenth to his eighteenth year he was without a piano, only being able to play occasionally. He also had the misfortune to lose his patron, but he soon found another aristocratic friend, through whose influence he received a stipend in Berlin, which enabled him to follow a course of theoretical studies under Dehn's guidance. At the same time Ingenheim was the means of procuring him several pupils of rank.

In 1842, Frau von Massow interceded on his behalf, and Friedrich Wilhelm iv. placed 400 thaler (£60) at his disposal to enable him to pursue his studies. He went to Vienna where he received pianoforte instruction from Czerny and theory from Sechter. After a trip in Austria he returned to Berlin in 1843. A Fräulein von Hellwig procured him the post of pianoforte teacher to Princess Anna, the daughter of Prince Karl. He then became the teacher of nearly all the princes and princesses of the Royal house as well as in many good families who were acquainted with his excellent teaching qualities.

In 1846, he became Pianist to the Prussian Court and received a salary. In 1850, he founded the Kullak institute afterwards known under the name of the Stern Conservatoire. He was actively connected with the former institute until the year 1855, retiring in order to originate the New Academy of Music, in which in the course of twenty-five years more than 1000 pupils have received instruction.

In 1844, Kullak was the originator of the

"Tonkünstler-Verein" in Berlin, and was president of it for many years.

In 1861, he was made Professor; and was also elected honorary member of the Royal Academy of Music in Florence, besides being the recipient of many other distinctions. He died March 1ˢᵗ 1882.

As a teacher of the pianoforte he wrote: "Schule der Fingerübungen und des Octavenspiels" and "Materialien für den Elementarunterricht". He published transcriptions and re-arrangements of the works of Mendelssohn, Schubert and Chopin, and composed very diligently. Among his works are 1 pianoforte Concerto, Fantasies, Drawin-groom pieces. "La Gazelle", "Les Danaïdes" and a re-arrangement of Aria from "Freischütz" are his best-known productions.

THEODOR LESCHETITZKY.

LITTLE is known of the childhood and musical training of this musician. He was the son of Polish parents and was born at Lemberg in the year 1831, (day unknown). He appeared in various Polish towns and . in Vienna, as a pianoforte player and teacher. In 1864, he was appointed teacher at the Conservatoire at St. Petersburg, where among other pupils he taught his future wife, with whom he travelled for a time, after having resigned his post at the Conservatoire in 1878, and then finally settled in Vienna as a private teacher. In the year 1880, he married Annette Essipoff with whom he then travelled giving concerts. They appeared together in London at the concerts of the Musical Union and met with brilliant success. During the time Leschetitzky was engaged at the Conservatoire in St. Petersburg he arranged excellent Chamber-Music Soirées assisted by Auer and Davidoff.

He composed several pieces for the piano and an opera called "Die erste Falte".

ERIKA LIE.

ERIKA Lie, of Scandinavian origin, was born on the 17th January, 1845, at Kongsvinger near Christiania. She received instruction from her father till her fifteenth year, and then for a year Hafdan Kjerulf was her teacher. From 1861 to 1866, she received her musical education at Th. Kullak's Institute in Berlin, and has become one of the best pianoforte players of the present day, her performance being characterized by masterly execution, grace, good taste and feeling. For two years she was pianoforte teacher at Kullak's Institute. After the completion of her studies she gave a concert in Berlin, and spent two years in visiting London, Stockholm, Copenhagen, Christiania, Leipzig, Cologne, Hamburg, Frankfort-on-the-Main, Bremen and Zürich, being fully acknowledged wherever she p'ayed as an excellent pianiste by all her critics.

Then following her own choice she relinquished her public career, and now devotes her time and talents exclusively to teaching.

FRANZ LISZT.

FOR years there have only been three great musicians who have stirred the world, not only by
their musical activity, but also in a literary sense;
and it is a strange dispensation of fate that these men
although working independently were connected by
ties of relationship; they are Liszt, and his two sons-
in-law, Bülow and Wagner. All three attained the
highest pinnacle of the modern German school, and
each one of them was entirely original in his own
way; it is therefore quite correct to say that Liszt was
without a rival in his day. Introducing new ideas into
pianoforte playing, and also in composition (having
been with Berlioz the principal representative of the

so called programme-music) he had in consequence
many opponents. As a man too he had also his
failings and as a politician he was paradoxical in the
extreme, yet notwithstanding he was much beloved,
and all his life was looked up to by the young generation, their sympathy for him always being most
enthusiastic. He was full of contratictions; for instance
in his earlier years he entertained the idea of becoming
a Roman Catholic priest and in ripe manhood he
carried out his intention so far as receiving the eccle-
siastical orders and also was made Abbé, yet he was
a man of the world, who enjoyed the pleasures of
life, and society was his element. He was at the same
time an advocate for freedom both in music and in
politics; from the year 1830, in Paris, he even went
to far in his immatured revolutionary tendencies as to
participate enthusiastically in the excesses of St. Simon
and developed strange freaks in following Enfentin
and his disciples. Chevalier, the most zealous follower
of Enfentin, with whom he even appeared at the
Assises, was Liszt's bosom friend, and the most
thorough socialist, exulting in the ideas of community
of property and womanhood, and especially in the
emancipation of woman; who, according to these views,
should be no longer bound by any moral obligation, but
should be able to say, wish and act exactly as she pleased.

Practically they confirmed these views in confidential
meetings, and communistic housekeeping; but in consequence of divergencies of opinion on St. Simonism,
violent conflicts took place, and eventually Liszt abandoned these fooleries: but for a long time after this he
cherished in his soul notions of a new formation of
Society, combined with a peculiar conversatism. He
even supported and aided revolutionaries like Wagner
and Röckel, yet simultaneously in 1851 he wrote:
"Germany will become Russian and for the great
majority of Germans there is little doubt as to

the only resolution which they can adopt." Then
again after the death of the exiled monarch at
Chislehurst he wrote: "Napoleon III is no more! A
great soul, an intelligence conceiving everything, a
gentle and noble character and an unblessed destiny!
He was gagged and bound like bound Caesar, who
was the ideal embodiment of earthly power. It is
still my belief that of all others, his government has
corresponded the best with the necessities and progress of our times. The day of justice will approach
when France will bring Napoleon the Third's coffin
and place it with all honours beside that of Napoleon I."

His character was full of beautiful and noble traits;
once he wrote thus to Pruckner: "Do not let us err
on the side of false modesty, but hold fast to all that
is true and real; this is far more difficult to practise
and but rarely met with." And he lived up to this
maxim. He continually spoke of his compositions
(which had met with much opposition) with that refined
graceful modesty which to use Liszt's own expression
comprehends a part of Schiller's "Menschheitswürde",
—"Dignity of Man" and was therefore not without
confidence in his talent, more fully developed by his
marvellous industry and the gradual acknowledgement
which he received. His utterance to Saint-Saens
when transmitting him the Mephisto Waltz also cor-
roborates this; he says "No one feels more acutely
than I do the incongruity between my good will and
the result attained by my compositions. Yet in spite
of it I persevere in writing, not without exertion—
arising from inward need and long habit. To strive
after higher things is not forbidden, but the attainment
of the end in view will always remain a question."

He encouraged numberless musicians of lesser
and greater talent, both in word and deed: wherever
he happened to be living, at Weimar, Rome,
Bayreuth or Paris the visits he received increased to

pilgrimages, and he was too kind-hearted to turn away a single person. A great number of modern pianists owe the good cultivation of their talents to his valuable guidance. He was the most patient man and did not feel himself weighed down by the continual claims made upon him until far advanced in years. In 1881 he wrote from Bayreuth to a friend: "My dislike to letters has become immense. How can I answer more than 2000 letters in a year without losing my reason!" And soon after, writing from Rome he says "I am honoured, flattered and oppressed by innumerable letters; during the last six weeks I have received more than a hundred; I should have to devote ten hours daily to my correspondence, but that is an impossibility. My health, although not bad, would not stand it." At last in 1862 he was obliged to announce in several musical papers that he must forbid the forwarding of scores and other writings. Yet it was still continued and he endured it with patience until his death.

Had this very popular and much honoured musician been of a selfish nature, he would without much trouble have soon amassed great riches and it is certain that he earned large sums of money but reserved none for himself. At his death he left little else but his silver laurel wreaths, jewelled bâtons, and gold snuff-boxes which he bequeathed to his great friend, Princess Wittgenstein. Unselfishness was one of his noblest qualities, this is noticeable from one of his letters which he wrote a short time before his death to Marie Lipsius as follows. "Since 1847 I have not made a 'farthing' by playing and conducting, on the contrary it has all cost me much time." Again it is apparent that Liszt even in his earlier years was by no means influenced by the love of money (often the case with musicians), this is evident from the history of Beethoven's statue at

Bonn. It vexed him that for years money should have been subscribed for this statue throughout Germany; he considered it an insult to the immortal genius, and in 1839 he wrote to the presiding committee that he would himself be responsible for the considerable sum still needed, so that the statue could then be immediately proceeded with. Franz Liszt's childhood is very similar to that of Mozart. His father Adam Liszt was at the time of his birth, 22nd Oct. 1811, accountant to Prince Esterhazy on his estate Raiding; he was himself very musical, played several instruments and often played the violincello in the performances of Esterhazy's private orchestra at Eisenstadt under Jos. Haydn's conductorship. He taught his son the piano and let him perform when nine years old for the first time in public at a concert at Oedenburg. After Prince Esterhazy had heard the child play, Adam Liszt arranged a concert for him at Pressburg which revealed the capabilities of the young musician to such an extent that several noblemen expressed themselves willing to place a yearly stipend of 600 guldens at his disposal for six years, to enable him to further his musical education. Adam Liszt then resigned his post at once, the whole family removed to Vienna, where Czerny undertook the boy's further tuition and the venerable Salieri is said to have instructed him in theory. The boy's extraordinary talents soon enabled him to attain to great perfection in pianoforte playing and in two year's time the "youthful prodigy" began his concert tours. At a farewell concert which he gave in Vienna in 1823 it is reported that Beethoven was present and was so delighted with the boy's playing that he hurried on to the platform and kissed him.*) This concert as also a former one were such a

---

*) This sounds very improbable as in 1823 Beethoven was already so deaf that he could not, according to Spohr's account, hear his own playing.

pecuniary success that all the travelling expenses were easily defrayed and from this period young Liszt became the bread-winner for the whole family, who travelled with him. As was the case with Mozart his father was his guide, introducer, and cashier, and his letters full of detail written to Czerny prove how successful all the concerts were when on a tour, both artistically and financially.

Their first visit was to Munich. Moscheles was at this time giving a concert, Liszt's succeeded his. In his first concert which was badly attended, the king and the princesses were present, and in writing about it Adam Liszt says: "The applause was tremendous and I was at once requested to give a second concert: In short, it was the greatest pity that the people, who could obtain no admittance on the second occasion, had not been present on the first.... Twice we had the privilege of a royal audience and were received most graciously and with much honour. At the first interview the king remarked "And now, little one, how did you venture to appear after Moscheles?" And when we were about to take leave His Majesty said: "Come here, little one, I must give you a kiss!" which he did.

From Munich they went on to Augsburg. Adam Liszt wrote from there: "We gave a small concert on the 30th Oct. which had been previously arranged when we were at Munich. On Nov, 1st he played at the Harmonie. The applause is general wherever we go. To-day Zizy (Franz) is to play at a concert arranged for the benefit of sufferers by a fire and to-morrow we leave for Stuttgart. Notwithstanding the fact that travelling-expenses, and board, especially wine amount to a large sum up to to-day after defraying all expenses we have a clear profit of 921 florins. We should have almost double the sum if I had not our reputation to keep up, and to try to benefit others."

The following remark contained in the same letter addressed to Czerny is characteristic of the partial father: "Moscheles has out-lived his fame at Munich, and is not spoken of with proper respect; I for my part must admit that he played magnificently at his concert; but the Fantasia was devoid of all beauty—in fact I cannot call it a Fantasia at all. He has especially lost all favour by charging double entrance."

The Augsburger Allgemeine Zeitung after the appearance of Liszt at Munich reported as follows: "A new Mozart has appeared among us. We have heard Hummel and Moscheles and are not afraid to say that this child's performance is equal to their's." The Schwabian Mercury mentioning the Stuttgart concerts had the following notice: "This boy now ranks as high as the best pianoforte player in Europe, perhaps even excels them all." They now went to to Paris, where the papers extolled "Le petit Litz." After his appearance at a concert at the Italian Opera they asserted: "Orpheus charmed the beasts of the forest and moved the stones, but little Litz charmes the orchestra to such a degree that it is silent." The musicians had forgotten to take up the ritornello at the right moment.

In March 1824 Adam Liszt wrote thus to Czerny: "Since our arrival here we have already accepted engagements for 36 soirées to be given by some of the best people, where never less than 100 francs, and often 150 francs are paid for the evening. He has played once at the house of Madame la duchesse de Berry, the whole of the royal family being present and improvised on four given themes. He has also played three times at the Duc d'Orleans'." The father then reckons that at the conclusion of the concert at the Italian Opera House and after settling all expenses amounting to 343 francs they had a surplus profit of

4711 francs. Thus the little virtuoso earned a tidy fortune for his family in the space of only a few months. "He who has talent" writes A. Liszt "ought to go to Paris; here the taste for art is of one accord and artist are valued, honoured, and rewarded."

Adam speaks almost contemptuously of the renowned pianist Peter Pixis, who at this time was also giving concerts in Paris, and repeatedly expresses rather spiteful opinions of other musicians, Hummel, Moscheles, Emilie Belleville (Oury)&c. He can scarcely have been actuated by any other motive than envy, in spite of the splendid talents of which his son gave evidence. Something resembling jealousy seems also to have reigned paramount in other quarters, for instance Hummel frequently treated Franz Liszt with intentional contempt, so at least A. Liszt asserts when writing to Vienna, and old Cherubini invented some paltry excuse for refusing to accept Liszt as a pupil at the Conservatoire.

The father and son made frequent trips from Paris to London with like success. Franz once had occasion to display his capabilities in transposing at a Philharmonie Concert in London. On account of the piano being tuned very low he had to play a concerto for piano and flute, in C sharp major instead of in C. From London they started on an excursion for pleasure to Boulogne-sur-mer, but here too the clever father understood the art of combining business with pleasure; he let his son give a Soirée in the salon of the Badehôtel, where a piano was to be had "in compliance with the urgent requests of the company", this not only cleared the heavy expenses of their visit but left them a profit of 600 francs. It was also in Paris that "Franzi" wrote his first opera "Don Sancho" or at least had it performed. An opera committee consisting of Cherubini, Berton, Boieldieu, Lesueur and Catel had it tried before the representation which took place on the 17th Oct. 1825, at the grand Opera and conducted by Kreutzer; Nourrit sang the principal rôle. At the conclusion the composer and Nourrit were called for and the latter appeared on the stage carrying Liszt, which of course greatly delighted the impulsive French audience. Yet it really seems as if almost too much had been said about this youthful work of Liszt's;— it is true that the opera was twice performed under official patronage, but it then disappeared from the stage, and finally the score with all the parts is said to have perished in a fire which took place in the library of the Opera House.

According to Ad. Liszt's letters to Czerny the former had made plans for a long artistic tour through the Netherlands and Germany, terminating with their return to Vienna but providence had decreed other-wise; on a concert from Paris through the northern French provinces A. Liszt died in 1827 at the much-loved and remunerative Boulogne-sur-mer. Liszt then took up his temporary abode in Paris where he taught, composed and gave concerts. Above all he sought to perfect himself as a pianoforte player, being con-tinually spurred on by the musical genius of others. Thalberg and Chopin are said to have greatly in-fluenced him. Then when Paganini played in Paris, Liszt is said to have made up his mind to become a Paginani on the piano. He showed much outward enthusiasm for Italian composers, but he had a genuine and more enthusiastic admiration for Chopin. Berlioz was his friend and fellow aspirant; the original ideas of Fétis were also eagerly embraced by Liszt. The Revolution of 1831 caused him to take an interest both in politics and philosophy; he freed himself more and more from the narrow bounds of art and morality existing during the monarchy of which his attachment and connection with the Comtesse D'Agoult bears sufficient testimony.

Until 1847 he continued his concert tours almost
without intermission and they brought him in both
fame and riches; his successes were unparalleled, and
he became a world wide favourite as pianist.

In 1847 he ceased his career as a virtuoso, and
accepted the appointment of conductor at Weimar; it
is said, but in some measure hyperbolically, that he
became the musical Goethe of Weimar. At any rate
all who recognised in him their musical ideal thronged
thither. He then made himself still more remarkable
by the energetic and self-sacrificing way in which he
took up the cause of Wagner's music dramas, and
Wagner proved himself fully grateful for his services.
On their first meeting in Paris he did not cherish the
best opinion of Liszt, as he thought the latter was of
a very different nature to his own. Later on when
his "Rienzi" began to attract attention, he changed
the opinion he had first formed on meeting him a
second time. When writing on the subject Wagner
says: "I am still deeply affected by the repeated
eager endeavours he has made to give me a better
opinion of himself. In doing this he was actuated
by no artistic sympathy, but only by a purely human
desire to set aside a supposed misunderstanding
existing between himself and another; perhaps too
he had a vague suspicion that unconsciously he might
have given me cause for offence. Those who have
experienced the egotism and want of feeling prevailing
in our social life ought to be filled with admiration
and delight at the treatment I received at the hands
of this extraordinary man..... I saw him last at
Weimar where I remained several days uncertain
whither I should be driven by the portending per-
secution. The same day on which I became aware
of my danger, I saw Liszt conduct a performance of
Tannhäuser and was astonished to recognize my second
self on this occasion. What I felt in the creation of this

music, Liszt felt in conducting it; what I had wished
to express in writing it down, he expressed in trans-
forming it and in giving it true expression. In the
love of this rare friend, at the moment when I lost
my home, I found a home for my art, which I had
long sought, and sought in vain, always searching in
the wrong direction.... When I was in Paris, ill,
wretched and in despair, grumbling at my fate my
eyes suddenly fell upon the pages of "Lohengrin"
which I had wholly forgotten. I felt grieved at the
thought that this music would never be brought forth
in sound from its paper-shroud. I wrote only two
words to Liszt, and the answer I received was, that
preparations were already begun for the performance
of Lohengrin in the most splendid style compatible
with the linited means at his disposal in Weimar.
Everything within the power of man was done to get
this work recognized.... The anticipated success was
only hindered by errors and false ideas on the part
of the public. Liszt at once saw what was still
wanting to lead to a correct conception and to ensure
the final success of the work. He represented to the
public with convincing eloquence the impression
which the opera had made on himself ... success was
his reward and owing to this success he came to me
and said: "You see we have attained so much, now
give us something else that we may attain still
higher."

Wagner writing with reference to Liszt's music
said: "Whoever has had the pleasure of hearing him
play Beethoven in society must confess that his playing was not only re-production, but that it was a
creation itself."... Another reliable critic characterizes
Liszt's playing briefly in a similar manner: "Liszt's
phenomenal execution enables him to direct his whole
attention to the intention of the composer." During
the time he spent at Weimar he wrote numerous im-

portant compositions, which however met with much
opposition, he also displayed great activity as an
author. His principal productions were "Symphonic
Poems an a programmatic groundwork", which have
at last supplied a want in orchestral art, being considered brilliant compositions. His pianoforte concertos
and in particular his Hungarian Rhapsodies give
evidence of great progress made in the direction of
genuinely artistic works for piano. A former biographer and critic says: "A pianoforte movement of
such extraordinary, and dazzling effect although it
may only have been extenorly was until then without
its equal and unexcelled in the history of pianoforte
music." Everything of his was original even to the
songs with pianoforte accompaniment to which he
added lyrical expression as well as a dramatic feeling.

A great deal in his personality was strange and
contradictory. Thus for instance we learn from his
letters which were not published until long after his
death that Schumann's compositions deeply interested
him, yet he never played a note of his music. He
and Adolf Henselt were the most intimate friends,
yet in his letters he mentions the latter's Etudes as
a "médiocrité dinstinguée."

All composers of sacred music who incline to the
immortal productions of classical times, hold in contempt that which is religious music with Liszt. His
life was rich with blessings to others in many respects.
Great musicians, Tausig, Bülow, Raff, Sophie Menter
are indebted to him for the success and fame to which
they aspired. Young musicians seeing or hearing
him play were either seized with despair at the
thought of their own inability, or they awoke to a
new life. His technical studies form a foundation for
modern pianoforte-playing. For many years he worked
with heart and soul on behalf of the "Universal
German Musical Union." It is rarely indeed that any

musician has ever been so honoured as he was; but one of the highest distinctions he received and valued the most was the diploma of honorary doctor of the Philosophical Faculty at Königsberg.

He was also honorary president of the Bayreuth Festivals, and it was at Bayreuth that he died on the 31st July 1886.

His principal compositions are the following: I. Pianoforte works: 2 Concertos (E-flat and A), "Danse macabre" (for piano and orchestra), 1 Concert-solo (Concert pathétique), 15 Hungarian Rhapsodies 1 Spanish Rhapsody, 1 Sonate (B-Minor), 1 Fantasia and Fugue on Bach, 6 Preludes and Fugues, Variations on a Theme from Bach's Mass in B-Minor, 2 Ballads, 1 Berceuse, 2 Legends, 2 Elegies, one for the Pianoforte, Violin and Cello, 1 Capriccio alla turca (on a motive from Beethoven's "Ruins of Athens"), 1 Idée fixe (after Berlioz), 1 Impromtu (F-sharp Major), "Consolations", "Apparitions", "Harmonies poétiques et religieuses", "Années de pélérinage", 3 Nocturnos ("Liebesträume"), chromatical Galop, 3 Caprice valses, Paraphrases on Motives from Meyerbeer's, Wagner's and Verdi's Operas &c., 1 Brilliant Fantasia on Paginani's "Clochette", 1 Tscherkessen March from Glinka's "Russlau and Ludmilla", 1 Wedding March, and Dance of the Elves from Mendelssohn's Midsummernight's Dream", Transcription of songs for the piano (very numerous, including 60 of Schubert's), Arrangements of Beethoven's Symphonies as solos, Berlioz' "Symphonie fantastique", and his "Pilgrim March" from "Harold in Italy", 1 Danse des Sylphes" from Faust's "Damnation", Pianoforte Overtures to "Fehmrichter", "King Lear", Wagner's "Tannhäuser" Overture, Saint-Saëns' "Danse Macabre", "Etudes d'execution transcendante", 3 Grandes Etudes de Concert, Etude de perfection "Ab irato"; for two pianos: Variations on a March from "I Puritani",

Arrangements, Andante religioso; melodramatic piano-forte works on Bürger's "Leonore", Strachwitz' "Helgo", Lenau's "Trauriger Mönch"; 3 Duets for piano and violin &c. II. Orchestral Works: Symphonic Poems: "Dante", "Faust-Symphony" "Ce qu'on entend sur la montagne" (Victor Hugo), "Tasso", "Les pré-ludes", "Orpheus", "Prometheus", "Mazeppa", "Fest-klänge", "Heroïde funèbre", "Hungaria", "Hamlet", "Hunnenschlacht", "Die Ideale", "Von der Wiege bis zum Grabe", Episodes from Lenau's "Faust", "Künstler-festzug", "Gaudeamus", (with chorus and solo), "Fest-marsch", "Festvorspiel", "Huldigungsmarsch", "Vom Fels zum Meer", Arrangements of Schubert's Marches, and of "Divertissement hongroise", and of the Rakoczy march. — III. Vocal works: "Grosse Festmesse", "Hungarian Coronation Mass", 2 Organ Masses, the 13th, 18th, 23d and 137th Psalms, Requiem, shorter hymns (Paternoster, Ave Maria, Ave Mario stella, Ave verum, Tantum ergo, O salutaris &c.), the ora-torios "Christus" and "Stanislaus", the "Legend of St. Elizabeth", the Cantatas "Glocken des Strassburger Münsters", "St. Cecilia", "An die Künstler", Choruses to Herder's "Prometheus Unbound", Festival Cantatas for secular occasions (Beethoven, Goethe, Herder), several books of quartets for male voices, numerous songs for solo voices and piano "Jeanne d'Arc an bucher", "The power of music" &c.

Liszt's compositions for the piano undoubtedly represent a step forward in the History of Music, but whether the same can be said of his orchestral compositions remains to be seen.

The most important of Liszt's writings are: "Lohengrin and Tannhäuser" (in French and German), "Frédéric Chopin", "The Hungarian Gipsies and their music" (in Hungarian, German and French), "On Field's Notturnes" (in French and German), "Robert Franz" &c.

One is accustomed to see portraits of Liszt taken in his later years, it will therefore be an agreeable surprise to our readers to see a carte de visite of the master which dates from about 1853 to 1854.

HENRY LITOLFF.

THAT a very slight circumstance may occasionally be the means of rescuing a musician from straitened means, and lead to success is exemplified in the life of Henry Litolff.

He was born in London as the son of a violinist, on the 6th February 1818, and taught by Moscheles. He was able to appear at the Covent Garden Theatre as a pianoforte-player at twelve years of age; but this premature independance was by no means of benefit to him. When scarcely seventeen years old he made a penniless marriage and started on a tour with his wife. He went to Paris, but was disappointed in his expectation of easily meeting with success there. He was very unfortunate, and it was

with great difficulty that he was able to support himself in French and Belgian provincial towns, and was
totally unable to maintain his wife. Quite by accident
in 1840 the singer Duprez, then on a tour, happened
to hear him play at a small charity concert; he was
astonished at such a talent which was in danger of
being lost among his miserable surroundings. He
took him to Paris, arranged for him to appear in
public, and thus brought about a change in his life.
Above all he was the means of restoring to Litolff
his self-reliance. He began to compose and among
other things he wrote a piano concerto and a
symphony in B-Minor. In 1841 he was appointed
conductor in Warsaw, where he remained until 1845.
Then he again started on tours and visited Leipzig,
Dresden, Prague and met with "tolerable but not
brilliant success." Fortune was more in his favour
in Berlin, the reports of that time state that he had
"maintained his position beside that of Jenny Lind."
In 1846 he re-appeared in London, left there for
Holland, and appealed, not without success, to the
patriotism of the Dutch by the performance of a
composition especially composed for them which he
called "Concerto symphonique national hollandais pour
Piano et Orchestre." In 1847 he spent some time
at Brunswick and there he made the acquaintance of
the poet Griepenkerl, and wrote concert overtures to
his dramas "Robespierre" and "Die Girondisten." In
doing this work he seems at the same time to have
become infected by politics, for in 1848 he suddenly
became mixed up in revolutionary affairs, and formed
one of the so-called academical legion. Luckily for
him he escaped just at the critical moment and returned to Brunswick for a time. He was divorced
from his first wife and married the widow of the
music-publisher Meyer, whose business he managed,
carrying it on under his own name. Litolff became

known throughout the world as a music-publisher and met with special success with his well-known collection of classical masters entitled "Collection Litolff." But here too there seem to have been domestic differences, for in 1860, he left the business in his step-son's hands and resumed his tours as a pianoforte player. In Paris he made the acquaintance of a Baroness Larochefoucald in 1861, obtained a divorce from his second wife, and married for the third time. Nothing further is known of his life; report says he settled down in Paris as a pianist and composer. He died in Paris on the 5th Aug. 1892.

In Sir George Grove's Dictionary the following opinion is given of Litolff's playing, which in England met with high recognition: "As a pianist Litolff's rank is high; fire, passion, and brilliancy of execution were combined with thought and taste in his playing. Had it also been correct, it would have reached the highest excellence." Litolff has written a good deal but nothing that is destined to last, 5 symphonic piano Concertos, Pianoforte Trios, Solos (the well known "Spinnlied" op. 81), also the Concerts Overtures already mentioned, String Quartett, "Illustrations to Goethe's Faust for solo, chorus and orchestra", an oratorio "Ruth and Boaz", and a number of operas, all of which were of no lasting importance.

————•❖❋❖•————

BERTHE MARX.

As a first-rate modern pianist and as the accompaniest of the violinist Sarasate, Frau Berthe Marx's reputation has become firmly established in both hemispheres. With Sarasate she has appeared at about 600 concerts, and has proved herself his equal as an accompaniest; and as a soloist her sweet, yet full and powerful expression, perfect touch, and complete devotion to the intentions of the older as well as the more modern composers, have received high praise. In England, especially with Clotilde Kleeberg, Sophie Menter, Teresa Carenno, Paderewski. Stavenhagen and others, she has become a favourite and popular pianiste.

She was born in Paris, on the 28th July 1859. Her father was a musician, who for 40 years was a violincello player at the Conservatoire and the Grand Opera in both orchestras. When scarcely fours years of age her father began with her instruction in music, and after one year's tuition she performed in public. During the next four years, she made such great progress, that in her ninth year she was introduced to the Director of the Paris Conservatoire, who expressed himself well satisfied with her playing, and without further examination he arranged for her to study at the Conservatoire. She was Henri Herz's pupil, and in his class when fifteen years of age, she gained the first prize.

Thus fully equipped for her artistic career, she began her concert tours in France and Belgium and met with a hearty reception everywhere. She played for the first time with Sarasate in Brussels, and recognizing her great talent he engaged her there and then for all his concerts; she shared his laurels in Europe and America, their tours in the latter country having extended to Mexico and California. She has composed some "Rhapsodies Espagnoles", and has arranged Sarasate's Spanish Dances for the piano.

DR. LOUIS MAAS.

DR. MAAS was born at Wiesbaden, Germany, in 1852. He inherited musical proclivities, and at the age of six could play proficiently. His father opposed professional musical life, but, through the persuasion of Joachim Raff, finally withheld his opposition. After study with Reinecke and Papperitz at Leipzig, he taught in Dr. Theodore Kullak's conservatory. He afterward became a teacher at the Leipzig Conservatory. He resigned this position in 1880 to go to America, where, after very successful concert tours, he was engaged to teach piano at the New England Conservatory. In connection with his teaching in Boston he continued his concert tours until his sudden death, which occurred Sept. 18, 1889.

CHARLES MAYER.

CHARLES Mayer has become distinguished both as a virtuoso and especially as composer by his numerous pianoforte compositions, (in number about 200) perfect in their style, effective, smooth, easily played and carefully written.

He was born on the 21st March 1799, at Königsberg; his father was an excellent clarionet-player, and his mother was also very musical. When Charles was barely four years old his parents went to Russia. The child first learned to play by ear, but when his father received a post in Moscow, and his mother established herself as a teacher of the piano, she then taught her son, and upon Field's coming to Moscow the child's instruction was continued by him, and he became his favourite pupil, (which by the way has been said of many of Field's pupils). In his ninth year Charles performing at concerts.

In the disturbed year, 1812, when Napoleon stormed Moscow, the Mayer family were forced to flee to St. Petersburg, where Charles again met Field, whose style of playing he now adopted.

In 1814, he made a long concert-tour with his father, visiting Warsaw, Germany, Holland and France. In Amsterdam he wrote his well-known variations on "God save the King".

In 1819 he made his reputation in St. Petersburg as a pianist composer and teacher, and since that time, in about twenty-five years, 800 pupils were taught by him.

On a second concert-tour he visited Stockholm, Hamburg, Copenhagen, Leipzig and Vienna, where he was received with great honour and distinction; being also made honorary member of the Musical Academy at Stockholm.

In the meantime a formidable rival had appeared in Russia, in the person of Adolf Henselt, who was a hindrance to his rending in Russia, he therefore removed to Dresden in 1846, where he remained until his death in 1862.

ANNA MEHLIG.

THIS excellent pianiste, who for a time also attracted attention in Germany, was born at Stuttgart on the 11th June 1846, where she had the advantage of Lebert's and Pruckner's instruction. She left Stuttgart for Weimar in 1864, and for a year became Liszt's pupil. In 1866, she went to England for the first time and made her debût on the 30th April, playing one of Hummel's concertos at a Philharmonic-concert.

She then played with great success in England, every season until the year 1869, at the Philharmonic concerts and at the Crystal Palace. During the

other months of the year, when not engaged in England,
she played in various German towns.

From 1869 to 1870, she went on a long tour
through America, establishing a considerable reputation
there. She re - appeared in London in 1875, and
played Chopin's Concerts in E minor on the 9th Oct.
at the Crystal Palace. Since then she has visited
London every year. Her repertoire is very extensive
and her poetic style and power of execution are much
admired.

Some years ago in London she married a merchant and now lives in Antwerp.

FELIX MENDELSSOHN-BARTHOLDY.

MENDELSSOHN is indisputably one of the most celebrated musicians of modern times, having had
the greatest influence on the development of music,
especially in that of a sentimental and melodious
nature. Few indeed can boast of such a wealth of
beautiful and effective compositions of the most varied
kind; many of them, even in the present day,
make a deep impression upon the feelings of both
players and listeners, and it is much to be lamented
that, in consequence of the introduction of more

modern music, his less important works are neglected. He received an excellent musical education and possessed a correct knowledge of the classical composers. The merit of having restored the works of Johann Sebastian Bach, to life again must be conceded to him. He was a masterly conductor, and was the means of making the Gewandhaus concerts in Leipzig, a lasting success, he also made the Leipzig Conservatoire a world-renowned institution. His style is little thought of by modern men of talent, but in all probability his music will be able to boast of a longer life than their's.

Felix Mendelssohn, was born at Hamburg, on the 3rd February 1809, but in 1812, his family removed to Berlin. He education was carefully carried out, befitting the son of wealthy parents, and he received good musical instruction. His mother was his first pianoforte teacher, Ludwig Berger succeeding her; Hennings was his instructor on the violin, and Zelter taught him theory. Paul Heyse's father gave lessons in languages to the Mendelssohn family. In 1818, Mendelssohn appeared for the first time in public, executing the pianoforte part of a Trio by Wolff, at a concert given by Gugel, and was much applauded. In 1819, he became a member of the Berlin Singing Academy, his voice being Alto. His second appearance in public in 1822, at one of Aloys Schmitt's concerts, on which occasion he performed a duet by Dussek for two pianos accompanied by the concert-giver. On the 5th December in the same year, he played one of his own pianoforte Concertos at a concert given by the vocalist Anna Milder.

The musical entertainments which were got up every Sunday in his own home, produced a very favourable effect upon his development as a musician.

When he was twelve years of age, he began to compose systematically, at least in this year he

wrote two pianoforte accompaniments, and he commenced the series of forty-four books, to which he
added autographical biographical copies of a great
many of his works, and which are now in the Royal
Library in Berlin.

In 1821, he was introduced to Karl Maria v. Weber
who had come to Berlin to witness a performance of
his "Freischütz", and his enthusiastic veneration for
this musician of the romantic school terminated only
with his life. The boy also met Goethe in the same
year, his teacher Zelter took him to Weimar, and
both of them lived for sixteen days in Goethe's
house.

Besides the Sunday Musical Soirées already
mentioned, there was music every evening in
Mendelssohn's home, often accompanied by theatrical
representations, impromtu or studied, when a number
of lively young people were invited to witness or to
take part in the proceedings. On such an occassion
one of his early operas "Die beiden Neffen" was
performed on his birthday in 1824, and at the conclusion his teacher Zelter adopting freemason phraseo-
logy promoted Felix from the rank of an "apprentice"
to that of an "assistant" in the name of Bach,
Haydn and Mozart.

In the same year he made the acquaintance of
Moscheles, who was already well known as a virtuoso,
and who called Mendelssohn's mother "the princess
of piano-players". For a month Moscheles gave
Mendelssohn daily lessons.

In 1825, Spohr visited Berlin on the occassion of
his "Jessonda" being performed, and was almost a
daily gaest in Mendelssohn's house, although this fact
is omitted in Spohr's autobiography. Two reliable
authorities expressed their opinion with regard to
Mendelssohn's playing in this year; Ferdinand Hiller,
who heard him with André at Frankfort, and thought

a great deal of his impromtus on Handel's and Bach's Choruses and Motets, also Dorn who said that he heard Mendelssohn accompanying the duet from "Fidelio" and was astonished at the way in which he brought out the cello and bass parts on the piano by playing them two octaves apart. "How often", says Dorn, "I have heard that duet sung, but have never again heard it accompanied in such a manner."

Even at this time Mendelssohn played the most comprehensive and difficult works without notes, showing marvellous powers of memory. He once played Beethoven's 9th Symphony, without a mistake and without notes in Spontini's presence, which is said to have awakened much envy in the breast of the old conductor.

Mendelssohn's opinion of Cherubini, whom he met on a visit to Paris in 1825, is very interesting; on this occasion he made the acquaintance of other important musicians; he called Cherubini "a dying volcano, giving forth occasional life, but entirely covered with ashes and stones."

On his homeward journey from Paris, he paid Goethe a short visit, and played one of his compositions to him, which he dedicated to the veteran prince of poets. In recognition of this honour Goethe gave him a rapidly written poem not conspicuous for inspiration.

When scarcely sixteen years of age Mendelssohn had became eminent as a composer, but he established the fame of his youth in the following year by the Overture of "A Midsummer Night's Dream", the rest of the music to Shakespeare's drama not being composed until fifteen years later.

From the year 1825, the Mendelssohn family inhabited a magnificent house newly bought, which had formerly belonged to a family 'von der Reck' by name, it contained spacious rooms, outhouses, a summer house, and extensive grounds. It was situated in the

Leipziger Strasse, where the Herrenhaus now stands.
Here the Berlin celebrities assembled; Humboldt,
Varnhagen, Lindblad, Steffens, Holtei, Gans, Marx,
Kugler, Droysen and Hegel. The garden parties
were particularly popular. A special paper was written
by the company, which in summer was entitled the
"Garten-Zeitung" and in winter the "Schnee- und
Thee-Zeitung" and of which Mendelssohn and Marx
were the editors. Any one who chose could contribute
to it, and even men like Zelter and Humboldt were
not above doing so. Young Mendelssohn was much
sought after, and ladies double his age were madly
in love with him. Yet even those happy days of his
life, otherwise so free of care, were not without
shadows. His youth, his Jewish origin, the position
which his family occupied, and his success gained
him many opponents in the musical world; there was
no want of malice, and it was carried to such an
extent that the royal orchestra at certain performances
in the Singing Academy refused to play under his
conductorship, and at concerts when his compositions
were on the programme, they were carelessly and
reluctantly played. And in later years he was often
not on the best of terms with Marx.

He composed his opera "the wedding of Gamacho"
in 1827, it was but once performed in Berlin, and
then laid aside at Spontini's instigation. In 1829, after
the most careful preparation, he arranged for the first
representation of Bach's Passion, according to St.
Matthew in the Berlin Sing Academie.

In the same year, at Moscheles' invitation he
went over to England, and had his symphony in
C minor performed in London, as also the Overture to
the Midsummer Night's Dream. This was the first time
these two works had been heard. From this period
his fame as a composer spread in musical circles. The
style of his compositions suited the English taste,

which resulted in his always finding a warm welcome in England. Thus in 1832, he had the "Hebrides Overture", his "concerto in Gminor" and his "Capriccio in B minor" also performed in London. In 1830, he travelled in Italy and on his return to Berlin, several of his compositions, and among them the "Hebrides Overture", "Meeresstille und Glückliche Fahrt" and the "Reformation Symphony" were heard in public. In 1833, he conducted the Musical Festival at Düsseldorf, this resulted in his being appointed Musical Director; in that town he remained only two years in this position, being in the meantime elected conductor of the Gewandhaus concerts in Leipzig, entering into office in 1835, after having conducted the Cologne Musical Festival. He called Leipzig, his Paradise, the Leipzig people made an idol of him, and even professional musicians honoured and esteemed him. In 1836, he was the cause of Ferdinand David's coming to Leipzig, and the same year the University conferred upon him the title of Doctor of Philosophy honoris causa.

His oratorio "St. Paul" was first performed at Düsseldorf on the 22nd May 1836, and in 1837, Mendelssohn married Cecilia Jeanrenaud at Frankfort-on-the-Main. From Spohr, one of Mendelssohn's friends, we learn what a happy marriage this proved to be. After a short visit paid to Leipzig, in 1840, he writes as follows: "We spent a lively evening with Mendelssohn, where everything was done to give me pleasure. In this family I seem to see something quite ideal, a union of interior and exterior qualities, and such beautiful domestic happiness, such as is rarely met with in ordinary life. With so much luxury and wealth, such a charming simplicily pervades their manner and mode of living, that it makes one feel entirely at home." On the same occasion, Spohr speaks very warmly of Mendelssohn's method of playing, he having performed Spohr's compositions with great effect on several occasions.

In the year 1843, Mendelssohn in conjunction with some eminent citizens and with such acknowledged masters as Moritz Hauptmann, Robert Schumann, Ferdinand David and Chr. A. Pohlenz, founded the Leipzig Conservatoire, and became its director. He and Schumann raised the Institutian to great eminence, but an interesting incident in Mendelssohn's life which occurred before the opening, and the explanation of which is due to his many admirers must not be omitted. At Zelter's death Mendelssohn had applied for his post, and it had been refused him, but later on when he became famous, and a monarch with taste for art had succeeded to the throne, great exertions were made to induce him to remove to Berlin. He received the title of Principal Musical Director, and after a long inward struggle and many consultations with his family in Berlin, and also with the ministers, he resolved reluctantly to exchange his pleasant post at Leipzig, for the one in Berlin. Yet he always longed for Leipzig, and even in the depth of winter he travelled thither to conduct a concert at the Gewandhaus. In general the reception he met with in Berlin was somewhat cool; at the concerts organized by the King, he received very scanty applause, and the old antagonism still prevailed on the part of the men in the orchestra. King Friedrich Wilhelm IV. was determined if possible to keep him in Berlin, and gave him, under the most favourable conditions, the task of forming a cathedral choir; but when Mendelssohn went to Dresden, he was persuaded at last to accept the post of Director of the newly established Conservatoire in Leipzig.

Thus the return to his beloved "Pleisse-Athen" was secured. Unfortunately he only enjoyed a few more happy years of life. He was far too premature for art, and his numerous friends had to lament his death on the 4th November, 1847. Spohr writing to Moritz Hauptmann on hearing of his death said: "What glorious works Mendelssohn could still have written in the height of his fame had Providence granted him a longer life! For his delicate constitution the mental effort was too great, and thus was injurious. The loss which art has sustained is very much to be lamented, for he was the most highly gifted of all living musicians,—and his efforts on behalf of art were in truth noble."

Of Mendelssohn's compositions Opus 1—72 were published during his life, and Opus 73—121 after his death. Many have also appeared without the number of the work. For the piano: 2 Concertos in G minor and D minor. The Capriccio in B minor, "Rondo brillant", "Serenade", Sextet, 3 Quartets, 2 Trios, Variations concertantes for the piano and cello, 8 books of "Lieder ohne Worte", 2 Capriccios, Characteristic pieces, 1 Rondo capriccioso, 2 Fantasias, Preludes, Studies, Album leaf, 1 "Duo concertant", "Perpetuum mobile", 4 Sonatas, 3 books of Variations, "Allegro brillant", 7 Preludes and Fugues. For orchestra, chorus and for various combinations of instruments: the oratorios "St. Paul" and "Elijah" and the fragment of an oratio "Cristus", the concert-overtures "Midsummer Night's Dream", "Hebrides", "Meeresstille und Glückliche Fahrt", "Schöne Melusine", "Ruy Blas", "Trumpet overture", the music to "Antigone", "Walpurgisnacht", "Athalia", "Midsummer Night's Dream", "Oedipus auf Kolonos"; 5 symphonies, 1 Violin concerto, 1 String Octet, 2 String Quintets, 7 String Quartets; for the Organ: 3 Preludes and Fugues, 6 Sonatas, 83 Songs for one voice with pianoforte accompaniment, 13 Duets, 28 Quartets for mixed voices, 21 Quartets for male voices, "Nachtgesang", "Stiftungsfeier", Concert Aria, 2 Festival Cantatas, 6 Anthems for 8 voices, 5 Psalms for solos, chorus, and orchestra, 3 Psalms a capella,

5 Motets, 1 Funeral Song, 1 Kyrie, 1 Lauda Sion",
1 Hymn, "Tu es Petrus", 2 sacred songs, 2 sacred
choral numbers for male voices; an operatic fragment
"Lorelei" the "Heimkehr aus der Fremde"; 2 concerted
pieces for the clarionet, Basset-horn, and piano, 1 song
without words for Violincello and piano; also the
arrangements of Bach's Chaconne in Dminor, Handels
"Dettinger Tedeum" and "Acis and Galathea". Early
works: 11 Symphonies, 5 small and operas &c.

Scholarships in Berlin and London, were founded
to Mendelssohn's memory, and at Leipzig, a statue
was erected in 1892, immediately opposite the new
Gewandhaus, 45 years after his death.

SOPHIE MENTER.

ALTHOUGH Franz Liszt often declared that Sophie Menter occupied "the highest position among contemporary pianistes", this opinion also being seconded by a large majority of people, yet it is impossible and scarcely fair to single out one among so many that are equally first rate. For instance, in the present work a great number of excellent musicians are mentioned: Emma Brandes, Teresa Carenno, Annette Essipoff, Arabella Goddard, Clotilde Kleeberg, Mary Krebs, Anna Mehlig, Berthe Marx, Clara Schumann, Frau Clauss-Szarvady &c. It is sufficient for us to add, that no lover of music will hesitate to admire Sophie Menter's masterly playing.

An interesting anecdote is related of Mary Krebs. When she went to Prague, Sophie Menter was also there, and the attraction that the two pianistes excited, naturally led to much party feeling, one faction recognizing Mary Krebs as an ideal pianiste, the other being all for Sophie Menter. Tales were carried backwards and forwards. First, it was reported that so and so had been said in Sophie Menter's disparagement at the "Blauen Stern" where Mary Krebs was lodging, and then in the "Schwarzen Ross" where Sophie Menter was staying, complaints were made that the scandal originated in that Hotel. Mary's mother, who was with her daughter, wished to put an end to all the gossip and ill-feeling, and called on Sophie Menter, (who at first was much surprised at receiving a visit from her), and said "Children, you must bear with each other." The end of the matter was, that they dined together, and in the afternoon their various admirers were not a little surprised to see the two supposed enemies walking arm in arm on the "Graben"; Count Waldstein then inaugurated the Festival hall of his palace with a large Soirée, both the artistes appeared, and each of them was greeted with hearty applause. They separated good friends. If one or the other pianist should make more impression by his or her performance, it will always depend on the taste of the audience; any special charm which an individual may possess, is never without its influence, and Sophie Menter certainly exercises a good deal of personal fascination.

She belongs to a very musical family; her father was the celebrated violoncello player, Joseph Menter, and her mother was also very musical; thus all their children were able to be instructed in the elements of music at home, needing no other teacher than their parents. Sophie was born at Munich on the 29th July, 1846, her mother was also her first instructess. Sigmund Levi, (or Lebert as he was called) a clever piano teacher and with Faisst, Speidel, Laiblin, Stark and Brachmann the joint founder of the Stuttgart Conservatoire became her instructors. When her father left Stuttgart on account of his health, this instruction was interrupted. She then continued her studies at home. Later on she was taught by various unimportant musicians but she was finally much influenced by Bülow, Tausig and Liszt and learned to overcome the greatest technical difficulties; her style of playing gained in grandeur, elegance, and evenness, she acquired feeling and expression.

She made Tausig's acquaintance in Leipzig, on one of her first concert-tours, when she appeared several times at the Gewandhaus concerts. He offered to arrange a concert for her in Berlin; she went there with her mother, and became a pupil of Tausig's, displaying great zeal and perseverance, practising ten hours daily.

In 1868, she was appointed Court Pianist to the Prince of Hohenzollern, a lover of art, at Löwenberg (Silesia). In 1869, she met Liszt in Vienna, and played his concerto in E-flat at a concert. At a private party she played his "Concert Pathétique" for two pianos with him, and from that time he became passionately devoted to her; he invited her to Pesth for several weeks, and she often appeared in public with him, he then accompanied her to Pressburg and again to Vienna, and distinguished her in every possible way. Their friendship was only severed by his death.

She has visited every country in Europe. In Stockholm the King told her she did not play, she made the piano sing. In Copenhagen, the students unharnessed her horses and drew her carriage. She was made honorary member of the London

Philharmonic Society. At Madrid, she became a favorite of the queen's. In Paris, the journalists called her "l'incarnation de Liszt", and in Prague, she became honorary professor of the Conservatoire. At Utrecht, the university even conferred upon her the title of "honorary student". In 1874, she was made pianiste to the Austrian court, in 1883, after repeated visits to St. Petersburg, she became Professor at the Conservatoire there; but when Anton Rubinstein was again appointed director of the institution she wrote to him: "Honoured Herr Colleague! As our esteemed president and also the directors, (nearly all of whom I may call my friends) have relinquished their positions, the Conservatoire seems very desolate to me", and she also resigned.

The banker Stieglitz, was one of her special friends and admirers in Vienna, and made her some of the most magnificent presents.

When not playing on tours she resides at her castle of Itter in Tyrol, which forms a charming residence.

LEOPOLD VON MEYER.

LEOPOLD von Meyer was an excellent pianist who carried on the good traditions of Czerny and Fischhof, and who also made a reputation by his long and numerous concert-tours.

He was born at Baden, near Vienna, on the 20th December 1816, and received instruction from the two musicians already mentioned. From the year 1835, thus from his nineteenth year, he travelled as pianist through the western countries of Europe, Russia, (remaining some time in Moscow) and Turkey.

Then in 1845, he started for the gold-country of all European pianists: America.

In 1847, he returned to Europe, and took up his residence in Vienna; but he died at Dresden on the 6th March 1883.

He was not a composer.

KARL MIKULI.

K ARL Mikuli, was born at Czernowitz, on the 20th Oct.
1821. Although he was a clever pianist belonging
to Chopin's school, yet he was little heard of except
in Austria; he has made a good reputation for himself by his publication of Chopin's works, which are
full of many corrections and different readings,
arranged according to the notes made by the immortal master himself.

He had originally commenced to study medicine
in Vienna, yet his love for music caused him to aban-
don his intention of becoming a physician, and in
1844, he went to Paris to begin a thorough course of

training under the guidance of Chopin and Weber. Chopin's notes were originally in the copy of his works used by Mikuli when teaching.

After the outbreak of the Paris Revolution in February 1848, Mikuli returned home, and gave concerts in various towns in Austria. In 1858, he became Director of the Galizian Musical Union at Lemberg, with which a conservatoire is connected.

SEBASTIAN BACH MILLS.

THE fact that Mills' father was a musician is very evident from the baptismal name he received, and it bears witness to his father's special preference for the great German composer. He was born on the 13th March 1838, at Cirencester, received his first musical tuition from his father, and then, in 1856, went to the conservatoire at Leipzig, where for three years Moscheles and Plaidy, were his teachers for piano.

Immediately after completing his studies. he went to the United States and Bergmann engaged him for his first concert in New York; he played Schumann's piano concerto, and Liszt's Fantasie "A Midsummer

Night's Dream" and with such brilliant success, that he determined to remain in the city as pianist and teacher, and in both capacities particularly in the latter, he has gained great esteem. He has composed some very pretty, although not important pianoforte pieces.

MORTIER DE FONTAINE.

Henry Louis Stanislaus Mortier de Fontaine, born on the 13ᵗʰ May 1818, at Wisnowisce (Wolhynien) was a fellow student of Chopin's; they were both taught by Elsner at Warsaw. Yet it soon became evident in their youth that Chopin was the greater of the two, and possessed great talent for composition which was not noticeable in Mortier's case. After the completion of his studies, Fontaine played in public in various western cities, meeting with great success, he lived in St. Petersburg from 1853 to 1860, (according to some authorities only five years) giving concerts and also teaching. He visited Paris and Munich, and went several times to London where he soon gained the position of a favourite pianoforte player and teacher.

His extraordinary execution was specially praised; yet he was also capable of entering into the spirit of the musical works he played, and did justice to the composer's intentions; he and Clara Schumann are said to have been the first to play in public Beethoven's celebrated sonata op. 106; Fontaine also performed the sonatas composed in the latter period of the great master's life, with intelligence and technical proficiency. He died in London, May 10th 1883.

IGNAZ MOSCHELES.

MOSCHELES artistic life can be divided into two
parts; his career as a pianist and as a teacher.
In both spheres and also as a composer, he has met
with great success, but his activity as a teacher seems
to have been of the longest duration, and he may be
reckoned among the most renowned, sympathetic and
practical pianoforte teachers of modern music. The
universal opinion of musical historians is, that he was
the most important pianist after Hummel's death, and
before Chopin's appearance.

Ignaz Moscheles, was born at Prague, on the
30th May 1794, in that city Dionysius Weber became
his piano-teacher. In his fourteenth year he appeared
in public as pianist playing one of his own compositions.

He then went to Vienna to continue his studies under
the guidance of Salieri and Albrechtsberger, main-
taining himself by giving lessons on the piano.
Moscheles has related the way in which, when he
was young he became acquainted with Beethoven's
works. "I was entrusted to Dyonisius Weber's guidance and tuition; fearing that in my eagerness to
play new music, I might damage my systematical
pianoforte education, he forbade me the use of the
music lending library and in the plan which he
had lay before my parents for their inspection, he
made one particular condition, that I was to study
no other composer's works than those of Mozart,
Clementi, and Sebastian Bach. Yet I must confess
that in spite of this order I made use of the library,
my pocket money enabling me to do so. At that
time I heard from some of my companions that a
young musician had appeared in Vienna, who wrote
the strangest things in the world, that no one could
either play or understand; this composer's name was
Beethoven. The next visit I paid to the library I
satified my curiosity with regard to this excentric
genius, and I found Beethoven's "Sonate pathétique".
That was in 1804. Not having sufficient money to
purchase it, I copied it in secret. The novelty of
his style was so fascinating, and I admired it so
enthusiastically, that I forgot what I was doing, and
spoke of my new treasure to my teacher. He reminded
me of his injunction and warned me not to play or
study such excentric works before I had completed
my musical education, and to take examples of a
more solid kind. However, paying no heed to his
wishes, I practised Beethoven's works in the order in
which they where published, and found in them such
consolation and pleasure which I have experienced
with no other music."

Some years later, Beethoven took him under his

special patronage, and in 1814, gave him permission to arrange the pianoforte edition of "Fidelio". A year later, Moscheles wrote the Variations on the Alexander March which gained great success. He became popular in the best society in Vienna. At this time also he wrote his "Polonaise" in E-flat and a sonata as a pianoforte duet in the same key. In 1816, he started on a concert-tour, visiting among other towns Munich, Leipzig, Dresden &c., and attracting much attention wherever he went by his great technical proficiency, the brilliant and finished style of his execution and his clever performance of the great classical works. His improvisation was also much admired.

He first visited Paris, in 1820, and there too he created a great sensation, if journalists of that time did not exaggerate. A year later he settled in London, became a very popular teacher, and made a good business with his pianoforte compositions, occasionally visiting the continent, where he formed a friendship with Spohr. In 1824, he stayed six weeks in Berlin, visited Mendelssohn's family daily, and gave him pianoforte lessons. This acquaintance resulted in Mendelssohn's coming to London, through Moscheles' invitation in 1829, and with his help the former met with a brilliant reception from the musical world; in later years Mendelssohn in his turn remembered Moscheles, and invited him to Leipzig. They were very intimate friends, and Mendelssohn was god-father to one of Moscheles' children in 1833. Their correspondence and some extracts from Moscheles' life published by his wife prove that theirs was a lasting friendship. In 1825, Moscheles was married at Hamburg, and the fact that he re-visited Paris in the same year, before again settling in England, is to be gathered from Adam Liszt's letters. The latter writing from Paris to Czerny on the 14th August 1825, in anything but a cordial manner, says: "Moscheles appeared during this time and many of the critics took a great deal of trouble to place him first and foremost, to the exclusion of all other talented men but they failed in the attempt. Herr Moscheles as well as Herr Hummel were obliged to seek an opening by calling on the best musicians for help and gave their concerts in insignificant concert-rooms, having to content themselves with small profits. These gentlemen believed they possess immense capabilities and imagined they would carry off large sums of money, but their expectations were not realized and no one thinks any more about them."

Finally in 1846 Moscheles removed to Leipzig, and became teacher at the Conservatoire and in this position he worked with great activity until his death on the 10th March 1870. He had a great many very good pupils.

Moscheles composed altogether 142 works, 7 pianoforte Concertos, Sextets, Duets, Sonatas, Variations, Rondos &c. Special works of his are the Concertos in C- and in G-minor, the duet "Hommage à Haendel", the variations on the Theme "Au clair de la lune", the "Sonate melancholique" a Sonata for piano and violincello, and his excellent Studies op. 70, 95 and 99.

MOZART.

As a Biography of Mozart cannot for want of space in this collection be very extensive, I propose extracting the principal points from Otto Jahn's great work on this eminent musician. This book is written in a truly thoughtful and reverential spirit, far excelling all other works on the same subject, namely; those of Schlichtegroll, Beyle, Niemetschek, Rochlitz, Cramer, Suard, Guattani, Arnold, Hormayr, Lichtenthal, Schlosser, Nissen, Fétis, Holmes, Goschler, Ulibischeff, Nohl, Köchel, Wurzbach, Meinardus, Wilder, Nottebohm &c. For although these authors were conscientious in what they wrote, yet no other writer was so competent to produce such an important work on the subject as Otto Jahn, his study of the life and works of the great composer being more profound and comprehensive. Although it is true that the speciality of this book is to speak of those eminent musicians who distinguished themselves as pianists and composers for the pianoforte, yet on account of the great influence Mozart exercised for all time on music, it will be impossible merely to take into consideration his work as a pianist and composer for the pianoforte. It will therefore be necessary to give a sketch of his whole life from the first development of his genius. To attempt to measure the growth of such a genius would be just as superfluous as it would be in the case of Schiller and Goethe. That Mozart was a youthful prodigy in pianoforte playing, is as well known as the fact that he reached the highest pinnacle of fame by his operas: "The magic Flute", "The marriage of Figaro" and "Don Juan." He always maintained a high position as a pianist. When he was twenty-one years of age, his mother wrote from Mannheim to her husband as follows: "Wolfgang is very much thought of everywhere; he plays quite differently to what he did at Salzburg; he has the choice of so many pianos here and his performance is quite matchless, nothing has been heard to equal it; in fact every one that hears him, says, he is without a rival. Although Beeké has been here and Schubart also, yet Wolfgang is said to excel them in beauty of expression and refinement; he causes great astonishment by his improvising as also by reading whatever is put before him." In a year's time he wrote to his father himself from Mannheim on the subject of pianoforte-playing: "I will willingly give lessons as a favour; particulary if the pupil is talented, and is anxious to learn. But to have to go out and give a lesson at a certain hour, or to be obliged to wait at home for a pupil, this I cannot do, even if it should bring me in a considerable sum. I cannot possibly do it, and therefore leave it to those who do nothing but play the piano. I am a composer and am born to be a conductor; God has so richly endowed me with a gift for composition (I may say this without boasting, as I feel it now more than ever) that I ought not to put it on one side, and yet this is sure to happen in constant teaching, which is very wearisome work. I would rather if I may say so, neglect piano playing than composition; the piano being only a secondary consideration with me, although a very important one."

Still from all accounts of his life, it is admitted that he still cultivated piano-playing, both from choice and necessity. Wolfgang Amadeus Mozart was born at Salzburg on the 27th of January 1756. His father Leopold Mozart was originally a lawyer, and musician for his own pleasure, then he entered the service of a canon, Count Thurn and Taxis, and became violinist and vice-conductor in the private chapel of the Prince Archbishop of Salzburg, he was an able composer and wrote Masses, Concertos, Sonatas, Trios, Marches, Dances, violin solos &c., and was also a clever pianist and organist, but always laboured under the disadvantage of having badly paid appointments. His son and a daughter were the only two that survived of a family of seven children, and he was therefore doubly anxious that the boy should advance much further than he himself had ever done; so he turned the child's attention in his earliest youth to music; nor was this at all difficult, as Wolfgang's inclination in that direction showed itself before even instruction was thought of. When he was four years old he could play the piano and also on a small violin. His father often played Trios at home with MM. Schachtner and Wenzl, one day he was unable to take part in the performance for want of time, and little Wolfgang begged to be allowed to take his place. His father chided him for his boldness thinking it a piece of childish nonsense; Wolfgang's pride was hurt and he forthwith began to cry, but as Schachtner interceded for him he was finally allowed to play. He took the second violin, and played so remarkably that the three men were thoroughly astonished. Wolfgang thought the second violin was too easy, and that he could take the first. He was able to do this also with such success that he moved his father to tears. The boy had a very sensitive ear for music, which made him so nervous, that he almost fainted at the sound of a trumpet. Father Scharl, professor at the school at Salzburg used to speak of the boy's piano playing at that time with great admiration: "The octaves that he could not stretch with his little hands, he would skip over with extraordinary rapidity and accuracy." Even at that time the boy loved to extemporise at the piano, and composed short pieces, one of them being a concerto for piano which he composed when he was five years old.

After Leopold Mozart had also given sufficient instruction in piano playing to his little daughter "Nannerl", he started on concert tours with the two children; the first journey brought them to Munich, where they played before the Elector, then went on to Vienna, where Wolfgang created a great sensation in the aristocratic world by his playing. On the 13th September 1762, Leopold Mozart was commanded to bring his two children to Schönbrunn, where they had to play before the Emperor and his children. The Emperor was highly delighted with "the little wizard" and made him play with one finger and also with the key-board covered, rewarding him richly—. Even at that time, little Mozart showed remarkable evidence of sensibility, which increased with years.

He was annoyed when he did not play before connoisseurs, and once when the Emperor and a number
of gentlemen of the Court stood round him, he looked
about him before beginning to play and then asked
aloud: "Is Herr Wagenseil not here?" Wagenseil
ranked as the best pianoforte-player in Vienna. The
Emperor sent for him and when he drew near the
piano, Mozart made this remark to him: "I am going
to play a concerts of yours, you must turn over for
me." In 1763, a long series of tours was begun, to
Munich (Nymphenburg), Augsburg, Ludwigsburg,
Schwetzingen, Heidelberg, Mayence, Frankfort, Coblentz,
Cologne, Bonn, Aachen, Brussels, Paris, London, the
Hague, Lille, Ghent, Antwerp, then again to Paris,
Dijon, Lyons, Geneva, Lausanne, Berne, Zürich,
Winterthur, Schaffhausen, Biberach, Ulm, Günzburg,
Dillingen, &c—. The expedition was a complete
triumph, Wolfgang's playing made the deepest impression on the very best connoisseurs, and the
throngs of people seeking admission to hear him were
so great, that three and four concerts were sometimes
given in one town. Goethe who was then seventeen
years old heard him in Frankfort—. In Paris, the
well-known Baron von Grimm did a great deal to
bring the children into notice. Amongst others,
Wolfgang was introduced to Madame Pompadour;
she had him placed on a table before her, but when
he bent down to kiss her she turned away from him;
whereupon he said angrily: "Wo does this person
think she is, that she should refuse to kiss me, when
even the Empress has seen fit to embrace me!"

On the other hand the King's daughters were
very sympathetic towards him.

When he was in London, George III caused him
to perform pieces by Bach, Händel, Abel, Wagenseil
and other composers, reading everything at sight.
And it was here that Wolfgang gave wonderful

examples of his organ-playing, which was even thought to excel his pianoforte performance. He had only learnt to play the organ at Wasserburg when on his travels with his parents, and when an accident happened to their carriage they were detained for one day. It was wonderful too to hear him accompanying French and Italian arias at sight and even transposing some of them, and to the bass part of one of Händel's Arias which he had never before seen he at once improvised a most lovely melody. Leopold Mozart writes thus from London: "It is more than the imagination can conceive. What Wolfgang knew when we left Salzburg is absolutely nothing compared to what he knows now ... My little girl is one of the cleverest players in Europe, although she is only twelve, and the great Wolfgang in his eighth year has the knowledge of a man of forty. It can only be believed, by those who both see and hear".

When he was in London, Wolfgang almost always played his own compositions, the first Symphony in E-flat, then three other Symphonies in B-flat, E-flat and D. His father had some of the boy's compositions printed in London, they were six sonatas for piano, violin and flute. In 1765, he composed the Aria for tenor, "Va dal furor portata". On his return journey at the Hague, he wrote the Aria for Soprano, "Conservati fedele", a Symphony in B-flat, six sonatas for piano and violin for the Princess of Weilburg, an orchestral piece with the following title, "Galimathias musicum"; in Mechlin, he composed a Kyrie in four parts for chorus with an accompaniement of stringed instruments; and at Munich while at the dinner-table he wrote a piece of music of several bars length on a theme which was sung to him by the Elector.

This entire journey, which was also undertaken by Leopold Mozart's wife, lasted for three years, then the family returned to Salzburg. As Leopold Mozart was still in the service of the Archbishop, the latter must have been particularly indulgent as regards the long leave of absence; this is worth mentioning, as later on the Prince changed his mode of conduct and was particularly rough towards Wolfgang. He seems to have had a certain satisfaction in the thought that the little son of one of his musicians had caused such a stir by his genius. He could not quite believe in the great wonders the boy wrought in music, and we are told that he had Wolfgang shut up for several days, so that he might compose an oratorio without any help. This the boy achieved to the Archbishop's satisfaction. Jahn says, respecting the 208 pages of the score of this oratorio, that, outwardly it bore unmistakeable traces of work done by a boy, but that the music itself contained nothing childish. "The whole work is in the style of Italian Oratorio, the form being handled with perfect certainty ... There is hardly a sign of inexperience throughout, everything is efficient; it is apparent that the composer has made good use of his experience."

The work was written in verse, which needed deep religious feeling; and this gives additional weight to the fact that the boy of ten thoroughly entered into the spirit of the words.

After Wolfgang returned home from the long musical tour, he went on a visit to a monastery at Seeon, "being on friendly terms with the monks there." During dinner, the prelate was deploring the lack of an offertory for the feast of St. Benedict. Wolfgang got up from the table and went into the adjoining room, where he at once wrote down on the window ledge the offertory "Scande coeli limina", which opens with a pleasing soprano solo, the flowing melody of which is carried along with an accompaniment of violins and is then followed by a vigorous chorus with trumpets and drums.

In 1767 he also wrote a dramatic scena: "Apollo et Hyacinthus", for a special occasion at the Salzburg University.

As a preparation for a musical tour to Vienna, he composed in the same year four Concertos for piano, in F, B flat, D and G; this journey, undertaken by the whole Mozart family, commenced on the 11th of September, but terminated very unfortunately. Small-pox broke out in Vienna, the Princess Josepha died of it, and consequently all court festivities (including the musical performance already arranged) had to be put off. Leopold Mozart fled with his family to Olmütz, but here Wolfgang became so ill with the dreadful disease, that he was blind for nine days. After his recovery they all returned to Salzburg, and the journey to Vienna was again undertaken in the following year, but this tour was also not a favorable one. Since the death of her husband, Francis I., the Empress lost all interest in music; the Emperor Joseph was very parsimonious; Prince Kaunitz was afraid to receive "Wolfgangerl" because he still bore the marks of his recent illness. The Vienna public had no taste for music in its noblest form, but only cared for balls and buffoonery. All musicians of consequence at that time were much against the youthful prodigy, they spread about the report that there was nothing in this great talent but tricks in playing, and that Mozart's father was at the bottom of it all. Leopold Mozart took the greatest trouble to give fresh proofs of Wolfgang's genius, but was not able to cope with the envious disparagement of these professional musicians, especially as the Emperor did not support him in the matter. At last, to avoid the possibility of sacrificing any of his own money, the Emperor proposed that Wolfgang should compose an opera, to be performed under the direction of Affligio, manager of a theatre. This man had formerly

led a life of swindling and imposture, and had managed
to attain to the rank of lieutenant-colonel; in Vienna,
among other exploits, he gave the following proof of
his feeling for art. During one of the dog-fights (then
still in vogue in Vienna) he said to a friend pointing
to two famous "Ochsenfänger": "I like those two
animals better than any of my best actors."

Finally this adventurer found his way to the
galleys as a convict.

It was with such a caracter as this that Mozart
and his son had to come in contact. Although
Wolfgang's first youthful opera "La finta semplice"
"was better than any of the thirty operas performed
in Vienna", yet Affligio put off the performance from
month to month, making all sorts of excuses in the
matter. The other composers were enraged to be
put on one side by a boy. Even Gluck himself,
perhaps unjustly, was said to have taken part in
these jealous intrigues. The Emperor continued to
interest himself in Mozart's work, but avoided interfering
with Affligio, on account of the free admission to the
theatre which was extended to the court, although
nothing was done in return towards the support of
the stage. At last driven to extremity by Leopold
Mozart, the impressario declared he intended giving
the opera, but he also intended it should prove an
entire failure. Wolfgang's father was obliged in
despair, to withdraw the opera after remaining nearly
a year in the city with his family and having had to
make many sacrifices.

The Italians at that time governed nearly the
whole musical world, and although Wolfgang himself
had not freed himself of the Italian fashion of
composing, yet in the main he was a German, his
power was making itself felt and for that reason not
allowed to come to the front.

These events in connection with Mozart's first

opera were only the prelude to numerous obstacles that were put in his way in Vienna during nearly the whole of his life. Still his life in that city was not altogether without artistic results: Wolfgang's little opera, "Bastien and Bastienne" was performed at a theatre belonging to a Dr. Messmer, supposed to be the well-known magnetizer; then on the 7th of December 1768, the court was present at a perfor- mance of Mozart's Offertory "Veni sancte spiritus" in C; this took place under the patronage of the Jesuit, Father Parhammer at the Waisenhaus Church in the Rennweg.

After Mozart's return home, the Archbishop had his opera "La finta" performed at a theatre in Salzburg. He spent the year 1767, in Salzburg, engaged in his own studies and in composing; then he made a tour in Italy, where he distinguished himself as pianist, organist and as composer; first at Innsbruck, then at Roveredo, Verona, Mantua; and here the Philharmonic Society gave a concert, at which musicians described Mozart as a "masterpiece of nature" which certainly implied that "the most experienced musicians were put to shame."

In Milan, the Governor General Count v. Firmian took him unders his protection, let him compose music to Metastasio's words and commissioned him to write an opera (Mitridate, Ré di Ponto,). He then played at concerts in Bologna, Florence (where Nardini accompanied him on the violin); at Rome he played before several aristocratic families; at Naples a very crowded public concert took place, and it was here that as the audience fancied Mozart's great execution of the left hand was due to a 'magic' ring he wore on that hand, he drew off the ring and played on with the same brilliancy; this occasioned a storm of applause.

During a second visit to Bologna, the Accademia

filarmonica admitted Mozart to the class of "compositori",
although he had not attained the required age, of
twenty years.

Then followed a great triumph, the performance
of "Mitridate" at Milan. Here too intrigues were set
on foot to prevent the performance of the opera, and
as this was not possible, reports were circulated
beforehand, proclaiming the work to be "a miserable
and youthful production" (as Leopold Mozart relates
in a letter); but the success was a grand one, the
most important musicians were very enthusiastic about
it and the opera was repeated over twenty times.
The public bestowed the honourable title of "Cavaliere
filarmonico" on the composer; this was confirmed
further by the Accademia filarmonica at Verona,
Mozart being made one of the members.

Mozart returned again to Salzburg on 28th March
1771, after having received a commission to write a
second opera for the theatre at Milan, and also making
a pleasant stay at Turin, as well as at Venice and
Padua. Here he was commissioned by the Empress
Maria Theresia to write a dramatic Serenade for the
occasion of the marriage of the Archduke Ferdinand
to the Princess of Modena, Maria Ricciarda Beatrice;
this serenade was to be performed at Milan. Hasse
had also to compose something for the same occasion,
the two composers therefore met at Milan. Mozart's
"Ascanio in Alba" quite put Hasse's "Ruggiero" in
the shade, so much so, that Hasse declared: "no one
will ever be remembered but this youth", and Leopold
Mozart wrote · home as follows: "I am sorry that
Wolfgang's serenade has so ruined Hasse's opera, to
such an extent that it is impossible to describe."

When he was in Milan, Wolfgang agreed to
write an opera for the theatre S. Benedetto in Venice,
to be ready for the carnival in 1773, but he did not
carry out his agreement. While travelling home

with his father, the Archbishop's death took place
and "to the general surprise and sorrow of the people",
the very unpopular Hieronymus Count Colloredo was
appointed his successor.

Mozart was barely seventeen at that time and
although his great works, entirely shorn of the
customary Italian style, belong to a later period of
his life, yet his two journeys to Italy and all that
took place during the time, must be considered as of
the greatest importance. He then became filled with
the self-consciousness and the knowledge of his task
in life, to devote himself to the compostition of great
works, namely to writing operas. If the musical value
of these youthful operas bear no comparison with
that of his later works, yet these compositions are a
significant transition as regards his development, and
show the position accorded then to operatic works.
The operas of Mozart's youth are: "Mitridate", "Il
Sogno di Scipione" (a work composed for the installation
of the Archbishop Hieronymus), "Lucio Silla" (for
Milan), "La finta giardiniera", "Ascanio in Alba"
(festival opera for Milan), "Il Ré pastore". Nevertheless Otto Jahn in his biography of Mozart makes
the following remarks with regard to certain elements
in "Ascanio": "In this work so much freedom and
precision are apparent, everything is kept so well
subdued, in order to get the proper effect, that it was
probably here that Hasse recognised the lion by
his claws."

The choice of Count Colloredo to be Archbishop
was of the greatest importanca in Mozart's life; this
this proud and arrogant nobleman, who thought nothing
of the dignity of art and cultivation of the mind,
behaved in such a manner to the two Mozarts and
particularly to Wolfgang, that the latter severed his
connection with him forthwith and took up an
independent position. Mozart had nevertheless striven

to obtain a position in the service of the new Archbishop and had received that of "conductor", at 150
Gulden a year; but his state of dependence became
unbearable, and notwithstanding all the efforts of a
self-denying father like Leopold Mozart, and the fact
that Wolfgang was far above the men of his day,
yet is was impossible for the latter ever to obtain a
post he had ardently longed for, namely that of
conductor of an orchestra. The principal obstacles
to this were, that the Emperor Joseph although he
was humane and just, yet lacked the ideal feeling
for art and was not open-handed; then Archbishop
Hieronymus was tyrannical and barbarous like the
feudal nobles of the middle ages; the two Electors
Maximilian and Karl Theodor could not understand
Mozart's genius and considered that music was better
represented at their courts by the musicians they
already had; Mozart although not of striking personal
appearance, was filled with a noble pride for his art
and an insatiable desire for liberty, he never cringed
to any one. The people were then sadly in need of
cultivation. Mozart's genius was wrecked, like that
of young Schiller, by trifling social circumstances,
although he was always of great note among people
of culture and high standing.

From 1772, his activity as a composer increased
more and more, he wrote symphonies, quartets, concertos
for wind instruments, but his principal compositions
at that time were sacred works. As regards the latter,
Otto Jahn says: "The inducement Mozart had to write
sacred music and instrumental music almost exclusively,
was due to circumstances at Salzburg, but he certainly
felt the great need to turn his mind to all forms of
composition." The same biographer also mentions that
in 1773, when the Archbishop was staying in Vienna,
Leopold Mozart made use of the opportunity to go
with his son to that city, to try and obtain an

appointment either at Vienna or at some other Court. The father and son had an audience of the Empress, who was very gracious to them, but that was all. At the end of their stay at Vienna, the Emperor came back from Poland unexpectedly; it seems they had never even spoken to him.

Then the performances of the new opera "La finta giardiniera", and of some sacred works in Munich in 1775, brought Mozart nothing but the commendation of the Court, the composer not altogether appreciating this. During Mozart's stay in Munich he played several times in public. Schubart, who was subsequently imprisoned in the "Hohenasperg" writes as follows: "Last winter in Munich I heard two of the greatest pianists, Mozart and v. Beecke; my host, Herr Albert, who is a great enthusiast for everything beautiful, possesses an excellent pianoforte, so I heard there two great performers. Mozart plays with great power, and reads whatever is put before him; but that is all that can be said; Beecke is far superior. His execution is wonderfully liquid, his playing full of grace and his taste is thoroughly original, no one can compete with him." On the other hand this opinion is refuted by the universal praise bestowed on Mozart's playing. However Mozart was not able to get a commission from the Elector to write an opera. On his return to Salzburg in the same year, he wrote five violin concertos, hoping to get employment more easily as a violin-player. In the following year he also composed a great deal for the piano, for instance, the concerto in C; most of the compositions were "for pupils and amateurs", and among other works, he wrote the Concerto for three pianos and a number of Sonatas, for some of which he received no remuneration. After 1773, he began to compose quartets and again in 1784, when he was in Vienna.

He took part in the court concerts in Salzburg

as violinist, and although violin playing was a burden
to him, yet at the instigation of his father, he studied
the instrument with a view to becoming a solo player.

In 1777, his father wrote thus to him: "You do
not know how well you play the violin; if yon would
only think a great deal of yourself and play boldly
with intelligence and fire, you might be the greatest
violinist in Europe." Justice was done him at Salzburg
by Brunetti, the greatest violin-player of that time
and a favourite of the Archbishop's.

In 1777, Mozart writes thus rather ironically from
Munich: "the audience was lost in wonder, I played
as if I had been the greatest violinist in Europe"; and
then again from Augsburg: "I composed a Symphony
and played Wanhall's violin concerto in B flat receiving
universal applause. In the evening after supper I
played the Strassburg concerto. It was a great
success, and everybody praised my beautiful pure
tone." Later on to the great grief of his father, he
gave up violin-playing and when he took part in
quartets in Vienna, he chose the viola in preference.
He only kept up his piano playing at home or among
a small circle of friends, as the piano was not
considered worthy of notice at Court; and at that
time he had very little inducement to busy himself with
piano compositions. He therefore made preparations
to leave Salzburg and commence another tour, taking
many new works for piano with him and often playing
during his journey, also in Paris. His father was very
loth to part with him, being afraid he would never
manage to get on alone, quite forgetting that he was
very much to blame for always exercising control
over his son, expecting entire obedience from him.
Therefore as a precaution, his mother accompanied
Wolfgang on this journey. It entirely broke up the
household, and was a great sacrifice on Leopold
Mozart's part, who only acted thus for his son's good.

At that time Wolfgang was never able to make a sufficient living for himself and his mother, and money had to be sent from time to time by his father, who fell into debt in consequence. In September 1777, at the beginning of this lengthened tour, the first halt was made at Munich. Mozart here applied to the Prince Bishop of Chiemsee, Count Zeil, to intercede for him at Court. After a few days, the Bishop said to him:

I do not think anything can be done at Court. At the dinner table at Nymphenburg, I had some private conversation with the Elector. He said: the time has not come yet. And his wife also had promised to do a great deal, but she would not give the subject any attention." Mozart then lay in wait for the Elector as he was returning from a hunting expedition; the account that Wolfgang gave of this meeting in a letter to his father, is so characteristic, that it is well worth recording: "As the Elector came near me, I said: „Will your Highness allow me to devote myself to your service'.—'What, entirely, away from Salzburg?' —'Yes, your Highness, quite away from there.'—'What is the reason of this?'

—'Oh, your Highness, I begged to be allowed to travel, this was at first refused to me, but I was forced to take this step; although I had long wished to leave, it is very certain that Salzburg is no place for me!— 'Good gracious, and such a young man! But your father is still in Salzburg?"—"Yes he is, your Highness, and is your humble servant. I have already been three times to Italy, I have written three operas, I am a member of the Academy at Bologna, and had to pass such an examination; so many others laboured hard for four and five hours, and I accomplished the work in one hour; that is a proof that I can be of use at any Court. But my sole wish your Highness, is to be with you, who are such a great . . . .", my dear child,

there is no vacancy now. I am sorry for it, if only
there was something for you."

"I can assure your Highness, that I would do honour
to Munich . . . ."—'That is of no use, there is no
vacancy". This he said as he moved away, and I
took my leave."—

Mozarts's efforts to make a better income were
unavailing.—Friends in Munich were full of empty
promises. Nothing came of a fresh journey to Italy.
The mother and son went from Munich to Augsburg,
Wolfgang created a great sensation by his organ and
piano playing, but the worthy inhabitants of the town
would sacrifice nothing for an "Akademie" there; when
Mozart not only took part in the orchestra in one of
his symphonies, but also played some of his piano
pieces, he only received two ducats.

Leopold Mozart on hearing of this, was in a fury
at such a beggarly proceeding. But at a public
concert $73^1/_2$ Gulden was made, all clear gain.

Then Mozart went to Mannheim, where the Elector,
Karl Theodor, was surrounded with musicians of the
first order, the orchestra consisting of first-rate players,
who soon made friends with Mozart.

There was an opera there, in which Italian music
was performed by German singers. Mozart surpassed all
expectation by his piano playing, although he could
not secure a position under the Elector. When the
latter moved the Court from Mannheim to Munich,
after the death of the Elector Max, and the end of
the Bavarian war, even then Mozart was not able to
get any appointment. He entered into negociations
with Wendling (flute-player) Ramm, (oboist) and Ritter,
(bassoon-player) to undertake a concert tour to Paris,
Leopold Mozart was strongly against this project,
although in the end he gave way. Suddenly Wolfgang
himself showed signs of hesitation; he had become very
much attached to a singer in Mannheim, Aloysia Weber,

and he had not strength of mind enough to separate himself from her. He concealed all this from his father, and even his mother, who was with him at the time, was not aware for a long time of the real reason of his change of plans. In a letter to his father at that time, he shows how difficult it was for him to decide anything definite; he begged Wendling, if he should follow him to Paris, "to try and arrange something of importance for him, especially if it concerned an opera. I think a great deal about writing operas, French in preference to German, but Italian rather than French or German". In the same letter to his father he goes on to say that he would be glad to give lessons "for nothing". This proposition appeared once before in the earlier part of the present biographical sketch. Then came Leopold Mozart's answer: "So you want to give lessons for nothing! Do you wish your old father to die of want? Is it too much trouble for a young man like you to work for your living? I suppose you think it more suitable for an old man of 58 like your father, to try and scrape together a miserable pittance to support himself and his daughter, and instead of paying his debts, to send even a small sum towards your maintenance, you, in the meantime amuse yourself by giving a girl lessons for nothing. My son, think this well over and be reasonable, you will see you are more cruel to me than the Prince."

Wolfgang wrote a reassuring letter in reply, saying the road to Paris was not closed to him &c., but he continued all the same to receive pecuniary help from his father, he also went on giving singing lessons to Aloysia Weber, who later on proved faithless to him. He instructed her in all his Arias; he planned a tour in Italy with the Weber family, and asked his father to facilitate matters for them. The latter wrote indignantly to him, showing him the folly of such an undertaking, how impossible it would be to introduce

a girl as a prima-donna when she had never appeared
on any stage, also how unfeasible a concert tour was
at a time when the country was threatened with war;
then a roving life with a stranger and his daughters
(Aloysia and Constance) would ruin his career and
disgrace his family. "It is quite in your own hands,
whether you wish to be an ordinary musician, soon
forgotten by the world, or to become celebrated for
all time: whether you prefer a life of poverty with a
woman of no character, and a pack of starving children,
or to end your days after a happy and well-spent life,
respected and honoured by all, your name made
immortal all over the world . . . . Away with you
to Paris and quickly too! Place yourself among those
that are really great—aut Cæsar aut nihil!"

After a severe struggle Mozart complied with his
father's wishes: "My motto as a child was, first God
and then my father; and I will keep to this even now."
But before he left with his mother, he did a great
deal to introduce Aloysia Weber in public, so much
so that she managed to get on without him, married
some one else, and became known as an opera singer.
When they arrived in Paris, Mozart and his mother
took very small poor rooms, which would not even
contain a piano; the poor woman suffered a good deal,
her son going into society, she was left very much
alone and often denied herself the necessities of life.
Mozart made a number of agreeable friends, composed
several things, played now and then at small parties,
and gave a few lessons for which he was badly
paid, but was not entirely successful. His mother then
fell ill, and after lingering several weeks, was released
by death from a sad life of privation, far from her
husband and daughter. After this heavy blow, Wolfgang could not content himself in Paris—he missed
his mother's tender care and resolved to go elsewhere;
he was very anxious to get employment with the

Elector Karl Theodor, but did not succeed in doing so. His father now worked untiringly for him in Salzburg, particurlarly as the organist Adlgasser and the conductor Lolli, both died about that time. Although Wolfgang wrote to his great friend Bullinger: "You know how I hate Salzburg, not only on account of the injustice done to my dear father and to me, which would be quite sufficient to make me forget the town and root it out of my mind", yet he expressed himself willing to accept an appointment from the Archbishop.

He left Paris in 1778, on the 26th of September. Otto Jahn, speaking of this episode, says: "Although Mozart's success in Paris was not great, and although he may not have accomplished all he wished, yet it was a distinct gain to his musical career; he freed himself from the Italian school, after a thorough experience of it, recognising and becoming instilled with the reality of the element of dramatic form."

On his protracted journey home, he gave three concerts at Strasburg without orchestra, (as he feared the expense), these concerts were so badly attended that altogether he only made 7 Louisd'or. He wrote as follows; "at any rate I took trouble about the concerts and they added to my reputation." When he reached Mannheim, he was again full of hope, and wavered in his determination to go to Salzburg; his father remonstrated seriously with him, and wrote to say how necessary it was for him to come at once, "surely you could not be so cruel and wicked as to make a laughing-stock of me, who am so constantly anxious about your welfare."

At last Wolfgang set out on his journey after months of hesitation; he passed through Munich, where he came across the beloved Aloysia Weber, etablished as an opera singer and completely changed. She appeared not to know the man about whom she had formerly wept so much. Therefore Mozart quickly sat down to the piano, and sang loudly: "I am glad to be rid of the girl that does not care for me"; this story is told by Nissen, Mozart's first biographer. Mozart returned to Salzburg against his will, and the Archbishop grudgingly gave him an appointment as "conductor and organist, at the Court and the cathedral". The father and son together were to receive a thousand Gulden a year, but afterwards Wolfgang's salary was four hundred Gulden instead of five hundred.

In 1780, he received a commission from Munich to write a great opera for the carnival, and Mozart, always hoping to be released from the slavery in Salzburg, composed "Idomeneo", partly in Salzburg, and partly when away on leave in Munich. After one of the rehearsals, the Elector spoke of the music as magnificent. The performance was a brilliant one, but the pay was very scanty, and there was no talk of an appointment. Before Mozart could return to Salzburg, he received notice from Archbishop Hieronymus to go to Vienna. The latter wished to make a sensation with his orchestra; it was the custom for the rich to have musicians to perform not only in their private houses but also to play at soirées; on these occasions the musicians were obliged to stand behind the door like servants, until their turn came to play. In fact they were treated the same as servants, having to take their meals with them. Mozart mentions who his companious were at table, namely, the cooks, the confectioners, valets, the quarter-master, also the two musicians Brunetti and Ceccarelli, the valets taking precedence of these three.

To the annoyance of his father, Mozart was indignant at such treatment, and when he was present at any performances in strange houses, he would not let the lacqueys show him to his place, but went straight into the music-room. If he ever wished to play in public, the Archbishop refused his permission.

The latter was universally disliked by the nobility and the Emperor did not care for his society.

Suddenly he gave orders through Count Arco, chief manager of the kitchen, that his musicians were to return to Salzburg. Mozart would not submit to this, as he wished to be properly recognised in Vienna as composer and pianist. The Archbishop hated him on account of his self-will, and often called him a good-for-nothing fellow; that he might go about his business, and that there were hundreds who would fill his place much better. As Mozart did not leave with the other musicians, he was called before the Archbishop who fell to abusing him: "When do you intend to go, fellow?" Mozart tried to excuse himself. But the Archbishop refused to let him speak and continued to abuse him; he considered him the most careless fellow he had ever known, no one could be such a bad servant, he advised him to leave at once or he would write and withdraw his salary. Mozart writing about this interview says: "He called me a scamp, a mean fellow . . . . Finally I could bear it no longer and said to him: "Is your Grace not satisfied with me?"—

"How dare you try to threaten me! You villain! There is the door—and remember, I will have nothing more to do with such a miserable fellow." In another letter to his father, he said; "I did not know I was a valet, and so I came to grief. I ought to have frittered away several hours every morning in the ante-room; I was often told I ought to put in an appearance,—but I never could remember my duties, and only obeyed the summons from the Archbishop whenever he required my presence."

He did all in his power to impress upon his father, who tried to dissuade him, that he must have his liberty; he was full of hope and could not be moved from his determination, not even when Leopold

Mozart explained that for the sake of his honour he must remain with the Archbishop. He heard that the Archbishop was thinking of going away, so he went to try and see him to ask for his formal dismissal. Count Arco refused to let him see the Archbishop, called him "a churl", "a fellow", &c. and had him kicked out at the door. This put an end to the connection, and notwithstanding all his father's protests, Mozart took up an independent position in Vienna. The beginning was poor. He soon got one pupil, Countess Rumbeck, (who later on became a very talented pianiste); he would not teach for less than 6 ducats for twelve lessons. For six new piano Sonatas of Mozart's, a few well-known ladies of rank with Countess Thun at their head, were only able to get together seventeen subscribers. He might have had better prospects as a composer of operas, as the Emperor Joseph had instituted a German opera as well as a German theatre, but preference was given to Salieri; so instead of entrusting Mozart with the composition of a German opera, he gave the commission to the Italian, who produced a work of great mediocrity, the "Rauchfangkehrer". Mozart wrote thus about the matter, "There is no one but Salieri for the Emperor." He then composed "Belmonte and Constanze" and was in hopes that this opera would be performed on the occasion of a visit of Prince Paul and his wife, but Gluck's "Iphigenia" in German had to be given instead, also "Alceste" by German singers in Italian. When a music master was being thought of for the Princess Elisabeth, bride of the Archduke Franz, the Emperor's brother, Archduke Max, proposed Mozart's name, but the Emperor decided in favour of — Salieri. He was also pleased to arrange a piano-playing competition between Clementi and Mozart. Clementi was enchanted with Mozart's playing, but the latter in one of his letters described him as a "charlatan" and as a purely mechanical player—"like all Italians." Clementi said about himself, that it was only later on that he acquired a broader and smoother style of playing. It was necessary at that time, to make use of very paltry means to get into favour with those in power, and Mozart took infinite pains to win the good-will of Strack, the imperial valet, even going so far as to compose a "Nachtmusik" for his fête-day. When his father wrote to tell him of the report in Salzburg, that the Emperor intended giving him an appointment, he wrote back in answer: "Up to the present I have heard nothing about it." He then went on to say that the valet "Herr von Strack" had spoken favorably of him to the Emperor, from motives of his own. "If things have gone so far without my assistance, all may end well. If I should move in the matter, my salary would at once be lowered. Besides the Emperor is mean. If he needs my services, he shall pay for them, for the honour alone is not sufficient for me."

Strack was the animating spirit as regards the Emperor's chamber music, he took charge of the scores, played the violincello himself, and gave precedence to bad compositions, Haydn, Mozart, Pleyel, Kozeluch and others of note were excluded. Joseph II, considered that only Hasse and Piccini moved in the right direction. Even Salieri himself dared not oppose the valet, "the Emperor's shadow", but rather sought his favour, so as to prevent the success of a dreaded rival like Mozart. The latter supported himself by his compositions and by teaching; by degress he got three ladies of rank as pupils, and at last after having successfully crushed all the intrigues that were on foot against him, his opera „Belmonte and Constanze" was performed for the first time, by command of the Emperor at the 'Burgtheater' on July 16th 1782; the theatre was crowded and the applause extraordinary, the opera was performed sixteen times in the course of a few

months, but the Emperor's judgment was not very
favorable: "It is too beautiful for our ears and there
are too many notes in it, dear Mozart."

The great vexation caused him by the want
of appreciation, is shewn by what he wrote to his
father, on the 17th August 1782, four weeks after
his brilliant success. "The Vienna people (among
whom the Emperor was especially meant) must not
imagine that I was sent into the world alone on their
account. There is no monarch in the world I esteem
as highly as the Emperor, but I will beg for no
situation. I believe I could do honour to any Court.
But if Germany, my beloved Fatherland, of which as
you know I am very proud, will not have me, then,
in God's name, France or England must become the
richer for an able German, and that to the shame of
the German nation! You know, that in all Arts it is
just the Germans who excell. But where do they
find good fortune? Where attain celebrity? Not in
Germany certainly! Even Gluck—Is it Germany that
has made a great man of him? Unfortunately, No.
Countess Thun, Count Zichy, Baron v. Swieten, even
Prince Kaunitz are discontented at the Emperor's
neglect of people of talent, allowing them to leave
the country. The Prince lately told the Archduke
Maximilian, when speaking of me, that such people
appear only once in a hundred years in the world,
and they should not be driven out of Germany,
especially when we are so fortunate as to have them
in the capital. You cannot think how kind and
courteously Prince Kaunitz behaved towards me
when I visited him. He even said: 'I am much
obliged to you, my dear Mozart, for the trouble you
have taken to pay me this visit', &c. You can
scarcely imagine, what very great pains the Countess
Thun, Baron von Swieten, and other high persons
have been at, to keep me here; but I cannot and

really will not wait so long for Charity; I find also that I am not dependent on favour (even though it be the Emperor's)."

And yet it all came about quite differently to what Mozart in his highmindedness anticipated.

During the following year, there were performances of the opera at Leipzig, Berlin, Salzburg, Prague, Mannheim, Cassel, Coblenz, Baden &c., but it seems that Mozart never received the smallest remuneration afterwards. A pianoforte score of the work was published at Augsburg without his consent, and he received no compensation for it.

Mozart was no business man, and he always took the most favorable view of people and of everything in general. It is not certain, in how far he was concerned as regards the removal of Frau Weber and her daughters from Mannheim to Vienna, but Mozart took up his abode with them, and finally, without much emotion, asked another of the daughters to be his wife. This time he chose Constance, notwithstanding his bad experience with Aloysia. The guardian of the daughters demanded a written promise from Mozart, the purport being as follows: that he was to marry Constance within three years' time, and if this did not take place, he was to pay her a yearly sum of 300 Gulden. But it is said that Constance tore up this document, because she felt she could trust Mozart without a written promise, yet he felt bound in honour to keep to his word, as he had got into such intimacy with the Weber family, specially with Constance. He never denied that Frau Weber was a very common person. When his father represented to him that she drank, he answered that it might be possible, but he had never seen her the worse for drink. He clung persistently to Constance, although during his engagement to her, his eyes ought to have been opened. In letters that passed between

them, she repeatedly told him "she would have nothing
more to do with him." As she frequently had quarrelsome
scenes with her worthless mother, Mozart arranged
for her to live for a lengthened period with the pianiste,
Baroness Waldstätter; from her he learnt that Constance led a frivolous life. He reproached her in one
of his letters, saying he considered she was too much
absorbed in pleasure, and behaved altogether in a
manner unworthy of her sex. All the same he married
her—ennobling her thereby—before his father could
give his consent.

This marriage does not seem to have been a
happy one. It is well known, that violent quarrels
frequently took place between them, Constance
was a constant invalid, and lived for several months
every year at Baden, away from her husband. Once
she remained for a long time with some one called
Flecksieder, "who did not know Mozart personally, but
was charmed with his music." She was ordered a
particular kind of bath for a lameness in the foot,
and this honest creature offered to procure them for
her in his house as long as they would be required.
At the end of this cure, "he refused any payment for
lodging and expenses."

Then Mozart was severely criticized for his mode
of life in Vienna, especially at the time when his
wife was absent in Baden, when on account of the
"Zauberflöte", he came into contact with the notorious
Schikaneder, who led him into a life of dissipation.

The pianist Hummel, who lived with Mozart as
a boy, and was his pupil for two years, declared in
1831, that it was untrue that Mozart had given way
to bad habits, excepting on the few occasions that
he followed Schikaneder's example. Nevertheless in
Mozart's day, manners and customs were not strict
in Vienna.

The young composer had a number of friends and

admirers, such as Prince Kaunitz, Baron van Swieten, Prince Lichnowsky, Counts Zichy, Esterhazy, Hatz- feld &c., they were all useful to him after his foolish marriage, but he was not happy and contented in Vienna, and often made plans to leave the city; once he thought of going to Paris, and then again he spoke of making a tour through Germany, and also of going to London; on this journey Constance was to accompany him and he proposed to his long-suffering father (who was heavily in debt on his son's account) that he should take charge of the children and servants in the meantime. But Leopold Mozart forcibly declined to do this. The son certainly possessed no firmness of character.

In 1788, Joseph II at last appointed Mozart as one of his musicians with a salary of 800 Gulden. This was never raised, not even under the following circumstances. When Mozart was invited to come to Berlin by the King Friedrich Wilhelm II and to take the post of conductor with a salary of 3000 Thalers, the Emperor said to him: "How is this, Mozart, are you going to leave me?"

The composer was touched, and replied: "Your Majesty, I will remain." Whereupon a friend asked him if he had not begged the Emperor to give him a better appointment; he said angrily: "How the devil could I approach the subject at such a moment!"

The Emperor Joseph died in 1790, without having advanced Mozart; he made an effort with his successor, Leopold II, to get a position as second conductor with Salieri, but it was unavailing. He then applied to the Town Council in Vienna, who made him assistant to the conductor Hofmann at St. Stephens Cathedral, but this brought him in nothing, as Hofmann survived him.

In May 1790, he only had two pupils who paid for their lessons, for notwithstanding his being such a virtuoso on the piano, the reason why he was not

much sought after as a teacher, was greatly owing
to the entire absence of the music-teaching element
in his nature. He only took pleasure in teaching if
he liked his pupil, as in the case of Barbara Ployer,
for whom he composed the E flat and G major concertos, the celebrated Dr. Joseph Frank, Freystädter,
Hummel and others. After his marriage he often
played succesfully at concerts in Vienna; on the other
hand, a scheme he undertook with Phil. Jac. Martin,
to give orchestral concerts in the "Augarten", did not
prosper at all, as only one concert was given.

He had regular musical performances at his own
house every Sunday, many amateurs as well as his
friends being present on these occasions. Sometimes he received rich rewards, for instance, the
King of Prussia sent him a gold box containing
100 Friedrichsd'or, for three of his Quartets, and the
publisher Artaria forwarded him 100 Ducats for the
Quartets, dedicated to Jos. Haydn. The publisher
Hoffmeister paid him well for the piano Quartets in
G minor and E flat, but then he cancelled the contract
because the public showed but little interest in them.
He said: "If you do not write in a more popular vein,
I cannot afford to publish anything more for you."
Mozart answered: "Very well, then I shall not earn
any more money and must starve, the devil take it all!"
Another publisher, well known at the time, Hummel
by name, sent several of Mozart's works back to him
as useless for publication. For each of the operas
named, "Belmonte und Constanze", "Cosi fan tutte",
"Hochzeit des Figaro", he received 100 ducats, for
"Don Giovanni" 225 Gulden; for "Clemenzo di Tito"
he got 100 ducats from the Bohemian States. Rochlitz
says, that Schikaneder deceived Mozart about the
"Zauberflöte", but Seyfried maintains he paid Mozart
160 ducats, the clear profit of the sale of the score
to be left to Mozart's widow. In many cases Mozart

received little for his compositions, either on account of his generosity, or owing to the prevailing abuses of his time. From the time he began housekeeping he was constantly in money di'ficulties, his wife's extravagance being frequently the cause, and he was exposed to the most painful humiliations from inconsiderate creditors. In such difficulties, a noble-minded woman would have been a great support and would willingly have helped to bear the burden, but from all accounts, Constance was indifferent to all this trouble, and after Mozart's death, her second husband, State Councillor Nissen, who knew her before Mozart died, told her coolly she had never loved him, although later on they both took advantage of his great renown.

Mozart became a Freemason—his "Zauberflöte" is an act of homage to freemasonery—for he was often obliged to turn to the Freemasons for help, especially to one, a merchant called Puchberg. Necessaries were often wanting, for instance, in winter they were sometimes in need of fuel for the fire; notwithstanding this, arrangements had to be made for Constance to pay her usual visits to the country. It has been proved that Mozart was very sociable and made many sacrifices for his wife's sake, he loved dancing, and used to go to masked balls &c., but how was he able to forego all the round of pleasures then so much in vogue in Vienna?

It was not from inclination, but absolute need that deprived him of all this, it was his penance. When at work, he liked to take strong drinks, and as he generally worked till very late at night, rising again early in the morning to be at the piano composing, it was no wonder that a life of such a description undermined his health. His doctor, Barisani, died in 1781, and Mozart wrote the following words in an album that had belonged to him: "To-day the 3th of September, of the same year I was so unfortunate as to lose quite unexpectedly my dearest and best friend,

who has done so much for my health. It is well with
him—but for me, for us all who knew him so well,
there can be no happiness—until we meet again in
another world, never to part."

Although Mozart possessed true friends, yet he
never failed to meet with hypocrites who pretended
to feel friendship for him, such as the clarionet player
Stadler, who deceived him most shamefully and abused
his good-nature. Without a doubt, Schikaneder also
belonged to those who injured his name and health,
causing a decrease in his income.

Important personages at the Vienna Court openly
slighted him and his financial difficulties had become
almost unbearable although he had given the very
highest proofs of his genius. He had completed "Die
Hochzeit des Figaro" in 1785, "Don Juan" in 1787, "Cosi
fan tutte" in 1790, and "La Clemenza di Tito" and "Die
Zauberflöte in 1791. Numerous works for orchestra,
for piano and for the voice, had been published most
of which surpassed any other compositions of the day;
he had proved himself in a thousand ways to be the
most gifted pianist of his time. On this point there
is very reliable testimony to be found. Ambros
Rieder in his reminiscences, says: "As a youth I
used to admire first-rate violin playing, as well as the
performance of many good pianists; but I cannot
describe my astonishment when I happened to be
so fortunate as to hear the immortal W. A. Mozart
playing before a large company of people; not only
did he vary with much skill what he was playing, but
he extemporised as well. I had never been accustomed
to hear anything so great or so wonderful. Such bold
flights of fancy that seemed to attain the highest
regions, were alike a marvel and a delight to the
most experienced of musicians. Even to this day,
although a very old man, I can still hear those
heavenly harmonies, and die in the firm conviction

that there has only been one Mozart." Niemetschek
writes in the same spirit to Aloys Fuchs: "If it
would please God to grant me more happiness on
earth, it would be to hear Mozart once more extem-
porising at the piano. No one, unless they had
heard him, could have the least idea of his power in
that art."

Dittersdorf, Rochlitz, Stiepanek, Schlichtegroll
and many other men of note spoke just as enthusiastically about Mozart's playing. Schlichtegroll says in
his necrology: "This absent-minded man quite changed
when he sat down to the piano, he became a higher
being. Then he seemed all absorbed, and his attention
became riveted on the object for which he was created,
the harmony of sounds."

It needed one who possessed power to place a
genius like this above the ordinary run of things,
and to free him from the cares of life, just as it
happened to Goethe, by means of Karl August; but
neither Joseph II, nor his successor Leopold II, even
in a lesser degree understood what was needful;
whoever had been fortunate enough to be in favour
with Joseph II, was intentionally put on one side by
his successor. Several musicians were dismissed or
sent away in disgrace. Salieri gave up the opera,
and instead of choosing Mozart as the most fitting
successor, Joseph Weigl was appointed. In very many
ways Mozart was thus neglected. In Vienna in 1790,
when the Neapolitan King and Queen were there on
a visit, Haydn was presented—Mozart was not even
asked to play, and instead of his master-pieces, Weigl's
"Caffetiera bizarra" and Salieri's "Axur" were put
forward for the festival performances. Stupidity and
capriciousness were doing their best to ruin the
young man's career. He lived to see the first performance of the "Zauberflöte" on the 30th of September
1791, at the theatre "Auf der Wieden", and worked

with feverish haste at the Requiem which he had
been commissioned anonymously to write by Count
Walsegg, when he was attacked by fatal illness.
Only at this juncture did his wife return from Baden.
Mozart said to her with tears in his eyes that he
was writing his own Requiem, as he felt he could
not live much longer. He also declared his suspicion
of having been poisoned. Several of his comrades
firmly believed this was true, but no one was
suspected, not even the much distrusted Salieri. If there
had been any truth in it—the symtoms of the illness
were swelling of the hands and feet, and vomiting—
the criminals would probably have been found elsewhere, and not in the artistic world. Dr. Closset,
the doctor in attendance, decided that death ensued
from inflammation of the brain. The great composer
died on the 5th of December 1791 ; his last thoughts
were for the "Zauberflöte" and the unfinished Requiem.
The circumstances of his burial are of an unworthy
and contemptible character. It is said that his wife
was so ill, that she was not able to be troubled
about anything ; nevertheless on the day of her husband's death, she was able to hasten forward to meet
her sister calling out to her: "Thank God that you
have come! Last night he was much worse, and I
thought he could not live through the day; if the
attack comes on again he will die to-night."

The Keeper of the house, Joseph Deiner, who
was always looked to in all domestic details of the
house, was with Mozart when he died. News of the
death was sent to Albrechtsberger. Count Deym came
and took the death mask. The day after Mozart died,
"crowds of people came to the house, lamenting and
weeping over him." The Viennese newspapers announced his death. Van Swieten came to condole
with the widow; but she left the house to go to
some friends, "so as to get away from the sad

surroundings"—she abandoned the house of death.
Van Swieten (who was rich) undertook the expenses
of the poor funeral which were 11 Gulden 36 Kreutzer
inclusive of the hearse. Some few "friends", Salieri,
Süssmayr, Roser, the violincellist Oxler, Swieten—
(the extortioner Stadler does not seem to have been
present)—accompained the hearse, but as the weather
was bad, they turned back—not a friend was present
when Mozart's body was lowered into the pauper's
grave, so that no one knew where the grave was.
When Deiner, who had only gone to the funeral
service, asked the widow if she would not have a
small cross placed on her husband's grave, so that
at least it might be known, she replied that in time
one would be placed there. Later on when the resting-
place could not be found, she made the miserable
excuse, she had thought the priest who performed the
funeral rite would have a cross erected!

Where was Schikaneder who owed so much to
Mozart? Where were the members of the Freemason's
Lodge, for whom Mozart had composed such wonderful music? Not one of them went to his funeral!
After several weeks, a pompous funeral speech was
delivered about him at the Lodge: "The everlasting
ruler of the world has been pleased to take away one
of our best beloved and most useful members. Could
there be any one who did not know him and value
him! No one could help loving him, our worthy
brother, Mozart &c." But not one of these Freemasons could say where this "worthy brother" had
been buried.

It has therefore come to pass, that the remains
of this immortal genius rest in an unknown spot,
and his grave is not distinguished by the least
monument.

The history of Mozart's life like that of Beethoven
is extremely instructive as regards the development

of musical education. What bitter warfare these great masters had to wage against representatives of the old Italian school; and how often were the greatest efforts of their splendid genius wrecked, owing to the dullness of musical comprehension on the part of those tone-giving circles which had not emanated from the middle classes of society. The enmity of a clique became of vital importance so long as it could be concealed by the humour or the ignorance of some influential personage.

This was clearly shewn especially by the treatment of Mozart's greatest work, "Don Juan", for whereas this opera, produced in Prague, by the aid of Dussek and Bucharz and with the enthusiasm of the performers, was crowned with brilliant success, this same opera, performed a year later in Vienna, was subjected to the worst ill-usage, and doomed through that, to utter failure.

The conductor took precedence with his hostility and the musicians and singers followed suit. The work was badly studied, played without understanding by the performers, and heard without comprehension by the public. The Emperor himself said to Mozart: "that is not a fit morsel for my Viennese"; to which the poor composer shrugging his shoulders, could only reply; "one must leave them time to digest the morsel"; a poor comfort for the great master, when he saw Salieri's "Azur" again preferred to his work. Don Juan was subject to the same ill-fortune in Berlin in 1790. The 'Chronik von Berlin" reported at that time in these terms: "That Mozart is a great composer is admitted by every one; but, whether nothing better than this Opera was written before him, or will be written after him, we must doubt. Not the art of overloading the instruments but the soul, the feelings and the passions, are what the composer must make speak. That is writing in grand style, and would make his name honoured by posterity. Grétry, Monsigni, Philidor are and will be proofs of this. Mozart intended in his "Don Juan" to write something extraordinary; and so much is certain, that it is extraordinary, but it is not the Inimitable, nor the Grand. Caprice, Whim and Pride were the creators of Don Juan, but not the heart; and we should prefer admiring the highest attainments of his composition in an Oratorium, or in solemn church music, rather than his 'Don Juan', the conclusion of which is nearly analogous to a description of the Last Judgment, the graves opening, the mountains splitting and the destroying Angel blowing the trumpet of horror and dissolution. Still at the same time this Opera brought large returns to the director, and the Galleries, Boxes & Pit, will not be empty in future."

The well-known author Fr. Jacobi, wrote thus to Herder, in Weimar, about the same performance: "So now I have seen 'Don Juan' which wearied me excessively. It is a most unbearable thing, and I am glad do have done with it."

On the other hand, how different was Göthe's judgment of it; a pity that this was only known seven years after, and in a certain sense Göthe was right: "Through Mozart's death, we may hope in vain for anything of a similar kind being again produced." Later times have reversed the judgment of the croakers of the eighteenth century. The Berlin and Vienna public in their true, strong and matured spirit, have done justice to the Genius of the Master who died in poverty. In such cases numbers decide; since 1790, 'Don Juan' has been given 600 times in Berlin: in Vienna since 1788, 550 times; in Prague 650, &c.; even at the present day, notwithstanding that many great works have been produced since his time, even

Mozart's earlier works, rank with them in the frequency of their performances.

Mozart's Works.

Of youthful compositions not quite authentic, the following is list: Sonatas for Piano and violin op. I. another set of the same, op. II., and a 3^d set op. III., 6 Sonatas op. IV. Variations for piano (Hague and Amsterdam), 2 books full of piano pieces written on the first journey, 1 Fugue for piano; 13 Symphonies for violin, horns, viola and bass; 1 Quodlibet; 1 Oratoria; 1 Music to a Latin comedy; 6 Divertimenti for different instruments; 6 Trios for violins and violincello; 1 Cantata; 1 Stabat mater; Solos for violin, violincello, gamba and flute; Pieces for two clarionets, 2 horns, 2 bassethorns; several minuets for different instruments; processional music for trumpets and drums; several marches; 1 Fugue with four voices; 1 Veni sancte spiritus for four voices and instruments, 1 Offertorium. List of compositions from Breitkopf & Härtel's catalogue: 1. Piano music: 27 concertos with an accompaniment of different instruments, also a Rondo with the same. 1 Quintet in E flat, 2 Quartets in G minor, and E flat, 8 Trios in B flat, D minor, G major, E flat, B flat, E major, C major, G major. 43 Sonatas for piano and violin, also 18 Variations for the same instruments. 5 Sonatas, pianoforte duets, 1 Sonata for two pianos, 1 Andante with 5 Variations, 1 Fugue for two pianos. 17 Sonatas for piano, 4 Fantasias for piano. 138 Variations. 1 Minuet and Trio. 5 Minuets, 3 Rondos, 1 Suite for piano, 1 Fugue, 3 Allegros, 1 Andantino, 1 Adagio, 1 Gigue, 36 Cadenzas for concertos.—Vocal music: 15 Masses, 4 Litanies, 1 Dixit and Magnificat, 2 Vespers, 5 Kyries, 1 "God is our refuge", 1 Veni Sancte Spiritus, 1 Miserere, 1 Antiphon, 3 Regina Cœli, 1 Te Deum, 2 Tantum ergo, 2 German

Kirchenlieder, 8 Offertories, 1 Psalm "De Profundis",
1 Recitative and air "Ergo inter est", 2 Motets,
1 Graduale, 2 Hymns, 5 Cantatas and oratorios. Operas:
1. "Die Schuldigkeit des ersten Gebotes (sacred Singspiel). 2. Apollo et Hyacinthus. 3. Bastien and Bastienne,
and La finta semplice.   4. Mitridate, Ré di Ponto.
5. Ascanio in Alba.   6. Il Sogno di Scipione.   7. Lucio
Silla. 8. La finta Giardiniera.   9. Il Ré pastore.   10. Zaïde
(German operetta).   11. Choral music and interludes to
"Thamos, King in Egypt".   12. Idomeneo.   13. Ballet
music for this opera.   14. Die Entführung aus dem
Serail (Belmonte und Konstanze).   15. Der Schauspiel-
direktor.   16. Die Hochzeit des Figaro.   17. Don Juan.
18. Cosi fan tutte (Weibertreue).   19. Die Zauberflöte.
20. La Clemenza di Tito.   21. Airs for soprano and
bass with instrumental accompaniment, 13 Songs
with recitative, 1 Scena for soprano, 1 Scena and Aria,
2 Recitatives and Rondo, 1 Rondo for tenor, 4 Trios,
1 Quartet, 1 German War Song.   1 Ariette for Bass,
1 Canzonet, 1 Duet, 36 Songs for one voice and for
several voices with piano accompaniment, 1 choral
work for three voices with organ accompaniment,
1 short German Cantata, 22 Canons.   Orchestral
works: 41 Symphonies, 31 Cassationen, Serenades and
Divertimenti for different instruments, 17 Marches,
movements of Symphonies and short pieces for different instruments, 1 Adagio for Harmonica, 1 Adagio
and Rondo for Harmonica, Flute, Oboe, Viola and
Violincello, 1 Fantasia for an organ, 1 Andante
for a small organ; 43 Minuets, 49 German Dances,
30 Contredances; 20 Concertos, Adagios, Rondos
for one stringed or wind instrument with orchestra;
9 String Quintets, 30 String Quartets, of which 2
are with flute, 1 with oboe, 3 String Duets and
1 String Trio; 15 Sonatas for several instruments
with organ.
    Then follow the unfinished and doubtful works:

The Requiem, 7 Symphonies, 3 Finales for Symphonies, 3 Finales for Symphonies, 1 Ballet for a Pantomime "Les petits riens", 1 Fugue for stringed and wind instruments, 1 Galimathias for piano and orchestra, 19 Minuets, 5 Contredanses, of which one is for piano, 6 Country Dances, Music for a Pantomime, 5 Concertos for different instruments, 5 Quintets for stringed and wind instruments, 1 string Quartet (fragment), 1 Trio for stringed instruments, 1 Fantasia, 2 Fugues, the first movement of a sonata for piano, 1 Adagio and Allegro for small organ arranged for piano, 2 Masses, 1 Lacrymosa, 1 Antiphon, 3 Kyries, 1 Credo, 1 Cantata; the unfinished operas "L'Oca del Cairo", and "Lo Sposo deluso", 9 Arias, partly with pianoforte accompaniment, and partly with accompaniment of stringed and wind instruments, 1 Duet, 2 Terzettos, 1 comic Quartet, 1 Solfeggi (Fragment), 3 Canons.

WLADIMIR DE PACHMANN.

IN spite of all the trouble taken, it has unfortunately
been impossible to learn very .much concerning
Pachmann. His artistic career belongs completely
to modern times, and like his countryman,
Paderewski, is therefore proportionally a short one,
and the critics up to the present have had to content
themselves with writing about the success of his
playing, no biography of him having been published.
It is well known that his first appearance in public
was not that of a finished pianist; unlike Pallas
Athene rising in perfection from the head of Zeus;
but his performances at important concerts, for instance in Berlin and London, must be mentioned as

being of great consequence and his talent as a pianist very much appreciated.

As he was born in Russia, he studied there during his youth, and has a great name in that country, especially in Moscow. There is no doubt that he is an excellent pianist, and concert agents experience no difficulty in procuring him good engagements in the very best society.

IGNAZ JOHANN PADEREWSKI.

UNTIL a little more than three years ago, Paderewski was not universally recognized as a great pianist; he came into notice through publishing some good pianoforte pieces, solos and duets. He was born on the 6th of November 1859, in Podolien; little is known of his youth; when he was twelve years old he went to the Conservatoire at Warsaw, where he was taught harmony by Roguski, and the piano by Janotha. Later on he went to Berlin, and received instruction from Wuerst and Urban at the New Academy of Music. In 1879, he was made pianoforte teacher at the Warsaw Conservatoire, remaining in that position till 1883. Then he commenced to travel, for a time in Slavonia, then in Roumania, Hungary

and Austria. After this he was made professor at
the Strasburg Conservatoire; but as he began to be
aware that his playing was not finished enough, he
relinquished the post and became a pupil again,
studying with Professor Leschetitzky at Vienna.
After seven months of truly gigantic industry he
made his first public appearance in Vienna 1887 He
left for Paris two years later, where he made a great
sensation by his playing of Chopin's compositions.
About three years ago he appeared for the first time
in London, and to show how difficult it is for the
greatest pianist to have any success there without
introductions or high reputation, Paderewski's first
concert in that city realized about 300 marks. But
soon things took a more favorable turn for him; he
was recognized as a pianist of the highest rank and
was acknowledged so by the critics; his masterly
execution, his playing full of fire and richness of tone,
as well as the originality of his slavonic nature per-
vading his performance, conquered all those that
heard him. He is now one of the greatest pianists
not only in Europe, but also in America. The reason
of this is not far to seek; apart from his executive
powers, he is a highly gifted musician, and is especially
great in his performance of compositions of the romantic school. For instance, as an exponent of
Chopin he is without a rival. In England he is a
favorite in the best society; one of his recent concerts
in St. James's Hall realized the sum of £1000,
His first tour in the United States was a triumph
from beginning to end; he went over there again not
long ago; for a concert-tour of eight days duration
in America he received £3,000, for 64 concerts within
three months, £35,000 were guaranteed to him, of
which sum he put aside £3,000 for charities.

Meanwhile Paderewski works hard at the piano,
practising day and night for many hours at a time.

He has been known to repeat certain passages in a
piece 200 times running, thus showing that perfection
is only to be attained by perseverance and industry.
Even when travelling, at least in England, he continues his practising in the train, Erard having con-
structed a miniature piano for the travelling carriage
which is placed at his disposal by the railway company.

As already mentioned, Paderewski has composed
several successful pianoforte pieces; Variations and
Fugues, Toccatas, Polish Dances, a Tatra-Album, a
Concert-Humoreske, &c.

ERNST PAUER.

THIS artist was born Dec. 1st 1826, at Vienna. His father was a Lutheran Superintendant - General. He received his musical education from Dirzka, W. A. Mozart (the son) und Simon Sechter, then from 1845 to 1846, he was taught by Franz Lachner in Munich. In the following year he was appointed musical director in Mayence, where he remained till 1851. Whilst there, he composed two operas: "Don Riego" and "The red mask", and a third opera in 1861, "The Bride", but they were only performed in Mannheim. At that time he played several times in public, but he only gained distinction as a pianist when he went to London in 1851. He was warmly received in London, and established himself there successfully as a teacher of the pianoforte. Having acquired a good position, he married Miss Andreä, a singer from Frankfort, and brought her to England. In 1861, he began his historical piano recitals with analytical programmes, which were the means of bringing into notice many classical compositions. He then travelled on the Continent with the same object, repeating his visit several times; in 1866, he was made pianist to the Austrian Court.

In 1870, he gave some successful lectures in London, on the history of pianoforte playing with musical illustrations. He was then made professor of the pianoforte, succeeding Potter, at the London Academy of Music, and in 1876, was also appointed pianoforte teacher at the National Training School for Music. The Cambridge University elected him in 1878, a member of the Board for Musical Studies. Later in life Ernst Pauer gained fresh distinctions for his zeal in the cultivation of good music, also for his publications of numerous works on classical music, as follows: "Alte Klaviermusik", "Alte Meister", "Old English composers for the virginal and harpsichord", "Volksausgabe der Klassiker von Bach bis Schumann", then "New gradus ad Parnassum", "Primer of the Pianoforte", Elements of the beautiful in Music", "Primer of musical forms". He has also composed several works for orchestra.

MAX PAUER.

Ernst Pauer's son Max, was born in London on the 31st October 1866, and was taught the pianoforte exclusively by his father, who guided him successfully in his studies. He then sent his son to Carlsruhe, to the conductor Vincenz Lachner for instruction in composition.—Max Pauer remained there from 1881 to 1885, during which time the young musician gave his first concerts, travelling through Germany, Holland and England, and then he settled in London.

But in 1887, he was appointed professor of the pianoforte at the Cologne Conservatoire. Since that time
he has frequently travelled as pianist in Germany,
Belgium, Holland, Austria, Hungary, England, Russia
&c. According to the very best opinions, his playing
is of a highly cultivated nature, and good musicianship
prevails throughout his performance, which is always
thoroughly classical in style, never exaggerated, but
careful and very exact, even in the most difficult
works, as for instance in Schumann's C-major Toccata,
Brahms' Sonata in C, and Chopin's compositions.

Although he has often had many brilliant offers
from the Conservatoires at Moscow and Prague, yet
he has preferred to keep his pleasant position in
Cologne.

Max Pauer who has surely a useful future before
him, has published several pianoforte pieces, both
solos and duets.

ERNST PERABO.

JOHN Ernst Perabo was born in Wiesbaden on the 14th of November 1845; he had nine brothers and sisters, who have all followed a musical career. His father taught him the elements of piano-playing when he was five years old. He practised a great deal, and at the age of nine was able to play Bach's "Wohltemperirtes Klavier" by heart.

In 1852, he went to New York with his parents, remaining in that city for two years. The family here made the acquaintance of Wilhelm Scharfenberg from Cassel, and this friendship was of the greatest importance as regards the development of his talents. During the second year of his residence in New York, he played for the first time in public at a concert of Professor Heinrich's.

Then the family went to Dover, New Hampshire, where they lived for two years, after which they spent one year in Boston, where the boy had violin lessons, and where he also appeared at a concert at the Music Hall under the direction of Karl Zerrahn; the family then lived some time in Chicago. The father, who had not been so successful in the United States as he could have wished, sent his son from Chicago to Washington, his mother accompanying him, to ask for assistance from the State towards the boy's musical education, but President Buchanan explained to her that neither the government nor congress took an interest in the development of the fine arts.

Ernst's mother then applied to Scharfenberg in New York, who became interested in the boy, and prevailed upon a number of wealthy men, (among others Henry C. Timm, Robert Goldbeck and Pyschowski) to take the entire charge of Ernst's musical development; in 1858, he was sent to Hamburg, from there he went to school for four years to a Professor Andresen at Eimsbüttel, for general education; then to the Conservatoire at Leipzig in October 1862, where he became the pupil of Moscheles and Wenzel; for harmony, Papperitz, Hauptmann and Richter, and finally Karl Reinecke for composition.

Having now become an excellent pianist, he returned to New York in 1865, where Scharfenberg shewed him how to advance in his career independently of the aid he had formerly received. He gave some concerts in Sandusky, Ohio, where his parents lived, he also played in Lafayette, Chicago and Cleveland.

In March 1866, he arrived in Boston on the invitation of Sebastion Schlesinger, and remaining there, soon played at the concerts of the Harvard Musical Association, also at the Chickering Hall, the Music Hall &c., achieving considerable success; he also gave lessons. The compositions he played were by Chopin, Mendelssohn, Mozart, Thalberg, Hummel, Schubert, Burgmüller, Gernsheim, Bennett, Rubinstein, Bargiel, Kirchner, Richter, Volkmann and Raff.

He published transcriptions of Loewe's Ballads, arrangements of Rubinstein's works, two transcriptions of Beethoven's Fidelio, as well as a number of his own compositions, partly in America and partly in Leipzig.

JOHANN PETER PIXIS.

I N the letters that Adam Liszt wrote to Czerny from
Paris, while on the first concert-tour with his son
"Franzi", there are many harsh criticisms regarding
Pixis. In one of the letters, the following occurs:
"I have to tell you something more about Herr Pixis.
This gentleman seems to be an enemy of ours. We
have only spoken once to him, when we met him
accidentally at the Palais royal; since then we have
often seen him in a music-seller's shop, but he has not
condescended to notice us. Although a rival like this
is not powerful enough to do us any harm, he will
be censured by others for such conduct." Adam

Liszt had hardly a favorable word to say for any pianist of that time, and declared there was no one like his "Putz" as he called his son Franz, so no importance is to be placed on his criticism of this "rival". Pixis had established his name in Paris as an excellent pianist and teacher of the pianoforte, and later on entered into friendly relations with Thalberg, Herz, Czerny and Chopin, as also with Franz Liszt; together they published a collection of their own compositions, called "Hexameron", Pixis contributing three variations to the work.

Johann Peter Pixis, was born in Mannheim in 1788; he went on his first concert-tours with his brother who was his senior by two years, the violinist Friedrich Wilhelm Pixis, a professor at the Prague Conservatoire. He first went to Paris in 1824, and then travelled in Belgium, Holland and Germany. In 1825, he visited Paris for the second time, remaining there for several years. It is not known how he came to adopt the Munich opera-singer, Francilla Göhringer (sometimes called Grüninger) as his daughter; they travelled together on extensive concert-tours.

Later on he bought a villa at Baden-Baden, giving lessons there; Baden-Baden was his permanent residence until his death which took place on the 21st December 1874.

Pixis trod in Haydn's, Beethoven's and Mozart's footsteps with regard to composition, although he also sought to be original; he published 150 Pianoforte compositions, Concertos, Sonatas, Quintets, Quartets, lighter pieces as well, but they are now forgotten. He also wrote several operas, but none of them were successful.

FRANÇOIS PLANTÉ.

Planté is considered the most important pianist of the present day in France, and was born on the 2d of March in 1839, at Orthez (Basses Pyrenées). His parents took him to Paris, where he was taught the piano by Madame Saint-Aubert. At ten years of age, and before he became a pupil at the Paris Conservatoire, he was allowed to appear in public. After seven months teaching in Marmontel's class he was awarded the first prize. Even at this tender age, he was said to possess excellent execution as well as a thorough understanding of classical music. He played at the Chamber concerts given by Alard and

Franchomme. But in 1853, he entered the Paris Conservatoire again, in order to pursue his studies in theory, and in 1854—1855, entered Bazin's class, also gaining the second prize for harmony and accompanying.

After he had appeared at several concerts, he left Paris, it was thought on account of a supposed insult, and returned to his native town, where he spent ten years in practising and studying. He then travelled, and during that time, perfected himself by listening to the performances of the most celebrated pianists, Rubinstein and Liszt; in 1872, he went again to Paris, and played at concerts for charitable purposes, being very well received.

He resumed his connection with Alard and Franchomme in the soirées for Chamber music, which became a great centre of attraction in Paris. He was created a Chevalier of the Legion of Honour. During his concert-tours, and particularly in Belgium, he created a great sensation by his faultless execution and beautiful interpretation.

DIONYS PRUCKNER.

BORN May 17th 1834 at Munich, Pruckner received instruction, up to his seventeenth year, from Fr. Niest. Then he became Liszt's pupil at Weimar until 1855, after which he took up his abode in Vienna, where Liszt's E-flat Concerto was played by him for the first time, and from there he went on several concert-tours. In 1859, he was appointed professor of the pianoforte at the Stuttgart Conservatoire and in 1864, was created pianist to the Wurtemberg Court and in 1868, professor. He instituted concerts for Chamber music together with Edmund Singer, which were very largely patronised.

In 1871 to 1872, he made a successful concert-tour in America, and at present resides at Stuttgart where he takes a first-class position as an artist of the highest rank and as a teacher of the pianoforte.

EMILE PRUDENT.

Emile Prudent was born in Angoulème on the 3^d of February 1817; he lost his parents in early childhood, but was cared for by his adopted father, a pianoforte tuner, who gave him his first instruction; then he was placed at the Paris Conservatoire, where he not only benefited by the good teaching of Lecouppey, Laurent and Zimmermann, but where he had the advantage of studying such models as Thalberg and Mendelssohn; the latter he particularly followed with great zeal, but he imitated Thalberg's style and in consequence of this competition had considerable difficulty in getting recognized. Although

it cannot be said that he was particularly original,
yet his playing was most painstaking, and he was
thoroughly at home in all the technical part of his
work, He was a musician of taste and devoted to
progress in music. As a proof of this it may be
mentioned that he was much sought after as a pianoforte teacher in Paris. His compositions, of which
there are about 70, for piano, partly with violin and
violincello, are correct and melodious and require
good execution. He especially made a name as a
clever composer of Fantasies on well-known operatic
airs.

JEAN PHILIPPE RAMEAU.

R AMEAU was an admirable pianist and organist, but he had a greater and more important influence on music in general, and especially on the pianist's art by his works on theory, as he is known to be the original founder of the newer teaching in harmony.

He was born at Dijon, on the 25th of September 1683, and went in early life to the Jesuit Fathers' school, but having little taste for lessons ran away after four years. The following years of his life were filled with adventure, for although he culti-vated music he did not make a profound study of it, and at the beginning of the eighteenth century

when he got entangled in an unfortunate love affair
at Dijon, and had to keep away from his native town.
He commenced a roving life as a musician; amongst
other things he became violinist of an orchestra which
played at theatres, and travelled about in the south
of France, returning to his home after several years.

In 1717, the post of organist in the Holy Chapel
at Dijon was offered to him, but he refused it, being
still attached to a wandering life. He went to Paris
with no special aim in view. Louis Marchand offered
to teach him, but later on through jealousy became
his enemy.

The truth was that Rameau was ashamed at
that time of his poor musical knowledge, and studied
with great zeal the works of Descartes, Mersenna,
Zarlino, Kircher &c. in doing which he conceived he
the idea of putting the theory of music on a sound
basis.

In order to make a living, he tried for an appointment, and was made organist at Lille, then at
Clermont; in his leisure hours he occupied himself in
writing his "Traité de l'harmonie", which he published
in 1721, in Paris. He now attracted general attention
both by his book and also by several Sonatas for
piano and Cantatas. He was appointed organist at
the church of Saint Croix de la Brétonnerie.

In 1737, the Academy made a trial of his works
on the theory of music. He was also fortunate in
finding a patron, in a landed proprietor, to whose wife
he had given some pianoforte lessons. He now had
time to compose operas. After some difficulties, he
was able to have his work "Hippolyte et Arricie"
performed at the Grand Opera, and this created such
a lively diversion of opinion, that even the King's
attention was attracted, and he bestowed a title on him.

Rameau now composed a number of operas, but
only a few of these works were done in public. As

years passed on he composed the following pianoforte pieces: Premier livre de pièces de clavecin, Pièces de clavecin avec une methode pour la mécanique des doigts, Pièces de clavecin avec une table pour les agréments, Nouvelles suites de pièces de clavecin avec des remarques sur les differents genres de musique, Pièces de clavecin en concerts.

In order to give weight to his ideas of reform which need not be discussed here, he brought out a number of theoretical works: Traitè d'harmonie reduite à ses principes naturels, Nouveau systéme de musique theorique, Plan abrégé d'une methode nouvelle d'accompagnement, Génération harmonique, Demonstration du principe de l'harmonie, Observations sur notre instinct pour la musique, Code de musique pratique &c. These works occasioned much opposition among musicians, the Encyklopædia writers strongly differing from his views; but, although much that was erroneous had to be ignored, yet the truth of his ideas took a lasting hold and established the great significance of this remarkable man.

He died in Paris at an advanced age on the 12th September, 1764.

WILLY REHBERG.

WILLY Rehberg who was born on the 2^d September 1863, at Morges, on the sunny shores of the Lake of Geneva, was taught in early childhood by his father, who was a music master at Morges; the boy played in public when he was five or six years of age. He was then sent to school for a few years, and after that he went to the Music School at Zürich, where Robert Freund was his pianoforte teacher.

In 1882, he entered the Conservatoire at Leipzig, and here Karl Reinecke and Zwintscher were his masters. After three years study, he was made professor of the piano at the same institution, having given evidence of a decided talent for teaching during these years of study.

At this time he acquired the name of being one of the best cultivated pianists of the young generation, in solo playing as well as in concerted music, and in accompanying. He played with success at the Leipzig Gewandhaus concerts, also at some of the musical Festivals in other countries, making a great point of performing new compositions, that were interesting and full of merit.

In the autumn of the year 1890, he received the appointment as first professor of the piano, at the Conservatoire at Geneva, and here he found opportunities both for solo and concerted playing.

At Leipzig, he shewed considerable talent for conducting. During two seasons he conducted the Abonnement-concerts and the Singakademie at Altenburg, and since 1892, besides teaching, he is the conductor of the principal concerts at the theatre in Geneva.

Besides a number of melodious pianoforte pieces, Willy Rehberg has published a Sonata for piano and violin.

———•❖•———

KARL REINECKE.

FOR a great number of years Reinecke's name has been intimately connected with the Gewandhaus concerts of world-wide reputation at Leipzig, also with the Conservatoire there. His musical life has been full of energy, in the direction of executive art, in teaching and in literature on music. Space will not allow of even an attempt to describe all the work he has been engaged in, and owing to the character of the present book, a biography must necessarily be condensed. It need only be noted that Reinecke has achieved great success as a pianist, his playing always satisfying all technical demands and his intrepretation being quiet and full of intelligence. In his rendering of classical compositions, particularly those of Mozart, these good qualities stand out prominently, the performance being always thoughtful and earnest. All striving after effect, which is so noticeable in the modern pianist par excellence, is totally absent in Reinecke's playing. As an accompaniist he is incomparable; his arrangements are the best of the present day, and among other works many of his pianoforte compositions have become exceedingly popular.

Unfortunately it has become the fashion for the young musical generation to look upon the school that Reinecke belongs to as antiquated, notwithstanding all the devotion and earnestness he brings to bear on his work. The reason of this is, that he refuses to follow blindly the modern school, either as conductor, composer or pianist; and it is fortunate that he maintains his influential position undisturbed by conflicting opinions.

His antipathy to the excentric efforts of modern art, joined to his extensive musical knowledge, render him a fitting representative of the traditions of such an important institution as the Leipzig Gewandhaus. Possibly the artistic position he has adopted may be thought too conservative, and a more liberal-minded comprehension, specially as regards the choice of compositions for performance, might be exercised; for there is no doubt that the music-loving public has a right to demand a hearing of all new compositions of importance, and in this respect the Gewandhaus at Leipzig is rather behind the time, having been surpassed by the large concert institutions in Berlin, Vienna, London, Paris, and even in America, where compositions by Liszt, Dvořák, Cowen, Mackenzie &c. are performed with success. At the same time it is a great advantage that an institution like the Gewandhaus should retain the artistic traditions of the old school.

Some of the modern examples of compositions

that vanish after a short existence are practically of no value as regards the furtherance of art, and those works that are only put forward for the purpose of creating a sensation at any price and are offensive to good taste are best ignored.

In this respect, Karl Reinecke is one of the strongest upholders of all that is beautiful in music, and of all those great works that time has no influence on.

All the world knows what Reinecke has accomplished by his teaching at the Conservatoire—he has completed the musical education of a large number of pupils, some of whom have become celebrated.

Reinecke was born at Altona on the 23^d of June 1824. He received all his musical instruction from his father, Johann Peter Rudolf Reinecke, who was a teacher of music and a writer on musical subjects. The son first devoted himself to violin-playing, but later on he turned his attention to the piano, and in 1843, went on his first concert-tour as pianist to Denmark, and Sweden, after which he lived for a long time in Leipzig, where he entered into friendly relations with Mendelssohn and Schumann. Then he travelled again, in 1846, was made Danish Court pianist, retaining this position till 1848. After living a long time in Paris, he received an appointment at the Cologne Conservatoire in 1850, was made conductor at Barmen from 1854 to 1859, and then musical director and conductor of the Singakademie in Breslau from 1859 to 1860.

In 1860, he was called to Leipzig to take up the joint positions of conductor of the Gewandhaus concerts and master at the Conservatoire; he was made professor, and received the honorary title of Doctor at the Leipzig University, besides becoming a member of several learned societies, and was the recipient of numerous distinctions.

Notwithstanding his active life at Leipzig, he was able to undertake several concert-tours, to Scandinavia, England, the Netherlands, and Switzerland, thus increasing his reputation.

His compositions number over two hundred, amongst them are several larger works for the piano: Concertos, Sonatas, Sonatinas, Fantasias, Caprices; also: 1 Fantasia for piano and violin, Quintets, Quartets, Trios, Violin and Violincello Sonatas, 1 Sonata for Flute, Concertos for Violin, Violincello and Harp; Symphonies, Overtures, 4 Operas, 1 Singspiel, 1 Oratorio, Music to Schiller's Wilhelm Tell, 1 Cantata for men's voices, Solos and orchestra, 3 Concert arias, 1 Chorus for male voices with orchestra, 1 choral work "Sommerbilder", 4 Märchendichtungen, 30 Canons, and among many other works some delightful songs for children.

ALFRED REISENAUER.

IT is easy to see that in the life of Franz Liszt,
certain facts and expressions that are alluded to
as regards his connection with musicians, must needs
be repeated. Such a master as Liszt, sought after
by so many talented musicians, either for his opinion
or his teaching, must naturally have had his pre-
ferences, and it cannot be wondered at that Alfred
Reisenauer was not the only one of whom he said,
that he approached him very closely in his manner
of playing, but without imitating him. It is true that

Liszt had a great influence on Reisenauer, and in a biographical notice of the latter the following incident is related, that when the boy at the age of eleven, played Hummel's B-minor concerto to Liszt, the great musician remarked; "Now, I always advise every one who asks me, against becoming a pianist; but with this boy it is useless to advise one way or another —his life will plainly be that of a musician."

Reisenauer was born on the 1ˢᵗ of November 1863, at Königsberg, East Prussia—. Before he studied with Liszt, he had been taught by his mother, also by the well-known piano teacher Louis Köhler. From the eleventh year of his age, he spent his summer holidays at Weimar with Liszt. When he was a little over fifteen, he neglected his University examination and went again to be with Liszt, following him to Rome. Whilst Liszt was absent for some time at Pesth, Herr von Keudell, the Prussian Ambassador in Rome took charge of Reisenauer's piano instruction, Professor Blum giving him lessons in composition.

In November, 1879, Liszt let him play at a concert got up for a charity in Rome; and in 1881, he played again at a public concert. As a finished pupil of Liszt's he now left for London, and from there went to Berlin and to Leipzig, playing with success at the Gewandhaus. The idea suddenly struck him, to give up the musical career and study law. But he soon abandoned this project, and through Liszt's interposition, he undertook the position of teacher at the Conservatoire in Sondershausen, where Felix Weingartner exercised considerable influence on his artistic career.

He then gave a series of concerts with the tenor singer, Heinrich Vogel, with the violincello-player David Popper, and with Teresina Tua; with the latter he went on concert tours through Sweden and Norway.

In 1887, he signed a contract with the Impresario Langewitz, for a tour of several years in length, through European and Asiatic Russia. He went as far as Siberia, and gave close upon 500 concerts with very great success. For his own pleasure, he travelled as an explorer along the coasts of the North Sea, to Bochara, China, Persia, Asia minor, &c.

From 1892 to 1893, he again came west, and played in Berlin, Dresden, Breslau, Vienna, Budapest, Prague, Copenhagen, Stockholm, Christiania, London, &c., and everywhere gained the reputation of being a very brillant pianist, his playing being of an intellectual order and very impassioned.

He has published "Wanderlieder", the words by Uhland.

MARTHA REMMERT.

MARTHA Remmert was born on the 13ᵗʰ of September 1854, at the village of Grossschwein near Glogau, and received her first musical education at home. Later on she was sent to Berlin, and was there taught by Theodor Kullak. During this time she enjoyed the patronage of the Princess Helene of Russia, who did a great deal for art. Martha Remmert received further instruction from Tausig and Liszt. This admirable instruction has rendered her capable of the very highest order of playing, and she receives much applause for her performances in almost all the countries where she travels.

ALFONSO RENDANO.

ALL the attributes of the German and the Italian
school are united in Rendano; apart from his
great technical execution, his playing is refined
and graceful, and in expression has a touch of melancholy. In the German school he has become a
specially good exponent of Bach.

He was born on the 5th of April 1853, at Carolei
near Cosenza and went to the Conservatoire at Naples
at the time when Thalberg was there, who became
his master. But this did not suffice for him, he
also entered the Leipzig Conservatoire.

In 1862, he played for the first time at the Leipzig
Gewandhaus and was received with favour. In the
same year he went to London, and played at one of

the concerts of the Musical Union; in 1873, at the Crystal Palace and at a Philharmonic concert. He then often took part in various concerts during the London season; but after having spent a considerable time in England, and going to Paris for a concert, he returned to his native country Italy, for a permanence.

Some very good compositions of his have been published.

FERDINAND RIES.

THIS musician was born on the 29th of November
1784, in Bonn, and was a son of the musical
director at Cologne, Franz Ries. He was taught by
his father when young, and afterwards had the
distinction of being a pupil of Beethoven's for the
piano, the great composer who was also born in Bonn
being a friend of Franz Ries. In consequence of
these intimate relations with Beethoven, Ries was well
able at a later period to publish the "biographical Notes"
on the great musician. Beethoven recommended him

to Albrechtsberger for lessons in composition, but as
the latter charged one ducat a lesson, after taking 28
lessons, the young student's means were exhausted and
he had to discontinue the instruction. He applied himself
all the more diligently to his work under Beethoven.
In 1805, this study also came to an end, because
meanwhile Napoleon's rule had extended to the Electo-
rate of Cologne, and all the young men of that part
of the country had been called in to serve in the
ranks. The consequence of non-appearance must have
been serious, as young Ries set off at once on
receiving the order, travelling by way of Prague,
Dresden and Leipzig towards the Rhine. Fortunately
when he presented himself to the military authorities
at Coblenz, he was not admitted to the army on
account of the sight of one of his eyes having been
rendered useless by small-pox.

He now commenced travelling as a pianist, going
to Paris, where he remained for two years; then
to Cassel, Hamburg, Copenhagen, Stockholm and
St. Petersburg. Here he again met Romberg the
violincello-player, who had once taught him that
instrument in Bonn; they started on concert tours
together, going to Riga, Reval, Kiew, Moscow &c.
Ries was obliged to flee from Moscow on account of
the advance of the French; he went over to London,
arriving there in March 1813, and was very warmly
welcomed, not only as a pianist, but as a composer
and teacher, so much so that he was enabled to take
up his permanent abode in that town; he married an
Englishwoman and acquired a fortune which he placed
in a bank, but subsequently he lost a great part of it.

When Spohr and his wife came to London for
the first time at the beginning of the year 1820, in
order to give concerts, Ries was of great advantage
to them. Ries, who had become almost thoroughly
English, introduced Spohr to the directors of the

Philharmonic Society, went about as his intrepeter with him, and smoothed over many difficulties, Spohr's rather rough manner and his ignorance of English customs being against him. Spohr made many acquaintances at Ries's house, the latter provided him with "old Johanning" as a servant, who proved a great acquisition to Spohr during his residence in London.

In 1823, Ries left London and retired to a country residence of his own at Godesberg on the Rhine, where he composed industriously and established a solid reputation. About 1830, he removed to Frankfort-on-the-Main, and from there went to England again in 1831, partly to write the music to an opera for a theatrical manager in London, partly to conduct at a musical festival in Dublin, then to Italy in 1832, where he gave concerts in several large towns. In 1834, he conducted the Rhenish Musical Festival at Aachen, and in consequence of this was made director of the town orchestra, and also of the Singakademie in that town, but as this work was not agreeable to him, he relinquished the appointment in 1836. After he had conducted the Festival at Aachen in 1837, he was made director of the Cæcilia Society in Frankfort in the same year, but died in 1838, at the age of 54.

Ferdinand Ries has composed more than 200 works: 9 Concertos for piano, 1 Octet, 1 Sextet, 2 Septets, 1 Quintet, 3 Quartets, 5 Trios with piano, 1 Trio for two pianos and harp, numerous Sonatas, Fantasias, Rondos &c. for piano only; 3 Operas, 2 Oratorios, 6 Symphonies, 3 Overtures, 1 violin concerto, 6 Quintets for different instruments, 14 String Quartets, 20 Violin Sonatas, 1 Sonata for violincello and many other works.

MORITZ ROSENTHAL.

ONLY the barest biographical notices exist about
Moritz Rosenthal; he was born in 1860, at Vienna,
and studied there. His execution is extraordinary,
particularly his playing of passages in thirds which
is most startling. Among the critics he has decided
friends, and great enemies. He was criticised in such
a way in the "Neuen Musik Zeitung" by Otto Lessmann,
that some of the other Berlin critics disputed the truth
of the statement. It ran as follows: "Unfinished musical students may think that they have witnessed the
greatest triumph of piano-playing in Herr Rosenthal's

heroic feats of execution, but every reasonable
person will be thoroughly convinced that beyond
this astounding performance, it is quite a different
question when a serious position is to be taken
up among real artists. The manner in which he
played the shorter pieces of Haydn, Mendelssohn
and Chopin, totally lacking poetry, the proper effect
being quite lost, only serves to show how unimportant
his performances are in an aesthetic sense." After
he had appeared at Frankfort-on-the-Main, some of
the critics found fault in a similar manner, with his
playing, saying that he altered rhythm and time, that
he had no Cantilene, and his playing often degene-
rated into such a chaos of sounds, particularly on
account of his unnecessary use of the pedals. On the
other hand, the accounts from Brussels were "that he
had roused the greatest enthusiasm". He was also
successful at the Gewandhaus in Leipzig, and at the
Alberthalle the deficiencies complained of were less
noticeable. A well-known critic, called him "a
Cagliostro among the young pianists." He gave
proofs of his incredible execution before large
audiences, having already created a sensation in
former years in Leipzig, at the Liszt Society concerts. At the same time this marvellous execution
was said to be his object, not his means to an
end. In Beethoven's "Appassionata" he played
certain passages with great emphasis and clearness, in such a way that would not be easy to
imitate, then again in the Allegro and Adagio and
Variations, all poetic feeling and expression was
missing. He was overpowering in the Finale, up
to the very last note.

Ed. Hanslick in Vienna calls Rosenthal "a pianoforte conjuror". His playing is very highly cultivated
as regards execution; Paderewski possesses the same
gift, and Rosenthal is at the present moment his rival in

America. His concert tours so successfully undertaken in France, Spain, Holland, England, &c. show that as well as his brilliancy of playing, Rosenthal directs his efforts towards an intelligent rendering of all he undertakes to perform.

ANTON RUBINSTEIN.

ANTON Rubinstein is one of the most remarkable men ever known among musicians. Genius in the full sense of the word, pervades his playing as well as his compositions, and the remark was once made, that not only is it like thunder and lightning, but, it is also like the fire, ashes and smoke of a volcano. No one is to be compared with him in piano playing; he has immense power and is very great in producing a deep impression; but his playing is full of contradictions. He has complete mastery of his instrument, but technical work does not seem

to be of the highest importance with him, he does
not adhere to absolute correctness and mechanical
accuracy, he turns all his attention irresistibly and
by instinct, to investing all compositions he plays
with the necessary life and power. Sometimes a
storm of passion and then the most delicate grace
and tenderness succeed each other; he at one moment
depicts thunder and tempests, at another, a sigh
like the breath of spring. With such immense creative power, he is never troubled if here and there a
note should be wrong.

It is now forty years since Rubinstein's playing
created such an enormous sensation wherever he
went, but even greater astonishment was caused by
a peculiarity of his which has been imitated in a
lesser degree by other great pianists, namely his
gigantic powers of memory; he played everything
by heart, Bach, Händel, Haydn, Mozart, Rameau,
Scarlatti, Beethoven, Mendelssohn, Schumann, Schulhoff, also his own compositions, in fact, the most
difficult piece he ever undertook to play; his colossal
memory has never forsaken him.

He was born on the 30th of November 1829, at
Wechwotinez near Jassy. In early childhood he went
to Moscow with his parents. He received his first
musical instruction from his mother, which was also
the case with his younger brother Nicholas. When he
was seven years old, he had lessons from a French
pianist, Villoing by name. He made such rapid
progress, that he was able to play in public at eight
years of age, and at ten, Villoing took him to Paris,
where he excited great interest among the best
musicians. Franz Liszt took great notice of him,
but was of opinion, that he ought to go through
a thorough course of teaching at a German school
of music. However Villoing arranged and carried
out an extensive concert tour in Holland, England,

Scandinavia and Germany; acknowledgments of all sorts and money were showered on them wherever they went.

In 1844, his mother took him and Nicholas to Berlin, where they both were by Meyerbeer's advice to study under the guidance of S. W. Dehn. Anton stayed some time in Berlin after the death of his father in 1846, but for want of means was obliged to give up his studies; he went to Vienna and there lived by giving lessons and subsequently, to Hungary, with the flute-player Heindl, to give concerts.

When the revolution broke out in Vienna, Rubinstein went back to Berlin, but here circumstances were not favorable and he removed to St. Petersburg. Here he was able to establish himself; the Princess Helene, a great patroness and lover of music, aided him, and appointed him as one of her musicians. In 1854, she provided him with the means to undertake a fresh concert tour in Europe; he visited Germany, Paris and London. While travelling, he composed among other things the oratorio "Paradise lost."

In 1858, he returned to St. Petersburg, was made Imperial pianist, and after that, musical director, and conductor of the Imperial Russian Opera. In 1861, he was placed at the head of the new Russian Philharmonic Society; in 1862, he was asked to found the Conservatoire at St. Petersburg and to become its Director.

In 1867, he again commenced to travel, this time going through the principal European towns on his way to America. His genius was triumphant everywhere. He was able to undertake all the concert programmes without any other help, and the concerts were never monotonous. In 1877, he again undertook the direction of the St. Petersburg Conservatoire, but his chief energy was devoted to concerts; for instance, he conducted a series of Russian historical

concerts in the larger towns in Russia, which brought
in a large fortune of which he devoted the greater
part to charitable purposes. He received the title of
"Imperial Russian Musical Director."

At the present time Anton Rubinstein lives * in
and near Dresden, apparently only playing in public
in aid of charities. Unfortunately his eye-sight is
very much affected. For piano his compositions are
as follows: 5 Concertos, 5 Trios, 1 Quartet, 1 Quintet,
1 Quintet with wind instruments, 1 Sextet, 4 Sonatas,
Variations, 6 Preludes, 2 Barcaroles, 3 Books of
"Soirées", Miscellanies, "Le bal", 1 Album of Popular
Dances, 1 Tarantella, Nocturnes, Etudes, Fantasia for
two piano, &c. Also; 1 Violin concerto, 2 Concertos
for violincello; then his operas are; "Kinder der
Haide", "Feramors", "Der Dämon", "Die Maccabäer",
"Nero", "Kalaschinkow", "Der Papagei", "Sulamith",
"Unter Räubern", the ballet "Die Rebe", oratorios;
"Der Thurm zu Babel", "Das verlorene Paradies";
5 Symphonies, 1 Fantasia, 3 Characteristic Pieces
(Faust, Ivan IV., Don Quixote); 2 Overtures for con-
cert performance, 3 Sonatas for violin, 1 Romance
and Caprice, 1 Sonata for viola, 2 Sonatas for violin-
cello, 1 String Quintet, 8 String Quartets, 1 String
Sextet; 2 Duets, 3 Choruses for male voices, 6 songs
for mixed voices, 2 Scenes with orchestra (Hecuba
Hagar), several Serenades, Songs &c. He has also
published some youthful, works for piano: the Etude
"Undine", "Hommage à Jenny Lind", "Voix interieurs",
"Trois Melodies caracteristiques à 4 mains", "Deux
Nocturnes", as well as some vocal music.

---

* Since the above was written Rubinstein died, November 20th, 1894,
at Peterhof, near St. Petersburg, of heart disease. He was within ten
days of 64 years of age. He received a state burial.

NICHOLAS RUBINSTEIN.

BEING the younger brother of such a remarkable character as Anton Rubinstein would necessarily rather put Nicholas in the shade, but Russians have been known to affirm that he was as a great a pianist as his brother, at any rate his artistic capabilities were as conspicuous, for the concerts that Nicholas played at in Russia were always as much favored as those of his brother.

But apart from their playing, which is of no moment, as their styles are so entirely different, Nicholas Rubinstein has gained as much distinction as Anton for his cultivation of music, in Russia.

The education of both the brothers was similar. Nicholas was born in Moscow in 1855, his mother teaching him the elements of pianoforte playing; and as in Anton's case, he also went to Berlin with his mother, to study with Kullak and Dehn. After two years, Nicholas went back to Russia with his mother, Anton continuing his studies in Berlin.

Nicholas' chief activity commenced in 1860, in connection with the Russian Musical Society in Moscow; he undertook the management of it, and conducted the Symphony concerts organised by this society. In 1864 (from other accounts, 1866) the above mentioned society added the founding of the Conservatoire at Moscow, Nicholas was also made director of this institution, and retained the appointment till his death, fulfilling his duties with zeal and intelligence.

During the war in the East, he organised 30 concerts in different towns in Russia for the benefit of the wounded soldiers. In 1865, he gave four Russian concerts in the Trocadero at Paris, during the exhibition there.

He died in Paris on the 23^d of March 1881.

FRANZ RUMMEL.

A<small>N</small> entire musical family of the name of Rummel belong to Brichenstadt in Bavaria. The head of this family was: Christian Franz Ludwig Friedrich Alexander, born in 1780, who led a very adventurous life before settling down to quieter days. His master was the Abbé Vogler; in 1806, he was made band-master of an infantry regiment in Nassau, and had to march with his regiment to Spain. Later on the Duke of Nassau made him conductor of an orchestra, he died at Wiesbaden in 1849. His daughter Josephine, born in Spain, became pianiste to the Court at Wies-baden, and died in 1877. The son Joseph, born in 1818, was conductor of an orchestra to a Princess

of Oldenburg, and lived sometimes in London, sometimes in Paris. He died in the latter city in 1880.
A second daughter, Franziska, received an education
in Paris as a singer, was engaged at the Court of
Wiesbaden and then married Schott the publisher
at Mayence.

Joseph Rummel's son Franz, was born on the
11th of January 1853, in London; his father was his
first teacher, and when he was fourteen, was sent to
Brussels to study the piano with Brassin, first taking
private lessons, and then at the Conservatoire. In
1872, he got the first prize at the examination in
pianoforte-playing, also an appointment at the Conservatoire in Brussels. On the 22d of December in
the same year, he played in public for the first time
at Antwerp, a concerto by Henselt. In the following
year he played in London, first at a concert in the
Albert Hall; his chief number being Schumann's concerto. On his return, he was honoured by an invitation
to play before the King and Queen of the Belgians,
and was then made professor at the Brussels Conservatoire. He continued his teaching there until 1876,
but then, on Anton Rubinstein's advice, he began
to travel and gave concerts in many countries, in
Holland, Germany, France and England, playing at
the Crystal Palace in London in 1877.

In 1878, he went to America, where his success
was great; but his concerts were interrupted by a
disaster. In 1881, he came back to London and
played again at the Crystal Palace. His repertoire
includes all the most important classical works and
many more modern compositions, like those of Rubinstein, Raff, Liszt, Tschaikowsky, &c.

After various concert tours he was made pianoforte teacher at the Stern Conservatoire in Berlin.
He is a prolific writer of pianoforte music.

CAMILLE SAINT SAENS.

ACCORDING to the opinion of his countrymen, Camillle
Saint-Saëns is considered a brilliant pianist, a composer full of genius, and a conductor possessing
thorough and perfect control over his orchestra. He
has made a great name as pianist and composer in
foreign countries. In his compositions he shows a
preference for the classical school, combining it very
cleverly with the modern effects in music; very severe
critics maintain that many of his works are very bizarre.
But it is certain that the composer is much in earnest
in his work, and full of the desire of the spirit of
real art, he also tries to keep free of everything

superficial, although all his compositions may not be equally successful.

He was born in Paris, on the 9th of October 1835, and received a thorough musical education; Stamaty was his master for the piano, and Benoist for the organ, in theory and composition he was taught by Reber, Halévy and Gounod.

In 1855, he was made organist at the church of St. Merry in Paris, three years later he had an appointment given him in the same capacity at the Madeleine in Paris. At the same time he gave organ and piano lessons at the Nadermann Institution. But after his compositions had begun to get a hearing, and brought him in a sufficient income, he gave up his teaching as also his post as organist; but he still retains the peculiarity of writing his serious compositions in the quiet of a church. Of his works for piano, the following must be mentioned; 4 Concertos 1 suite algérienne, Variations and Tarantella, Marches for four hands; 1 Sextet for piano, stringed instruments and trumpet (said to be a quaint and pleasing combination) &c. He also wrote, 1 Violin concerto, 1 concerto for violincello, 4 Symphonies, 4 Symphonic Poems, 6 operas, one of which on a sacred subject, 2 Masses, 1 Oratorio, 1 Requiem, 1 Psalm for solo, chorus and orchestra, motets, choral works, Cantatas, 1 Ode, Songs, Marches for orchestra &c.—

EMIL SAUER.

SAUER was born at Hamburg, on the 8th of October 1862, and there received his first musical instruction in the piano from his mother, later on he went to St. Petersburg and from 1876 to 1881, was Nicholas Rubinstein's pupil. In 1884 he finished his studies as pianist with Liszt.

He has played with great success in almost all European countries, and is recognized as a most excellent executant, as well as a very good teacher, in consequence of this he has bound himself to spend some months every year in giving lessons at the Conservatoire at Dresden.

DOMENICO SCARLATTI.

A LESSANDRO Scarlatti, was remarkable as a composer
of oratorio and opera; and his son Domenico was
almost as remarkable with respect to the piano; he
did a great deal to promote technical study. In a
certain sense he was the originator of modern playing,
and his influence can be traced in Liszt, Mendelssohn
and other more modern musicians. He made much
use of the crossing of hands in playing.

His relations with Händel are interesting, they
met in 1708, at Venice, and seem to have travelled
together to Rome by way of Florence. At Rome,

Cardinal Ottoboni arranged a competition between
Händel and Scarlatti, first on the harpsichord when
the result was undecided, and then on the organ,
when Händel was proclaimed' victorious.

Domenico Scarlatti, was born in Naples in 1683
or 1685, and was taught partly by his father and
partly by Gasparini at Rome. The harpsichord
(Arpicordo or Harpichord) in wing shape was his
favourite instrument, but at that time in Italy preference was given to the Clavicembalo, dulcimer, with
keys added, and for examples of the old traditional style,
the organ reigned supreme. Domenico, notwithstanding his masterly playing was not properly recognized
in Italy. On the other hand he attracted attention
when travelling in England and Spain. In 1720, he
had a friendly meeting with Händel in London.

He remained some time at the Court at Lisbon,
but the love of his country attracted him so strongly
that he returned to Italy in 1725.

In 1729, he was again invited to the Court in
Spain, and was then appointed music master to the
Princess of Asturias. He only went back to Naples
in 1754, and died there in the following year. He
was passionately fond of the game of hazard, but
this was the means of impoverishing his family to a
great extent.

Domenico Scarlatti, was a very prolific composer.
His pieces were all short ones. Abbé Santini possessed
349 of them, but Scarlatti only published 30 of these
pieces in Venice, as "Esercizii per Clavicembalo".
Czerny's edition in 1839, contained 300 pieces. In
Farrenc's Trésor des Pianistes (Paris, 1864) there are
130 numbers. 60 Sonatas were published by Breitkopf
& Härtel, 18 Suites, edited by von Bülow and
published by Peters.

XAVER SCHARWENKA.

SCHARWENKA's career as a pianist is devided
into two periods, when he was not engaged
in teaching; but these intervals of teaching were of
decided use in advancing his playing to a state of
greater perfection, and perhaps the example of his
elder brother Philip, who had entirely devoted himself
to theory and composition, helped to influence him in
adopting the musical profession.

Xaver was born on the 6th January 1850, at
Samter, a little town in Polish Prussia. In early childhood he went to Posen with his father who settled

there; the boy then went to school, and was also
taught the piano, but not as a serious study. In
1865, when his father moved to Berlin, the idea
was entertained that Xaver should study music in
earnest. Like his brother Philip, he now entered
Kullak's Conservatoire, and made rapid progress in
piano playing, so that in three years' time he was
able to accept an appointment as teacher at this same
school of music. He now had a good opportunity to
control his somewhat hasty Polish nature by confor-
ming to the stringent rules at the Conservatoire, and
he was also able to improve his playing to a great
extent.

In 1869, he played for the first time in public,
at a concert in the Berlin Singakademie, and received
great commendation from all musicians. His playing
combined clearness and brilliancy, with great
smoothness and power. The critics ascribed a peculiar quality to his playing, and he retained this at a
later date. But his work as a teacher prevented him
almost entirely from playing in public. In order to
be more at liberty, he resigned his position in 1874,
and commenced his concert-tours, and became much
appreciated. In nearly all the larger towns in
Germany he received the highest praise, his concerts
were very crowded and were of great profit to him.

In 1881, he again gave up his life of travelling
and in October of that year he founded a Con-
servatoire of his own in Berlin, his brother, Albert
Becker and W. Jähns being on the teaching staff.
The rapid way this school has grown, testifies to
Xaver Scharwenka's excellent capabilities as a teacher.

He was made pianist to the Prussian Court, and
from this time turned his attention more to composition. Franz Liszt considered Scharwenka's piano
concerto in B-flat-minor a remarkable addition to
pianoforte music.

In 1891, he entrusted his Conservatoire in Berlin, to his brother Philip and Dr. Hugo Goldschmidt, who then combined it with Klindworth's former School of Music. Xaver Scharwenka went to New York, and there established the "Scharwenka Conservatoire of Music", the management of this school now takes up the chief part of his time. Still he travels occasionally, giving concerts in Western America.

The compositions of his that are known, are as follows: 2 Piano Trios, 2 Sonatas for piano, 1 Piano Quartet as well as numerous shorter pianoforte pieces in a lighter style. He has also written for violin and violincello. Following Liszt's example, as well as that of other composers in respect to Hungarian music, Scharwenka made use of his national music, in his "Polish Dances", that have become very popular. His newest work is an opera "Mataswintha" with words from Felix Dahn's romance "Ein Kampf um Rom". The pianoforte score of this opera was published by Breitkopf & Härtel.

ALOYS SCHMITT.

ALTHOUGH Aloys Schmitt travelled for some little time giving concerts, and was also proved to be a pianist of great excellence, yet his work as a teacher and composer for the piano was of much more consequence. His instructive pianoforte works are of the greatest value for teaching purposes even to the present day.

He was born on the 26th of August 1788, at Erlenbach am Main, (Bavaria), where his father was Cantor. He taught his son the elements of pianoforte playing. Then J. A. André, at Offenbach, became his master for the piano and theory. After having been heard several times in public at some of the towns in Central Germany, he settled as a teacher in Frankfort-on-the-Main in 1816. In 1820, he went to Berlin, remaining there till 1824, and making a name more especially as a composer.

In 1825, he was made pianist at the Court of the Duke of Cambridge at Hanover; he retained this post until 1829, and then resumed his teaching at Frankfort with success, continuing this work until his death, the 25th of July 1866.

He composed 4 pianoforte concertos, about 80 Studies, a Method of piano-playing, Sonatas, Sonatinas, Rondos, Variations, concerted pieces; besides these, String Quartets, Overtures, Oratorios, Masses, Operas &c.

Not only his nephew George Aloys, (born the 2nd February 1827 in Hanover) but also his younger brother Jakob, both excellent pianists, were indebted to him for their musical education. Jakob Schmitt published Etudes, Sonatas, Variations and lighter pieces for piano, and his son played often in public at concerts in Germany, Belgium, France, England, Algeria &c., in 1857, he was made conductor at Schwerin, and had a number of pupils, one of whom was Emma Brandes.

JULIUS SCHULHOFF.

SCHULHOFF spent a considerable part of his life in playing in public, and attained great success by his refined interpretation of modern and classical pianoforte works. Chopin encouraged him in becoming a professional pianist.

J. Schulhoff was born at Prague, the 2^d August 1825. He was there taught the piano by Kisch and Tedesco, Tomaschek being his master in theory.

In his eighteenth year he played in public, both at Dresden and at the Gewandhaus in Leipzig. He then went to Paris, where Chopin did a great deal for him, and induced him to give some concerts; these were so successful, that he was enabled to go to

London, appearing there in public with success. He also travelled more extensively in Spain, Russia &c,

After this he returned to Paris, resigning the career of a pianist, and employing his time in composition and teaching then.

In 1870, he settled in Dresden where his mother was living. He married there in 1878. About four years ago he settled in Berlin and has been living there since.

The following are a few of his compositions, which all belong to the best style of light music: 1 Sonata, 12 Etudes, a series of Caprices, Impromptus, Waltzes, Mazurkas &c.

CLARA SCHUMANN.

THE immortal composer's widow, Clara Schumann, occupies a very high position among the greatest pianists and the best pianoforte teachers. She was born in Leipzig, September the 13th 1819, and was the daughter of the well-known music-teacher Friedrich Wieck. Both she and her sister Marie went through a course of severe and arduous study, the plan of which was laid down by their father. From the fifth year of her age, she was obliged to practise a great deal on the piano, and at six years old, owing to her father's systematic teaching, such success was achieved with his method, that it made his name as a teacher, widely known. When Paganini first heard little Clara play in Leipzig, his remark was a prophetic one: "This child has a great future before her and she will put many great musicians in the shade."

When she was nine years of age she used to play pieces by Mozart, Hummel, Beethoven &c. with great cleverness and intelligence. In 1828, she played at a Gewandhaus concert in Leipzig the F-minor concerto by Chopin and Variations on a theme from "Don Juan".

After that Wieck travelled with his daughter; in Weimar the veteran Goethe heard her play at a concert, and after it was over he presented her with a picture of himself with the following inscription: "To the little genius and musician, Clara Wieck." In Weimar she was only able to play at the houses of some people of rank, because Hummel, together with the concert director Eberwein did all they could to prevent the child's playing with orchestra at the Court theatre, although she played Hummel's own compositions.

At Cassel, she completely gained Spohr's good-will; his best pupil for singing, Wilhelmine Baldewin took part at a concert of Clara's, and long afterwards she used often to speak of the great charm in the young girl's playing.

In Paris, the greatest interest was taken in her by great musicians like Meyerbeer, Chopin, Mendelssohn, Kalkbrenner, Wilhelmine Schröder-Devrient and others. The latter sang at a concert which Wieck arranged for his daughter, who was received with immense applause. She was stimulated by this success to make a serious study of J. S. Bach, Beethoven, Chopin, Mendelssohn &c. and she thus learnt to play classical as well as more modern music with equal intelligence. On her return home, she continued her theoretical studies with Weinlig, Kupsch and Dorn, took lessons in singing from Mieksch and also learnt the violin with Prinz, thus becoming generally educated in music. All the greatest musicians in Germany who heard her, were highly interested in her career. In 1835, in Leipzig, Mendelssohn and Moscheles played Bach's Triple Concerto with her. After she had appeared in Vienna in 1837, she received the title of Imperial pianiste, and Franz Liszt who heard her play at that time, and who had not himself reached the zenith of his artistic career, spoke thus of her: "I was enchanted with her talent, she has great capabilities, deep, genuine feeling, and she shows great elevation of mind." Her playing combined all the qualities necessary for a fine performance; great intelligence and feeling, power, fire and tenderness; yet never sought after effect alone.

Robert Schumann had known her well long before he married her; he wrote about her and talked of her with great enthusiasm, which awakened in her, gratitude and love, such a love that proved capable of overcoming the greatest difficulties. There were many obstacles in the way, for Friedrich Wieck from purely selfish motives was very strongly opposed to the marriage. Clara had to appeal to a Court of justice against her father, and she was fully justified in the course she followed, as Wieck had deserted her mother in order to marry again. In September 1840, Clara was married to Robert Schumann, and the marriage proved to be a decidedly happy one. They were perfectly in harmony with each other; Clara interpreted her gifted husband's compositions and he was stimulated to new creations by his life of love and happiness; it was thus his most beautiful songs were produced. Clara was at the same time a thoroughly good manager, and kept her husband free of all household cares.

It is universally known, that after Schumann had been made musical director at Düsseldorf in 1850, his nervous system gave way through over-work, and in 1854, this developed into complete insanity. The happiness of their married life thus came to an end; but Clara remained with her suffering husband until 1856, when his eyes were closed for ever in death. She then went to Berlin, where her mother, formerly separated from Friedrich Wieck, was now married to Bargiel; from here Clara commenced her concert-tours again, and during that time she introduced her husband's works to public notice. She played with equal finish the works of Chopin and Mendelssohn, as also those of great classical composers. As time went on she acquired an intellectual style of playing which was peculiarly her own.

In 1878, she was made first teacher of the pianoforte at the Hoch Conservatoire at Frankfort-on-the-Main, and she has retained this position up to the present day, her inimitable teaching qualities being thoroughly acknowledged.

Clara Schumann has also been assiduous as a composer, for piano, she has written a concerto (op. 7), a Trio, Preludes and Fugues, Variations on a theme by Robert Schumann, also Romances for piano and violin, songs, &c. Besides this, she revised her husband's works, also the Finger Exercises from Czerny's Pianoforte School.

ISIDOR SEISS.

THE excellent course of instruction by means of which Seiss was taught, has placed him in the foremost rank of modern teachers, and among the most notable pianists. Combined with his natural gifts he has a fine feeling for true art, and has attracted notice as a composer of much taste.

He was born in Dresden on the 27th of December, 1840, being the son of a musician there; his father gave him his first instruction, and then Friedrich Wieck and L. Niedermeyer were his pianoforte teachers, Julius Otto and later on C. Riccius, laying the foundation of his knowledge in theory; these theoretical studies being continued from 1859 to 1860, under the guidance of one of the greatest teachers of counterpoint, Moritz Hauptmann.

At that time Seiss brought out some of his first compositions, and in 1861, he travelled on concert-tours to several of the larger towns in Germany. The critics always praised the refinement and smoothness of his execution, also his endeavours to make the composer's meaning perfectly clear, and to give a faithful rendering, down to the smallest detail of every work he performed. His preference was given to classical composers, and then to Schumann, Mendelssohn, Chopin, Brahms, and Rubinstein.

On passing through Cologne on one of his tours, when Ferdinand Hiller heard him play, he at once engaged him to teach at the Conservatoire. Seiss occupies this position up to the present time and in 1878, he was formally appointed professor. A number of excellent pupils are indebted to him for their musical cultivation.

As regards teaching purposes, Seiss's compositions for piano are of great value. He has gained much merit by his excellent arrangement of Haydn's Quartets for the piano, and of Beethoven's German Dances, a new edition of C. M. von Weber's Concerto in E-flat, as well as some of his own compositions: Sonatinas, Bravoura Studies, Preludes, a Toccata, &c.

GIOVANNI SGAMBATI.

SGAMBATI, a composer of the modern Italian school, has been strongly influenced in composition by two great men: Liszt and Richard Wagner, and he is undoubtedly one of the first Italian musicians of the present day.

He was born in Rome on May the 18th 1843, and was the son of a lawyer, his mother being a native of England. As he showed great inclination for music in his early childhood and also an aptitude for the piano, it was decided that he should take up music as a profession, and Barberi, Natalucci and Aldega gave him instruction.

Fortunately for him, he was pursuing his studies

during Liszt's long residence in Rome, and it thus came about that the latter undertook to give him lessons. He was able to appear as a pianist in 1860, and his first composition, a pianoforte quartet, was successfully performed in 1866. In the same year in Rome, he also conducted Liszt's Dante Symphony and Beethoven's Eroica Symphony.

Since then he has become known during his concert-tours in Italy, as also in Germany, France, England &c. In 1877, he was appointed first pianoforte teacher at the Music School of the Cecilia Academy in Rome. Richard Wagner had long been interested in him and advanced his cause as a composer, by inducing him to publish some of his best pianoforte compositions, as well as Symphonies, String Quartets &c.

ALEXANDER SILOTI.

SILOTI, who is the possessor of very remarkable talents, is considered by his Russian compatriots to be one of the very best of their modern pianists. He has as much execution as any performer of the present day, and is also known to be a very good musician. His playing of Liszt's music is splendid, and he is looked on as one of Liszt's most remarkable pupils.

He has brought himself advantageously into notice in Germany, and since 1883, again in Leipzig, by the elegance, refinement and brilliancy of his performance of the most difficult compositions. At his last appearance in Leipzig, he created a sensation by his masterly and spirited performance of Edward Grieg's brilliant

Concerto in A-minor. He was born on the 10th of October 1863, near Charkow (South Russia) on his father's estate: from 1875 to 1881, he was at the Conservatoire in Moscow, and was taught there by Swereff, Nicholas Rubinstein and Tschaikowsky, and from 1883 until 1886, he was a pupil of Liszt's.

He has played much in public since 1880, as also lately at a concert of the Russian Imperial Musical Society in St. Petersburg, since which time he has travelled extensively.

Quite lately, in 1893, he was offered an appointment as professor of the pianoforte at the Conservatoire at St. Petersburg, but has refused the post, in order to be more at liberty as pianist and teacher; he resides mostly in Paris.

BERNHARD STAVENHAGEN.

STAVENHAGEN takes high rank among those pianists of modern times, who, in consequence of earnest study are able to combine all the qualities necessary for an executant with the true cultivation of good music. He has been received on the continent, also in England, with decided approbation, and has been singled out for many distinctions which could only be awarded to musicians of the best reputation.

He is one of the youngest among musicians, and was born at Greiz 1872, he received his musical education in Berlin with Friedrich Kiel and Ernst

Rudorff. After this he had lessons from Liszt, and as one of his last pupils, Liszt helped him on and showed him special favour. For the last two years of Liszt's life, Stavenhagen accompanied him everywhere; to Rome, Pesth, Paris, London and lastly to Bayreuth, where he was with him at the time of his death.

In 1880, Stavenhagen had already received the Mendelssohn prize for executive music. In 1890, he was made pianist at the Weimar Ducal Court, and the Society of Music in Edinburgh elected him one of their members.

DANIEL STEIBELT.

D ANIEL Steibelt, who was much thought of as a
pianist about one hundred years ago, was a remarkable genius, but his mode of life in many
respects was not well-regulated, such an example
being the reverse of encouraging. The date of his
birth is quite uncertain: some say, he was born in
1755, others again 1756, while Fétis fixes the date
as 1765. His father was a pianoforte maker in Berlin,
and taught him the elements of piano playing. His
musical talent was noticeable early in life, and the
Crown Prince, a great lover of music, (afterwards

King Frederick William II.) took an interest in him, so much so, that by his means, Kirnberger, who at that time directed the music at the Court in Berlin, instructed Steibelt in piano and theory. It is not known how long and to what extent this instruction was continued, but there was certainly no trace of Kirnberger's pedantic method to be found in Steibelt's style of playing and composition. The musical life in Berlin during Frederick the Great's despotic reign, seems rather to have had an undesirable influence on Steibelt's peculiarities, producing a bad effect throughout his life.

It has also been proved that young Steibelt studied the technical part of the pianoforte very thoroughly at his father's manufactory, and was able to exhibit the perfections of the instruments to the best advantage.

In the later years of his life, he has been found fault with on account of his unpolished manners as well as his unsteadiness; this roughness of behaviour may partly be explained by the fact, that Steibelt was obliged to enter the Prussian army, which was strongly imbued with much that was barbarous and servile. About 1784, when he was able to leave the army, it appeared to him like a release from bondage, as he then led a restless, roving life. He gave concerts in several large towns in Germany: Dresden, Hanover, Munich, Waldheim &c., and achieved great success. It is not certain when he first appeared in Paris, but it must have been before the outbreak of the Revolution, as he figured at Louis XVI's gay Court and was very much favoured by Marie Antoinette. The latter arranged a competition between him and Hermann, a pianist of note at that time, and who had taken Seb. Bach as his model; Steibelt was declared the greater of the two pianists. His manners which were then anything but those of a courtier, were overlooked at this pleasure-loving Court. He had many aristocratic pupils. He imposed upon the publisher Boyer, having sold him as new, some of his successful compositions that had already been published in Munich.

Induced by Count Ségur who had written a libretto after Shakespeare's Romeo and Juliet, he commenced to write the music for it. The Academy refused this opera, but a performance of it took p'ace in 1793, at the Théâtre Feydeau, and was a success, notwithstanding much unfavourable criticism. This opera was performed there 19 times; at the Opera Comique 22 times; and in Stockholm there were fifteen performances of it. If Steibe't had led a quieter life he would have become very great, but he could not control his tendency to disorderly conduct, and finally had to leave Paris, owing to many wild adventures, as also on account of debts incurred there. In 1796, he went to London, his rivals there being Dussek, Clementi, Cramer, &c.; but he was received with favour, more as a composer than as a pianist:—his pianoforte concerto in C, No. 3 with the Storm Rondo and which was first played at Salomon's concert in 1798, became the favorite piece of the season.

In 1799, he travelled on the continent, and was enthusiastically received at Dresden and Hamburg; in Berlin and Prague, he made but little impression at the concerts; in Vienna he was compared to Beethoven, but there is no doubt that he was inferior.

He now arranged a French translation of Haydn's Creation; this work brought him in at least 10,000 Marks, and at the performance in Paris in 1800, at Christmas time, there was not a seat to be had, the success being very great.

Steibelt now lived alternately in London and Paris, he was mostly in a good position and much sought after; he played at concerts and wrote the music for two Ballets for the Haymarket Theatre. In 1806, his festival cantata, written to celebrate the battle of Austerlitz, made a great impression in London. But the life he led in London again forced him to leave that city, as he had been obliged to quit Paris; he went to Frankfort, and then to Leipzig, where his impositions in re-selling his own compositions already published became known; then he went to Breslau, and Warsaw, and about the year 1809, to St. Petersburg. Here he was fortunate enough to receive an appointment for life as Director of the French Opera, thus taking Boieldieu's place who went to Paris. Steibelt's wanderings now came to an end, and this good position steadied him for the future. Until 1814, he played in public; his performance was weak in slow movements, but in quick movements his playing was great, and always correct. He exaggerated in the use of the pedal, but his playing was attractive for the moment. At his death in 1823, there was accorded him a pompous funeral, and his friends headed by the Governor of St. Petersburg organised a benefit concert for his family.

Steibelt has written many larger and smaller pianoforte works, partly with accompaniment of other instruments, but these compositions are mostly forgotten. He also wrote 60 violin Sonatas, 40 Sonatas for harp and piano, several overtures, and four or five operas, that were all performed, but with the exception of "Romeo and Juliet" none of them were heard of afterwards.

———— ❖❖❖ ————

WILHELMINE SZARVADY.

THIS distinguished pianiste is more universally known by her maiden name Clauss. On the numerous concert-tours she has made, she was always favorably received by the public, on account of her brilliant execution, her refined feeling and tasteful interpretation.

She was the daughter of a merchant and was born at Prague on the 13th of December 1834, and as she showed aptitude and taste for music in early childhood, she was placed under the excellent tuition of Professor Proksch, who gave her lessons that fitted her for the career of a pianiste.

In 1849, accompanied by her mother, she made

her first concert-tour, which proved such a success that Wilhelmine Clauss was often able to re-visit the principal towns on the continent, and always played to crowded audiences. The critics in Vienna, Berlin, Leipzig &c. praised her playing very highly.

In 1852, she played for the first time in Paris, at a concert got up by Berlioz, where she introduced Beethoven's first pianoforte concerto and had a brilliant success. She made a point of including works by Schumann and Liszt, as well as classical compositions in her concert programmes.

Her mother having died in Paris, Wilhelmine discontinued her performances for a year; she then went for the second time to South Germany, Hungary, and later on to London. She married the author, Fr. Syarvady and settled permanently in Paris, but since that time has given proofs of still greater perfection and knowledge of classical music in her performances in public. She has further shewn this by editing and performing a concerto by Philip Emanuel Bach, which had not previously been published, and which she arranged exclusively for the piano.

WILHELM TAUBERT.

WILHELM Taubert was a devoted follower of
Mendelssohn's, being a friend and colleague of
his, and he faithfully upheld the cause of classical
music. From this point of view and in his own capacity as pianist and composer, he has not been surpassed. Everything was bad in his eyes if it did
not advance the pursuit of real art in any way. He
was eminently successful during his extensive concert-
tours in Germany, Holland, England, Scotland, &c.,

by his conscientious and delightful rendering of classical works, as also by his very careful execution. Favored by fortune, he has received more marks of distinction that many other musician of equal talent.

He was the son of a military official, and was born at Berlin on the 23^d of March 1811; although the times were rather troubled, Taubert's parents were in easy circumstances, so that his early life was a peaceful one. Neithardt, Bernhard Klein and L. Berger taught him music; he and Mendelssohn at the same time finished studying the pianoforte with Berger, who was an excellent master. Taubert also attended the University in Berlin in order to extend his knowledge by attending those lectures that dealt chiefly with the science of music.

When he was twenty years of age, he was made director of the Court concerts. In 1836, he commenced a series of concert-tours, and in 1839, he was made a regular member of the Academy of Arts in Berlin. In 1841, he was obliged to give up concert-tours, having been appointed conductor at the Royal Opera House in Berlin. When Mendelssohn was persuaded to leave Leipzig again and go to Berlin, Taubert and he organised together a series of Symphony concerts in the winter of 1842. These concerts were a great source of pleasure to him, as they gave him a good opportunity of proving his enthusiasm for classical music.

In 1845, the title of Hofkapellmeister (Conductor to the Court) was bestowed upon him. In 1869, he became principal director, and in 1882, was appointed President of the musical branch of the Academy of Arts. During the last twenty years of his life, he was only heard as pianist on special occasions, either to play some classical concerto, or to accompany.

Universally esteemed and beloved, he lived to a good age and died on the 7th of January 1891.

He has written a number of melodious pieces for the piano; among them are 6 Sonatas; also Symphonies, overtures, choral works, chamber music &c. In his very numerous vocal compositions, the Children's Songs (numbering about 150 in 12 collections) have especially become widely popular, and are included in nearly all books for singing in German schools. Other works to be enumerated are as follows: Choruses to "Medea", Music to Shakespeare's "Tempest" and "Macbeth", to Schiller's "Phädra", to Tieck's "Blaubart" and "Joggeli", and also three operas: "Die Kirmess", "Der Zigeuner" and "Marquis und Dieb", but they have not had any lasting success.

CARL TAUSIG.

Tausig was one of the most highly-gifted of modern pianists, and it is much to be regretted that he was removed so early when at the zenith of his artistic career. During the process of development which in Tausig's case was uncommonly interesting and instructive, he finally was able to attain to a high degree of clearness and self-possession; and this undoubtedly made him the most perfect interpreter of pianoforte compositions. As regards execution, he reached the same height that his master Franz Liszt had attained before him; no one of the modern school has surpassed him, and although Anton Rubinstein is an incomparable pianist, yet his playing is not always faultless which never occurred to Tausig notwithstanding the magical brilliancy of his execution.

He was born either in or near Warsaw on the 4th of November 1841; his father taught him the piano until he was fourteen, then he had the instruction which is considered the best for pianoforte playing of the present day; namely that of Franz Liszt, and this talented pupil developed marvellously under such guidance. Between Tausig and Liszt there existed singular relations; the former had an unbounded admiration for Liszt's playing, for after having benefited by his teaching, he said: "Compared to Liszt we are all worth nothing!" In talking of his pupil, Liszt was heard to say: "Tausig is one of my best pupils, he has surpassed me in his playing which is full of deep feeling; he has great inborn musical talent."

When Tausig appeared for the first time in public towards the end of the fifties, his execution was quite extraordinary, his playing was so fiery and impassioned, that he aroused great enthusiasm as well as violent censure among the critics, particularly in Vienna and Berlin. Tausig did not trouble himself about the criticisms, and continued his triumphal progress to all those towns where he was subsequently heard at concerts. The public were in his favour. A young genius will not allow itself to be crushed by cold criticism, it passes through certain phases, of which the earlier ones are perhaps the most valuable, and at any rate they make the most impression.

However the change in Tausig came about by itself, he was no mere mechanical imitator, but rather a thinker, who knew how to govern himself. After many successful concert-tours, staying some time in Dresden, Vienna and Berlin, he took advantage of the name he had made for himself, and established

an "Academy for the higher development of pianoforte
playing" in 1865, in Berlin; there seems to be a
superfluity of words in this title, because an Academy
is understood to comprise the development of playing.

Tausig appears to have shown a remarkable
aptitude for teaching in this institution, and his
marvellous execution was an excellent example for
the more advanced pupils. Moreover the young
master kept on improving himself by further study
while imparting instruction to others, and he was
able thus, after several repeated appearances in
public, to make friends of his former opponents. It
was said, that his concerts and musical soirées were
like festivals to the music-loving public.

In 1870, his Academy was given up; but it was
not to be wondered at—there was no need for it;
the unfinished piano player requires systematic
teaching, such as can be found at the Conservatoires,
but the finished player does not stand in need of an
"Academy", as he can school himself.

Tausig began to travel again, and again created a
sensation. But for some years the gifted pianist had
become an unhappy and melancholy man. Many
people said this change in him was due to philosophical researches, and others again said, it was on
account of his marriage with the pianiste Seraphine
Vrabely, from whom he very shortly separated.

A friend of Tausig's in Berlin, Count Karl von
Krockow relates, that Tausig was much troubled by
many lady admirers, that he always avoided them
with a certain shyness, and always refused to speak
of his marriage. His freshness of intellect seemed to
forsake him from that time. When meeting with a
friend at Berlin some years before his death, he said:
„I am becoming an o'd man", at the same time showing
that the hair on his temples had become perfectly
white. It has been further asserted that already at

that time Tausig prophesied his early death with great certainty, his whole outward appearance being that of an old man, though young in years.

In the summer of 1871, he felt very ill, and decided to go to Ragaz for his health. He travelled by way of Leipzig, in order to meet Liszt. He arrived there on the 2ᵈ of July, and went immediately to a sacred concert given by the Riedel Verein, two of Liszt's works being performed. After the concert was over he went to pass an hour or two sociably with Liszt and some other friends, but the following night he fell seriously ill with typhus fever and was taken to the hospital. He endured tortures with the fever for fourteen days. Countess Krockow was at his bed-side; in certain memoirs, a Russian lady, Countess Moukhanoff-Nesselrode, a former admirer is mentioned as Tausig's "devoted nurse"; this is however contradicted by Count Krockow, who describes the following scene: "My wife just entered the sick-room as the hospital nurse was trying to soothe the patient in his excitement. He lay on his couch with a troubled countenance and closed eyes, and when he heard a well-known voice addressing him, he asked (being very short-sighted): "Are we alone?" When he was assured no one was present, he said: "Thank God!— Never leave me alone again with Madame von Moukhanoff, she may mean very well towards me, but she has tormented me very much with over-zealous attempts to convert me." After the sick man had quieted down a little, he stretched his hand out to my wife saying: "You are a true friend to me, you know and understand my thoughts and opinions, I beg of you not to leave me!"

He died on the 17ᵗʰ of July 1871, and his remains were brought to Berlin.

Tausig arranged Wagner's operas for the piano, also Clementi's well-known "Gradus ad Parnassum",

Studies, that were published after his death by Heinrich Ehrlich. He composed several short pianoforte pieces, published the "Soirées de Vienne" and also edited several classical pianoforte works.

SIGISMUND THALBERG.

As an exponent of outward effects and of the most refined execution, Thalberg was one of the most successful pianists of modern times. His appearance in the musical world was like that of a meteor, vanishing again without leaving any light behind. But he is universally credited with having done away with all that was antiquated in pianoforte playing by his method and style.

Musical historians of note agreed that until 1830, all living pianists, (Moscheles being of the number) used to place the principal elements of pianoforte music side by side: namely, harmony and melody on the one hand and groups of passages on the other. Those who performed Mozart's and Beethoven's works as well as other important compositions, had to subordinate their talents to the composer's intentions, but a brilliant performance had thus to be sacrificed. New ideas appeared with the cultivation of technical work. Clementi introduced effects into his playing, but Thalberg was in reality the representative of this newer system; he carried out the plan of combining the melody with the groups of passages in such a manner, that the technical part of his playing took the form of an accompaniment in such variety, that the greatest astonishment was created not only in this respect, but also by the powerful tone which he obtained from the instrument by the clever use of the pedal. At first musical connoisseurs thought that these innovations would present insurmountable difficulties, but on careful examination it was found, that performers with moderate executive ability were able to carry out Thalberg's method without any great difficulty, his compositions requiring a knowledge of this method. It was also said: that Thalberg understood the art of composing so as to make his works appear more difficult than they really were. His Etudes were easier than those by Chopin and Moscheles, but they sounded so brilliant that it seemed as if they had required very hard work in order to perform them. The only thing Thalberg had in view was to produce a brilliant effect, and he knew how to attain this object in a marvellous manner.

Catalani made the following remark to Henriette Sontag: "Thalberg's genre is not great, but he is great in his own genre."

His fingers were very wonderful, the foremost joints lay like small soft cushions on the keys, his legato playing being thus very beautiful. Liszt in speaking of this said: "Thalberg is the only pianist who can play the violin on the piano."

It is interesting to hear some more opinions of musicians on this subject. Anton Rubinstein said: "Liszt was a god at the piano, Thalberg a shop-keeper". Mendelssohn gave utterance to the following opinions about the "heathenish scandal" that was occasioned in Leipzig when Liszt played there: he declared that Thalberg's quiet self-control was to be more valued than his actual playing. Chopin agreed in this also. When Liszt played, his hair flew about and his body moved very much, and therefore Chopin said of him, that when he was not able to charm the public, he could at least astonish the people to a very great degree.

Thalberg was wonderfully quiet at the piano, excepting the movement of his fingers and elbows, he was perfectly still, even in the most difficult passages.

Thalberg knew how to delight his audience, and the ladies in particular were very enthusiastic about him, so that Schumann (of whom Thalberg was a great admirer) made the following remarks on the subject: "If any one were to criticize Thalberg, all the girls in Germany, France and other European countries would rise up in arms. An army of young women declare, that he is a god when he begins to play."

Proofs of this feminine enthusiasm were often heard of. If Thalberg left a glove lying on the piano, the ladies would pounce on it like furies, tear the glove to pieces, keeping the bits as relics. But Thalberg was a very handsome man into the bargain, fine-looking and gallant.

He was the natural son of a wealthy Austrian Prince, Dietrichstein, and of a lady of rank. He was born at Geneva in 1812, on the 7th of January, 1812 and passed the early years of his life in that town with his mother. He was then sent to Vienna, where his father who was proud of him, placed him under Hummel and Sechter's tuition. Later on Thalberg refused to allow he had learnt anything from either of these masters, he insisted that the first valuable teaching he ever received was from the first bassoon-player in the Vienna orchestra.

When he was fifteen, he was heard in public for the first time, and even then attracted the attention and interest of all connoisseurs and lovers of music, and charming the feminine world. Soon after that, he published his first composition, but later on he considered it worthless. In 1830, he began his first more important concert-tour in Germany, playing his first pianoforte concerto op. 5; of this concerto it was said that "the composer still adhered to the classical form introduced by Mozart and Beethoven and carried on by Dussek, Kalkbrenner, Hummel and others".

Thalberg's triumphs and successes in later years were very great and quite unique in a way, in 1835 in Paris, in Belgium, Holland, England and Russia; in the last-named country in 1839, he acquired fortunes by his playing. Then he made an unfortunate attempt to compose an opera "Florinde", libretto by Scribe. It was performed at the Italian Opera in London with the assistance of the very best vocalists: Cruvelli, Calzolari, Lablache (whose daughter Thalberg afterwards married) Sims Reeves, Coletti, &c., but the work did not succeed. Nitwithstanding this, Thalberg wrote another opera: "Cristina di Suezia", which was also a failure.

Thalberg made extensive concert-tours that brought him in thousands, he went to Brazil and North America, returning later on to Brazil. Paris and London were great sources of revenue to him.

In 1858, he bought a charming villa with garden and vineyard at Posilippo near Naples, and lived there, absenting himself for a shorter or longer period at a time, but from 1863, without any interruption until his death on the 26th April 1871.

Thalberg has composed 83 shorter and longer pianoforte pieces: Valses-Caprices, Fantasias, Divertissements, Variations on operatic airs, Nocturnes, Andantes, Impromptus, Etudes, Sonatas, Marches &c.; at the present day a few of these are still popular, without possessing great musical value.

WILLI THERN.

I N the history of music it very seldom happens that
the genius of the father descends to the children,
the sons are never famous if the father has become
celebrated; although it often happens that the sons
surpass the father.

This is the case with Karl Thern and his sons
Willi and Louis. The father was a master of pianoforte
and composition at the Conservatoire in Pesth, he
was a very good musician, and a very popular composer for the piano in Hungary. Greatly to his delight,
his two sons who were very talented took up the
pianist's career; they were both so equal in their

playing, that they are now called the Siamese Twins of the pianoforte; this is not a mere nick-name, but it must be understood in the full sense of the word. There is not much difference in age between them (Willi was born on the 22$^\mathrm{d}$ of June 1847 at Ofen), their tastes and inclinations were very similar, which made their education an easy matter for their father. As soon as one of them could play a piece thoroughly well, the other would never rest until he did the same. They would accompany each other sometimes, or both play the same piece at once on two pianos. Under their father's careful supervision, the two brothers developed a marvellous unisono in playing, which is thoroughly astonishing to all who hear them.

When Karl Thern thought his sons had studied long enough, he resigned his own position in 1864, and travelled with them. But being a capable musician himself, he soon realized that with the present modern requirements, it was not possible to become justly famous without very thorough teaching; he therefore placed his sons for another year and a half at the Leipzig Conservatoire, where they completed their studies under Moscheles.

After having gained the decided favour of the public and the press at the Leipzig Gewandhaus, they commenced their more important concert-tours in 1866, and thus legitimately acquired a universal reputation.

LOUIS THERN.

L OUIS Thern who was born on the 18th December
1848 at Pesth, showed the same taste and love
for music in childhood as his brother, they were
thoroughly united in everything, and attained equal
perfection in their art.

In Leipzig, after they had both thoroughly im-
bibed and entered into the spirit of their work, they
understood each other so completely in their playing,
their execution being well up to the modern standard,
that it always sounded as if one pianist was performing instead of two. It was phenomenal, but there

was more in the playing than mere practice. They created great enthusiasm everywhere by their marvellous unity of playing. From Germany they went to Brussels, then to Paris, where they made a great furore at concerts of their own, and by playing in the salons of musicians and artists: Rossini, Berlioz, Vieuxtemps, Szarvady, also men of note and influence, Prince Metternich, Baron Erlanger &c.

The two brothers then went to England, played with immense success at the Crystal Palace in London, the Musical Union, the Philharmonic concerts, Leslie's concerts, and at Liverpool at the Philharmonic concerts—returning there each year.

In Germany they played at concerts of their own, also at the best soirées in Berlin, Weimar, Altenburg, Dresden &c.

Their performance of the works of Bach, Mozart, Beethoven, Liszt and other modern composers, display perfect execution with a clear and well-defined interpretation.

JOHANN WENZEL TOMASCHEK.

Although Tomaschek did not, strictly speaking, follow the career of a pianist, still he was an excellent organist and pianoforte player, and became known by his influence on the development of musical life, also by several of his pupils, who afterwards became celebrated.

He was born at Skutch (Bohemia) on the 17th of April 1774, and in his youth received two years instruction in singing and the violin from the choirmaster Wolf at Chrudim. In 1787, he was placed in the convent school at Iglau for studies in science. He had no other master for music, and taught himself for nine years, with the help of books by Marpurg, Kirnberger, Mattheson, Türk, &c. He thus became a finished pianist and a skilful composer.

While studying law at the University of Prague,

he shewed a greater taste for music than anything else. He gave piano lessons, and a young Count Buquoy who was one of his pupils, became his patron and made it possible for him to devote himself to the musical profession only. He became composer to the Count, received a considerable salary and took up his abode with him. Even later, when Tomaschek married the sister of the well-known Austrian poet Egon Ebert, he retained the benefit of the Count's protection as also his independent position.

His house in Prague was the centre of musical life at that time. He was called "the Schiller of Music", which shows how highly he was thought of. The following were among his most important pupils: Dreyschock, Schulhoff, Kuhe, Tedesco, Worziszek, Würfel &c.

He died on the 3^d of April 1850.

His compositions are 110 in number. Among them for piano there are, 5 Sonatas, 1 Concerto, Dithyrambe op. 65 and Eclogues op. 35, 39, 43, 51, 57, 66, 83, all these pieces are worth the attention of pianists; besides these compositions, Tomaschek wrote 1 opera, 1 Symphony, 1 String Quartet, 1 Trio, 2 Requiems, 1 Mass, Hymns, Cantatas, Songs &c.

KARL MARIA VON WEBER.

VERY few of those who derive great pleasure and delight from Weber's music, have an idea of the troubled life he led and what vicissitudes he went through, from the depths of misery to final recognition. Franz Anton Weber was a good violinist, also viola and bass player, and of all his children, Karl Maria was the one of least promise. The sons and daughters of Franz A. Weber's first marriage distinguished themselves in one or other branch of art; the two elder sons became very good musicians; the father always hoped that one of his family would be a prodigy like

Mozart, and when he had a son born to him by his second wife, the name Karl Maria being given to the child, it was just this delicate and sensitive boy that showed so little taste for music. He was scoffed at by all the family, and his eldest brother Fritz used often to say to him: "Karl, you may be great some day, but you will never be a musician!"

The boy, with the other children of the family, received their musical education from their father. Karl was also taught partly by his elder brothers, but he made so little progress that his father thought it would be better to make a painter or a sculptor of him. But all these attempts were unsuccessful and the boy was reproached with: "Karl, you are utterly without talent!"

His young life was anything but peaceful and regular. A year after his birth (at Eutin on the 18th of December 1786) his father commenced a wandering life as director of a theatrical company, having already tried many professions, that of clerk, officer, band-master, musical director, &c. The company in question consisted really of members of his family; his wife Genoveva, who was then barely nineteen, was a good singer, and he and all the children by his first wife, played and sang at many performances. The company was not at all a poor one, as they gave performances in several large towns, as Meiningen, Kassel, Nürnberg, Erlangen, Augsburg, Vienna &c. In 1794, after much travelling about, the Webers seemed to be on the point of settling for some time in Weimar, in consequence of Frau Weber's being engaged at the theatre there; but from some unknown cause this engagement soon came to an end, and the travelling was renewed.

In 1796, the family remained for some time at Hildburghausen; this was so far favorable to Karl Maria who was then ten years old, that he was able to have piano lessons from an oboe-player, Heuschkel by name.

The family then stayed at Salzburg; during their wanderings in 1797, Michael Haydn, who was there at the time (as he held an appointment in the Bishop's orchestra), gave young Weber instruction in composition. In 1798, six short Fugues, op. 1 by Weber were brought out, dedicated to Michael Haydn.

At Salzburg, the organist Kalcher taught him theory, and Valesi gave him singing lessons. In the meantime the family arrived in Munich in 1800; and here young Weber began to study the practical use of lithography, invented by Sennefelder; he soon made such progress that he was able to lithograph his Variations for piano, Op. 2.

The mode of travelling at that time was very difficult and particularly so for the Weber's, who had to make many long journeys. In that same year, 1800, they appeared in Freiburg (Saxony), and Weber wanted to institute a school of lithography here, but it was not successful, and the family moved on to Salzburg again in 1801; Michael Haydn was again Weber's master here for some time. He then went to Hamburg in 1802, to Augsburg in 1803, and from there to Vienna. Joseph Haydn declined to teach him, not considering him a genius, but it was at this time that Karl Maria wrote his first youthful opera: "Das Waldmädchen", which is said to have been performed at Vienna, Prague, Chemnitz, St. Petersburg &c.

The instruction which he then received from Abbé Vogler cannot have lasted long, as in the winter of 1804—1805, he became conductor at the theatre in Breslau. There is an inscription on a house in Breslau in the Taschenstrasse No. 31: "Karl Maria von Weber lived in this house in 1805." The old house does not exist any longer, but the tablet with inscription has been replaced on the building erected on the same site.

In 1806, Weber gave up his appointment in Breslau for the position of manager of music to Prince Eugene of Württemberg in Karlsruhe (Silesia). But Weber did not retain this post very long either, on account of Napoleon's impending war with Prussia, when Prince Eugene was summoned to the army. But he sent the Weber family to Stuttgart, where young Weber became secretary to Prince Ludwig, and also gave music lessons to the Prince's daughters. Spohr gives an account of this, when speaking of the extraordinary things that happened at a concert which he gave at Court, and he also describes the despotic government which oppressed Württemberg at that time: "I got to know the famous Karl Maria von Weber for the first time at Stuttgart, and I remained friends with him until his death. Weber was then secretary to a Prince of Württemberg, and only cultivated music for pleasure. But this did not prevent him from applying himself industriously to composition, and I remember very well hearing specimens of his work at that time, some parts of his opera "The Ruler of the Spirits". In dramatic work I was always accustomed to rank Mozart as the highest in order, therefore these extracts of Weber's opera seemed to me unimportant and amateurish, and I never thought for a moment that it would be possible for him to make an impression with any opera."

In Stuttgart he changed the name of his "Wald-mädchen" to "Silvana" and finished the one act opera "Abu Hassan"; this was performed at Munich in 1811.

Weber lost his appointment at Stuttgart in 1810; some biographers say; on account of the imprudence of his father, but the real reason was owing to his patriotic sentiments: he felt revolted by the

treacherous and servile conduct of the Württemberg
Government with regard to Napoleon, and by the
contemptible abuse of liberty on the part of the
German soldiers, also the immeasurable slavery of
the Württemberg people. Those in power were so
furious, that both the father and son were banished
from the Württemberg territory.

After Weber left Stuttgart, the accounts given
of his life by several biographers are calculated to
give a wrong impression; namely that he continued
studying with Abbé Vogler in Darmstadt, and then
got to know Meyerbeer, Gänsbacher, Gottfried Weber
&c., and that he stayed at Munich, Leipzig, and
Berlin, going to the courts of Gotha, Weimar, &c.,
his life being made very pleasant and easy for
him; but all this is very misleading. The fact was,
that for years Weber earned a poor and uncertain
livelihood. It was only in 1813, that this kind of life
came to an end by a sudden stroke of luck, through
the intervention of a man of intelligence. The excellent conductor at the opera in Prague, Wenzel
Müller had died, and the manager of the theatre,
clearly appreciating Weber's talents as a musician
and composer, and feeling sure he had found a
worthy successor to Müller, he offered the position
to Weber with a yearly salary of 2000 Gulden, and
thus the composer's future was assured.

He filled this appointment in Prague very successfully until 1816, and at that period received a Royal
order from Dresden, to organize a German opera there,
of which he was to be the principal conductor; this work
he undertook, meeting with general approbation. After
having married the singer Caroline Brandt, he lived
in Dresden in easy circumstances, and enjoyed great
popularity on account of his spirited composition to
Theodor Körner's "Leyer und Schwert". It was at
Dresden also that he composed his famous opera,

"Der Freischütz", the fantastic libretto by Friedrich Kind, and he completed the music to "Preciosa" which was as national in its way as the first-named opera.

Preziosa was first performed at Copenhagen in 1820, amid great applause; "Der Freischütz" was producedat Berlin in 1821, and the success was enormous. Weber now became celebrated in the fullest sense of the word.

The opera which succeeded these, namely "Euryanthe", and which in many respects was musically greater than the Freischütz, had a strange fate; Weber wrote it as a commission for the Kärntnerthor Theatre in Vienna, and it was first performed there in 1823, and although the work was highly approved of by critics, it did not please those accustomed to Rossini's light music, and was soon taken off the repertoire. On the other hand Weber achieved lasting fame by the performance of this opera in Berlin, in 1825.

In 1821, when Spohr went with his family to Dresden, he criticized Weber's Freischütz in a manner that certainly did not agree with the general idea of the composer's artistic intentions. Hauptmann and Weber gave the great violin composer a warm welcome to Dresden, and introduced him to many musicians, taking him about wherever good music was to be heard. Spohr after relating all this then goes on to say: "After the brilliant success achieved by the Freischütz in Berlin and Vienna, Karl Maria von Weber has also been able to arrange for a performance of the opera in Dresden, and the private rehearsals have already begun. As I had never thought very highly of Weber's talent for composition, I was naturally very auxious to hear this opera, so as to understand why it had created such enthusiasm in the two principal cities in Germany. I was doubly interested, on account of my having had the same subject (from Apel's Ghost Stories) worked into a libretto for an opera several years ago in Frankfort, and I now relinquished my composition on hearing that Weber was busy with the same work. I therefore begged to allowed to be present at the rehearsals, a request which was at once complied with. Although an intimate knowledge of the opera, I could still not understand the reason of its enormous success, and thought it more probable that it was owing to Weber's facility in being able to write for the masses."

In the same year, Weber was offered the post of conductor at Kassel, but he very urgently recommended Spohr for the appointment instead of himself.

In addition to his two great operas, Weber was commissioned to write one for the Covent Garden Opera in London. Whilst working at this third opera, "Oberon", he was often interrupted by serious illness. In the spring of 1826, when he went to England to conduct "Oberon", he was very ill with consumption, and he died six weeks afterwards in London. He was buried in the Moorfields Chapel, and in 1844, his remains were brought to Dresden, at the instigation of Richard Wager, who delivered a funeral oration and introduced an Elegy of his own on this occasion.

From the description of Weber's life, it is evident, he was not allowed to enjoy the fruits of his celebrity in ease and peace. This was owing partly to the political and artistic conditions of the times, but also to his not over agreeable manners. At the period of his first appearance, the old German Empire was in the throes of dissolution. Not a single feature of national uprising was apparent. The olympian quiet of small communities was deeply stirred. They cringed at the feet of the allpowerful Corsican, and were only anxious servilely to please him in order to escape destruction. The sentiment of an artistic ideal scarcely awakened by a few genial spirits was drowned by the howlings of War.

In the theatre, the antiquated musical potentates reigned supreme, and with great obstinacy, excluding younger talent in every possible way. It was only by the greatest exertion that Weber could get his 'Abu Hassan' performed at all.

Spontini at Berlin was for years the bitterest enemy of all his creations and was frightened at the prospect of any rays of light piercing his gloom. In Dresden there was no lack of conflicts against the adherents of Morlachi and his Italians. Weber found opponents especially amongst the performers. Envy, ill-humour, and sluggishness opposed him at every step. The instrumentalists often made his life irksome, so that he told them they would drive him mad with worry. But in rehearsals and directing, his violence went beyond all bounds even to using bad language; he found fault with them on the slightest occasion or for not understanding his intentions and worried them into opposition or even to wilful misreading.

Whereas in common life he was very quiet and spoke little, at the director's desk he became an exacting and extremely disagreeable person. The complaints of the singers and musicians were endless and gave rise to violent conflicts.

Once in Dresden, he was obliged to apologize and ask pardon of the members of the choir for insulting words he had used towards them.

Weber was small and of spare build of body, the lower part being also somewhat ill-formed, knock-kneed, with knees projecting forwards; but he had long arms and fingers, which appeared as though expressly made to stretch over the key board, and of course this peculiar formation enabled him to arrive at a high degree of excellence as a pianist.

In order to comply with the object of this book,

mention must be made of Weber having been a remarkable pianist, with a style peculiar to himself. His friends related how he made special studies in order to acquire a better expansion of his hands.

For piano he has composed: 4 Sonatas, (in C-, A-flat, D-minor and E-minor), 1 Sonata as a pianoforte duet, 2 Concertos (C- and E-flat), 1 Concertstück, 1 Polonaise, 1 Rondo brillant, 4 Variations, 1 Invitation à la Valse, several Dances and other shorter pieces; 1 Pianoforte Quartet, 1 Pianoforte Trio; also, Variations for piano and violin, 1 Duo concertant for piano and clarionet, Variations for clarionet and piano; 6 Violin Sonatas, 2 Clarionet concertos, 1 Concertino for clarionet, 1 Quintet for clarionet and stringed in-stringed instruments, 1 Concerto for bassoon, 1 Andante and Rondo for bassoon and orchestra, 1 Concertino for horn. For orchestra: 2 Symphonies, Overture and March to "Turandot", Jubel-Overture. Vocal-music: Der erste Ton, Kampf und Sieg (to commemorate the battle of Waterloo), part-songs for men's voices, "Leyer und Schwert", Natur und Liebe for 2 sopranos, 2 tenors and 2 basses, Quartets for mixed voices, Duets, Hymns, Children's Songs, 2 Masses with orchestra, 8 Arias and Scenas, also numerous songs. His operas have been already mentioned. "Die drei Pintos", Weber's comic opera, which was lately put on the stage again, was finished by Gustav Mahler and a descendant of Weber's.

In 1860, a monument by Rietschel was erected to the immortal composer in Dresden.

The portrait at the beginning of this sketch is from an oil painting which was formerly in Mendelssohn's possession.

MARIE WIECK.

MARIE Wieck, like her celebrated sister Clara Schumann, had great natural gifts and was thoroughly well taught under her father's care, and all her life has been devoted to the cultivation of music in the true sense of the word.

Friedrich Wieck, whose pianoforte teaching was so highly valued, lived at Leipzig at the time of Marie's birth, January the 17th, 1832, and their house was a place of meeting for artists and lovers of music. With her two sisters Clara and Cecilia, she was most carefully trained by her father for the musical profession, her playing was refined and intelligent, delighting her hearers at the numerous

concerts in which she appeared.—She played for the
first time in public in 1842, together with Clara at
Dresden, then in company with her father at the
Gewandhaus at Leipzig. As Friedrich Wieck had
settled in Dresden in 1840, the two sisters gave
concerts in that town, after which they went to play
in other towns in Germany.

For five seasons, Marie Wieck played at concerts
in London, where she did a great deal of good in
bringing forward German music; she also gave piano
and singing lessons there, using her father's method.
She had a good soprano voice and sometimes sang
at her sister Clara's concerts. On some of these
occasions Madame Joachim also appeared, and they
made a great impression in Schumann's duets.

As a pianiste, she took part at concerts in Dresden,
Berlin, Gotha, Karlsruhe, Schwerin, Detmold,
Sigmaringen, &c. The Prince of Hohenzollern appointed
her as pianiste to the chamber concerts.

Later on she travelled in the Eastern provinces,
South Germany, Sweden, Denmark, Switzerland, Italy,
Austria, Croatia &c. Critics praised her playing and
admired her beautiful soft touch as also her earnest
rendering of classical compositions.

She developed great talent for teaching, and
taught principally in Dresden, but also in other towns
during her numerous tours, both singing and piano.

She has published a number of short pianoforte
compositions of her own, and has also edited her
father's works, studies for the pianoforte and the voice.

JOSEPH WIENIAWSKI.

JOSEPH Wieniawski was almost as remarkable as
pianist and teacher, as his brother Henri the
violinist.

Both the brothers often played together at concerts and won the applause they so richly deserved,
their studies having been long and thorough.

Joseph Wieniawski was born at Lublin on the
on the 23ᵈ of May 1837. For seven years he was
taught music in his native town by Müller and Synck,
in 1847 he was admitted into the Paris Conservatoire,
first in Zimmermann's pianoforte class, and then in
Alkan's solfeggio class, after which he entered a class

newly formed by Marmontel, receiving there the first prize in 1849, and also the solfeggio prize. In the following year he studied harmony and accompaniment under Bazin. After leaving the Conservatoire, he had instruction from Ed. Wolf, Hallé and Alkan.

Edward Wolff, an excellent concert player, composer and teacher was his uncle who no doubt had the greatest influence on his artistic education and especially in its peculiar direction. Wolff had composed, in the style of Chopin who was his intimate friend, more than 300 works for the piano, and these were looked on at that time as models for study. His sister who had taken her two sons to Paris for their further musical development was very anxious that Joseph should have the benefit of her brother's superintendance the effect of which was afterwards evident.

In 1853, he went to Weimar, where Liszt became greatly interested in him and gave him lessons.

Afterwards he travelled with his brother through Germany and Russia. They were able to give twelve concerts in Berlin alone, having met with a good reception everywhere. When in Berlin in 1856, Joseph Wieniawski took lessons in theory from Marx for three years, so as to finish his musical education.

He went to Paris by way of Brussels, and took up his abode in the first-named town; he was warmly welcomed there and became a great favorite at the concerts at Napoleon's Court. Through Auber's, influence he was made examining professor of the pianoforte at the Conservatoire; but in 1866, he again left Paris and went to Moscow, where he became a professor at the Conservatoire. He however soon gave up this position, establishing a pianoforte school of his own, which prospered wonderfully, and within a short time it numbered 720 pupils.

In 1877, he and Wislicki founded the Warsaw

Musical Society, and Wieniawski undertook the direction of it. Since his brother's death (1880) he has
played oftener in concerts.

Joseph Wieniawski, who is at present master
at the Brussels Conservatoire, has written the following compositions: 1 Concerto for piano, Idylles,
Sonatas, Tarantelles, Waltzes, Polonaises, Etudes,
Caprices, Rondos, Songs without words, Impromptus,
Fantasias, Fugues, Cadences for Beethoven's C-minor
concerts &c.

ALEXANDER ZARZYCKI.

ALTHOUGH one of the last to be mentioned in this book, yet Zarzycki is not the least in the estimation of musicians critics, and is entitled to a more exhaustive notice but unfortunately it has been impossible to collect more material for his biography.

Although born in Moscow in 1840 he is doubtless of Polish nationality and in this respect is an instance of the fact that in the present century, the Polish nation has produced an unusually large number of artists. With his natural gifts he worked hard and industriously, and was considered a good pianist twenty years ago, and in 1879 he was made Appolinary von Kontski's successor as manager of the Conservatoire in Warsaw. Since then he has almost entirely given up his career as a solo player.

Strangely enough name has become best known lately by a brillant Mazurka for violin which is played by nearly all violin soloists.

GÉZA GRAF ZICHY.

IT is certainly a very rare occurrence in the musical world, that a man with only one arm should have devoted himself to pianoforte playing and achieved an extraordinary success. But such was the case with Count Géza Zichy (Gesa Sitschy). In 1878, he had great success when he played in Austria, and in 1882, Ed. Hanslick wrote as follows about him: "A pianist with one hand, Count Géza Zichy, has performed the greatest marvels of modern times on the piano. Many people can play, and some can delight their audience, but Zichy's playing works like magic. He only plays in public for charitable purposes; on this occasion he divided the considerable profits between the Billroth Rudolfiner Society and a Hungarian Institute for students. Since we first heard this left-handed pianist in Vienna and then admired his playing, he has made still greater progress in his art, although this might seem impossible. When Count Zichy lately played an Etude de concert, then a Hungarian Rhapsody of his own composition, and Bach's Chaconne arranged for the left hand, the listeners could hardly believe their ears or eyes, so great was the marvellous fulness of tone, with such wonderful execution, all parts of the composition being clearly defined and interpreted."

Fétis also in his Biographie universelle, pronounces him "one of the most remarkable pianists", and all those that have heard him will agree with this opinion.

It must have required great perseverance and exertion to attain to such a degree of perfection, especially taking into consideration the fact that Count Géza only began to study the piano at a relatively advanced age. He was the son of a wealthy Hungarian magnate and was born at Sztára on the 22^d of July 1849: at fifteen years of age he had the misfortune to lose his right arm on a shooting expedition. He had talent and taste for music, and decided to cultivate himself in this art, but not to make a living by it. He studied law at Pressburg, at the same time taking piano and composition lessons of Mayrberger and Robert Volkmann. His great endeavour was to accomplish that with the left hand which great pianists have achieved with two. This difficult aim he eventually attained after several years tuition under Franz Liszt. Connoisseurs, who heard him play after the completion of these studies, declared, that Dreyschock with his phenomenal culture of the left hand, was eclipsed, for of course the latter could always supply any want with his right hand. But Count Géza, by his clever arpeggio work, by the sliding and springing of chords and careful shading from piano to forte, made his playing appear as if he had ten fingers at work, instead of only five. It was quite impossible to understad at first how such technical difficulties could be overcome with one hand only. Count Géza is not only a brilliant pianist, but his playing is very expressive; whatever he performs is always full of taste and intellect.

He has been heard in public in a great many towns, and always in aid of charities: in Vienna, Pesth, Graz, Stuttgart, Mannheim, Frankfort, Cologne, Wiesbaden, Giessen, Karlsruhe, Munich, Berlin, Leipzig, Breslau, Paris &c., and has earned for those charitable institutions several hundred thousand marks; in 1886, the Paris newspapers said, the sum amounted to even 1,200,000 Frcs. He continues to play in his native country for charitible objects, although, in consequence of his having undertaken the post of manager of the Royal opera, and of the National theatre at Budapest, he has less time for this than formerly.

AGNES ZIMMERMANN.

Miss Agnes Zimmermann, who was born on the
5th of July, 1847, at Cologne, was brought to
England in early childhood. She occupies a high
position in this country as a concert player, and also
takes part in the best of classical concerts. From
the commencement of her musical career, she was
devoted to the classical school of music, and never
deviated in her allegiance to it. In December 1872,
she played a transcription of Beethoven's violin concerto for the first time at a Crystal Palace concert
in London; her own compositions are written for the
most part in classical style.

At nine years of age she was a pupil at the Royal
Academy of Music, Cipriani Potter and Steggall being

her masters. Later on she was taught by Pauer and Sir George MacFarren. Although she was sometimes heard at other places, she never discontinued her lessons, and her compositions were often heard at the pupils' concerts at the Academy.

In 1860—1862, she gained a scholarship, and in December 1863, she played for the first time in public at a Crystal Palace concert.

In 1864, she played in several towns in Germany, and at the Gewandhaus in Leipzig, where as on many other concert-tours (1879—1880 and 1882—1883) she won the decided approbation of the public and the press. England has become her home, where she is very well known and her name is a great attraction on concert programmes.

Her compositions are as follows: 1 Sonata (op. 22), 1 Mazurka (op. 11), 1 Presto alla Tarantella (op. 15), 3 Sonatas for piano and violin (op. 16, 21, 23), 1 Trio for piano, violin and violincello (op. 19), several songs, arrangements of instrumental works &c. She has published editions in London, of Mozart's and Beethoven's Sonatas, also of Schumann's works.

MADAME JULIE RIVÉ-KING.

A MONG the few women who have reached celebrity in the pianistic world none have excelled Julie Rivé-King. She is conceded to be one of the first pianists of America and is equaled by few of her sex in the world.

She was born October 31, 1857, at Cincinnati, Ohio. Her genius for music was inherited from her mother, an eminent teacher, and became evident when she was little more than an infant. Her mother carefully instructed her from the first, and to this careful, rightly grounded instruction much of her present success is due. At the age of eight years she played at one of her mother's concerts a Thalberg transcription of themes from "Don Juan."

Soon after she was taken to New York where she

studied with Wm. Mason, S. B. Mills, De Korbay, and Pruckner. For the completion of her education she was sent to Europe at the age of fifteen, receiving instruction from Reinecke, at Leipsic, Blassman and Rischpister, of Dresden. Her professional début was made under Reinecke's direction at one of the Euterpe concerts, before a cultured and critical audience, when she was seventeen years old, with great success, her playing creating a *furore*. The sudden death of her father recalled her to America and cut short a contemplated concert tour of Europe. Her first appearance after her return home was in Cincinnati in 1873–74. Her American reputation began at once and was emphasized by her performance at a concert of the Philharmonic Society in New York, in the spring of 1875. She played again at the concerts of the same society and further enhanced her already rapidly growing reputation.

An appearance during the second season of the Apollo Club of Chicago, was her first in that city, and was the occasion of the most pronounced triumph she had made up to this time.

Her career as a soloist is a remarkable one. Since her return to her native land the career of Mme. King has been a continuous succession of brilliant triumphs, from the Atlantic to the Pacific; her versatility being such that she has been enabled to present to her audiences a *repertoire* incomparably greater than that of any pianist now before the public, with the exception of Rubinstein and Von Bülow, and her enormous technique (which seems to have no limit, but rather to be only seeking new directions in which to unfold itself), placing her equally at home in the entire range of pianoforte literature, from the severely classical school of Bach and Händel, through the romantic styles of Chopin and Schumann, to the brilliant and sensational inspirations of Liszt and his followers. During the past twelve years Mme. Rivé-King has performed at over eighteen hundred concerts and recitals, having played with grand orchestra under almost every conductor in the United States. She was the soloist with the Thomas orchestra in his tour across the continent, and has been engaged as soloist of all the principal concerts given by the most distinguished musical societies throughout the Eastern and Western States.

Her success, great as it has been, has only kept pace with her steady advancement and artistic development. Madame Rivé-King has composed quite extensively, but it is as a pianiste that she has won her eminent position among musicians.

EDWARD ALEXANDER MacDOWELL.

AMONG those musicians who have gained reputation and success as pianists may be found some who have added to their pianistic laurels by their creative genius. These have, in addition to the interpretative powers of the piano virtuoso, been blessed in an unusual degree with the faculty of creating art works in their own individuality. Such artists have an increased scope for musical activity and can leave a more indelible impression upon the art life surrounding them.

It is a thing to be desired, this combined talent of piano virtuosity and composition; and it is rare that the combination exists in one individual to so great a degree as it does in the person of Mr. MacDowell.

A young man, with a past already filled with honor and artistic success, abundant promise is given of yet more far-reaching results to come.

Mr. MacDowell was born December 18, 1861, in New York City, and began early the study of the piano, at one time being a pupil of Teresa Carreño. He went to Paris in 1876 and was admitted to the Conservatory in 1877, studying piano while there under Marmontel, and theory under Savard. In 1879 he went to Wiesbaden and studied for a time with Louis Ehlert, thence to Frankfort-on-the-Main, where he enjoyed the privilege of studying composition with Joachim Raff and piano with Carl Heymann, the celebrated pianist. In 1881, on Raff's recommendation, Mr. MacDowell accepted the position of first piano teacher at the Darmstadt Conservatory. In 1882, at Raff's suggestion, he went to Weimar to play his compositions for Liszt, who became so much interested in the young American that he had him play at the convention of the *Allgemeine Deutscher Musik-Verein*, in Zurich, his (Mac-Dowell's) first suite for piano, Op. 10, which met with great success. After considerable successful concertizing, Mr. MacDowell, in 1884, took up his residence in Wiesbaden, composing and giving piano and composition lessons. He returned to America in the autumn of 1888, and is now a resident of Boston.

Since his return to his native country he has not traveled as a virtuoso, but has devoted himself to teaching and to composition. He has been heard, however, frequently in public, and has won high encomiums as an artist who is equal to all the requirements of concert work. Especially has he been praised for the playing of his own works.

He has appeared in Boston with the Boston Symphony Orchestra and the New York Philharmonic, under Seidl, in New York, playing his own concerto.

Of his work as a composer it may be said that he is a master of orchestral coloring, second to no living author;

and Mr. Anton Seidl has, in the *Forum*, expressed his personal preference for Mr. MacDowell's works to those of Brahms. His music for piano has been no less successful. His two concertos, Opus 15 and 23, for piano and orchestra, Sonata Tragica, Opus 45, for piano, two modern suites, Opus 10 and 14, for piano, and Twelve Studies, Opus 46, for modern pianoforte virtuosity, with Technical Exercises, Parts I, II, and III, all of which take their place in the foremost rank of piano music, the major portion having won exalted praise abroad, give him place as a piano writer of the highest class.

He has had the enviable fortune of a wide and favorable hearing abroad. In addition to his personal successes his compositions have been played at St. Petersburg, Amsterdam, Paris, Berlin, Dresden, Leipzig, Vienna, Frankfort, Wiesbaden, Darmstadt, Sondershausen, Cologne, Baden-Baden, Breslau, etc. Mr. MacDowell is doing much for the disciples of the piano in the threefold rôle of pianist, teacher, and composer of artistic and pedagogic piano works.

EMIL LIEBLING.

EMIL Liebling was born April 12, 1851, at Pless, near the Austrian frontier. His first piano studies were pursued under Adam Kong, a blind pianist, and, later, under Ehrlich, of Berlin. He appeared in public at the age of twelve years as pianist of Liebeg's symphony concerts. He came to this country in 1867 and taught in a Kentucky school for young ladies from that time until 1871 when he returned to Germany for further study.

He returned, however, in 1872 and settled in Chicago. In 1874 he again went abroad for study. His teachers in this instance were Kullak at Berlin, Dachs and Kreun at Vienna. During his stay with Kullak he was engaged as teacher of the piano in Kullak's celebrated school. He was also with Liszt, at Weimar, for a short time.

While in Berlin he won the commendation of the critics for his finely developed technique, excellent touch and true interpretation of works of the masters. He returned to Chicago in 1876, and in 1877 was heard in New York and other principal cities. He also played with Thomas' orchestra and took two trips with Wilhelmj, the violinist.

For the last twenty years Mr. Liebling has been engaged in teaching piano in Chicago. During this time, however, he has won a fame that is cosmopolite. Despite his activity as a teacher,—and he stands at the head of one of the largest and most active musical clienteles possessed by any American piano teacher,—he is known as a concert pianist throughout the country and has at his command an enormous repertory. During his career as an artist, he has played probably four hundred different compositions, the vast majority of which he could play for you off-hand at a moment's notice. In this respect he stands almost alone among artists, as few of them will undertake to play compositions they have not lately studied. This readiness is largely due to the quickness and tenacity of his memory, but it is also a growth from his daily life as a teacher.

He is constantly called upon to give illustrative readings of every work in the whole piano playing repertory. For this, the notes brought by the pupil are naturally at hand, but it is rarely necessary for Mr. Liebling to refer to them; he is ready, on the instant, to show all the hundred little *nuances* which go to make up a "reading" of a great work.

Another remarkable fact is the unusual musical activity his pupils show in their own fields of labor, where a vast majority of them are leading teachers. They found amateur clubs, circles for musical reading, and get up series of recitals of their own and visiting artists. It can be readily understood how wide a range his musical personality is given by these things.

Since his return to America he has given a large number of pianoforte recitals and chamber music concerts. The musical and educational importance of these performances cannot be over-estimated, for by them all the best works in pianoforte and chamber music literature have been presented. American writers have also received a generous share of Mr. Liebling's attention, he having given programmes from the works of MacDowell, Nevins, Foote, W. G. Smith, Mattoon, Wm. Mason, and others.

As a pianist he brings to the interpretation of his vast repertory, which embraces the very cream of modern pianoforte literature, intelligence, repose, and refinement. His fine technique is equal to all demands that may be made upon it. He has been very successful in lectures with pianoforte illustrations. A ready talker, *en courant* with musical tradition and personality, as well as musical history, knowing by heart almost the whole of the compositions of all the great writers, and able to play extracts at a moment's warning, he is in a position to do the highest work in this feature of musical life. Hence for educational recitals he is one of the very best artists possible to secure.

His compositions belong to the highest order of salon music and rank with those of Bendel, Loeschhorn, and Mason.

Especially notable are the Concert Romances, Opus 20 and 21, a charming Gavotte Moderne, Op. 11, the brilliant Florence Concert Valse, and a very pleasing Albumblatt. He has also edited a special edition of the Heller and Loeschhorn Etudes.

Of a pleasing, incisive, and highly stimulating personality, Mr. Liebling is abundantly endowed with the elements of artistic and commanding success.

CARLYLE PETERSILEA.

THIS musician, whose home is in Boston, stands high both as a teacher and a pianist. He was born on the 18th of July, 1844, at Boston, Mass. His father, an excellent and finely educated teacher, who had made some reputation as the author of the Petersilea system of teaching music, took charge of his early musical education. The result was surprisingly rapid progress, so that, when only twelve years old, he was qualified to appear in conceit and to teach. His extraordinaiy endowment was such that, in 1856, when Thalberg met him, he predicted a bright future for him.

His memory was remarkable even at a very early age, and he played sonatas, fugues, whole concertos, and fantasias from memory.

His powers of memory, however, did not interfere with his ability as a sight reader.

He went to Leipzig when he was eighteen years of age and soon attracted general attention. He was acknowledged to be the favorite of Moscheles, who always chose him to play on important occasions. After remaining for three years at the conservatory, Mr. Petersilea graduated with higher honors than had been conferred upon any piano pupil that had left that institution previous to that time. Before returning to his native country he visited the principal cities of Germany, giving concerts and meeting everywhere with a hearty reception. While at Munich he met Hans von Bülow, from whom he derived much benefit. He also played at the famous Gewandhaus concerts, an honor never before enjoyed by any American.

After being prostrated with a severe attack of typhoid fever, his physician advised him to return to his home. He received a cordial reception, and soon after appeared in a concert, when his playing of Henselt's Concerto won for him the most favorable impression. In Boston he was heard in public under the direction of Charles Koppitz, with great success. He also played at the Harvard symphony concerts

In 1867 he inaugurated his Schumann soirees, at which he introduced several works not then known to Boston audiences. In these soirees Mr. Petersilea was supported by the best artists in Boston. As a performer of classic music he has few peers. His technique is almost faultless, while his conception of the great tone-masters is original and inspiring. His recitals of Beethoven's Sonatas, playing three or four at each recital, were novel in their way, and had never been attempted in Boston before. So great was the satisfaction which they gave that he was prevailed upon to repeat them.

Mr. Petersilea's success as a pianist has been so pronounced as to make him a prominent figure before the musical world. He has chosen to leave the concert field, however, for that of teaching. Inheriting his father's talent as a teacher, he has united to this his powers as a pianist, and has sent out many proficient students.

ROBERT GOLDBECK.

ROBERT Goldbeck was born at Potsdam, near Berlin, Prussia, April 19, 1839. He gave evidence of striking musical talent when a boy. His first teacher of piano and harmony was his uncle, Louis Kohler. Attracting the attention of Alexander von Humboldt, he was, through von Humboldt's efforts, sent to the great master of piano, Henry Litolff, under whom he pursued the higher branches of piano playing and composition.

With letters of introduction from Humboldt to members of the highest circles of Parisian and London society he went to Paris where he spent three years. He was a great favorite here and became acquainted with such eminent musicians as Berlioz, Halévy, Henry Herz, and others. He then went to London where he stayed eighteen months. While here, the Duke of Devonshire threw open the famous picture gallery of Devonshire House, in his honor, there to have him appear in a concert. In 1861 he came to New York, where he wrote the greater number of his larger compositions. Among them may be named the five symphonic pieces for piano and orchestra, two piano concertos, and a large number of piano pieces and songs. Beside these he has written two trios for piano, violin, and 'cello, and a quintette for piano and strings.

He went to Chicago before the great fire, taking charge of the Chicago Conservatory of Music. The fire destroyed many of his manuscripts. From Chicago he removed to St. Louis, where he founded the Goldbeck College of Music. From here he also issued his well-known " Musical Instructor" and " Musical Art." Some years ago he returned to Germany, where he was very successful in teaching and concertizing. He has recently returned to this country and is again located in Chicago.

As a teacher he is unusually successful, numbering his pupils by the thousands. As a composer he is one of the few who have a style of their own. His compositions have won very great success and have been given again and again by the leading orchestras of the country.

As a pianist his playing is characterized by clearness of execution, great expression, and high spirit. His mastery of the piano is complete. He has gained a cosmopolitan reputation both as a pianist and composer, and takes high rank among the musicians of the world. Although much engaged in his teaching, Mr. Goldbeck has found time for frequent piano recitals, when his powers as an artist have shown to full advantage.

ALEXANDER LAMBERT.

A MONG the many pianists who have gained reputation
for themselves as pianists, and who, after successful
work in the concert field, have devoted their talents to the
making of pianists, is the subject of this sketch. Mr.
Lambert was born in Warsaw, Russian Poland, on November 1, 1862. His musical talent was first developed
by his father, a very good musician and violinist, who was
his first teacher. He began his lessons with his father
when he was ten years old. In 1874, when in his twelfth
year, he played before Rubinstein, who advised his parents
to send him to Vienna for further study. Accordingly,
that same year he went to Vienna with a letter of recom-

mendation which Rubinstein had written for him, and entered the conservatory there.

Here he remained four years, earnestly prosecuting his musical studies. At the end of this time he graduated under Professor Epstein. He remained in Europe until 1881, when he came to America and gave some concerts. In 1883 he returned to Europe under an engagement with Hermann Wolff, of Berlin, under whose management he gave concerts in conjunction with Joachim and Sarasate. His successful work with these great artists gave him place among the foremost artists of the day. His concertizing, however, was principally confined to Germany. Although very successful, he went, in 1884, to Liszt, with whom he remained five months. In 1885 he returned to America. His reappearance in America was in New York, with Van der Stucken. In this year (1885) he played with orchestra five times in New York, Boston, Chicago and Montreal. His record as a concert pianist includes many prominent concerts with the orchestras of Seidl and Damrosch.

In addition to these leading concerts he spent his time, until 1887, in concertizing and teaching. In 1887 he was offered, and accepted, the position of Director of the New York College of Music, which post he has held since. While principally engaged in teaching and directing the affairs of this institution, he is still often heard in concert. Mr. Lambert has at his command abundant technical resources, united to an experience as an artist only to be gained from a wide acquaintance with the masters of musical form.

MISS NEALLY STEVENS.

MISS Stevens was born in Illinois in 1861. The first mention we have of her early study is that she began her studies in Germany under the direction of the late Dr. Hans von Bülow, in 1879. After she had been with him for a year, in 1880, Dr. von Bülow placed her under the tutelage of Prof. Theodore Kullak, with whom she remained until his death. She also devoted herself to study, during the seasons of 1879 and 1883, with Liszt, in Weimar, from whom she has a testimonial in the master's autograph. During the year previous to her return to America Miss Stevens placed herself under the artistic care of the distinguished composer and pianist, Moritz Moszkowski. Miss Stevens' first appearance of importance in this country was before the Ohio State Music Teachers' Association, in 1886.

The success of her playing here led to an invitation to play before the Music Teachers' National Association, in 1887. A second hearing was had before that organization with orchestra, in Philadelphia, in 1889.

Her initial appearance in Boston took place the same season. She made a success here which at once won the unanimous approval of the press and gave her rank among the foremost artists. So pronounced was her Boston success that it was followed by engagements in all our leading cities. The close of the season of 1888–89 found Miss Stevens firmly established as a much sought-for concert pianist. Her career since has been one of artistic triumph. She is still before the public and is constantly adding to her laurels.

CHARLES H. JARVIS.

TO Philadelphia belongs the honor of this musician's birth. It was here he first saw the light in 1837. Coming from a family whose ancestors for several generations back were musical, his talents were inherited.

His father, a native of Leicester, England, was a well-known teacher of music in Philadelphia from 1834 to 1855. He was organist of the Church of the Epiphany during the rectorship of the late Rev. S. K. Tyng, of New York. He was also a composer of considerable ability, producing an opera in the winter of 1846.

His son, Charles H. Jarvis, began at an early age the study of piano and violin under his father's instruction. The progress was so great that the boy appeared at a concert given in the Musical Fund Hall, Philadelphia, in

December, 1844, being then only seven years old. He played at this concert a duo arranged from a fantasie by Rosellen on themes from " Don Pasquale." He appeared several times at the same place during his early years, and in January, 1854, he played Thalberg's Fantasia on themes from " Lucrezia Borgia," at the last concert of the Philadelphia Philharmonic Society, Natale Peretli, conductor. His success in playing so difficult a work at an early age and under such exacting circumstances was very marked.

The visit of Sigismund Thalberg to this country in 1857, when the superb pianistic methods of this artist electrified all who heard him, had a great influence upon Mr. Jarvis. The wonderful performances of Thalberg so impressed him as to greatly sway his musical tendencies, and since beginning, in 1862, his series of chamber concerts, he has made it a point to include one or two of this writer's fantasias in nearly every season's soiree prospectus.

He holds that were Thalberg's music more used and studied, a much more musical tone and touch would prevail among pianists generally.

The series of chamber concerts, already alluded to, has been continued, and the prospectus for this season (1894–95), being the thirty-first annual series, is now before the public.

Mr. Jarvis has covered in the programmes of these concerts the entire range of classical and modern music, both piano solo and concerted music of all description, numbering in the aggregate nearly 1000 different compositions. He has also given twenty historical piano recitals, at which he has played over 300 piano pieces, large and small. Mr. Jarvis has played the great concertos of Beethoven, Schumann, Chopin, Hummel, and Mendelssohn, with the New York Philharmonic, in 1869, under Carl Bergmann's direction, and under the same conductor with the Brooklyn Philharmonic, and during the Centennial he played with

Theodore Thomas.   In addition to these important engagements, Mr. Jarvis has appeared in numerous other orchestral concerts in Philadelphia and elsewhere.   He has been closely identified with Philadelphia musical progress for forty years, both as a teacher and pianist.   His place as a pianist is fully determined, his technique being remarkably great, and his interpretation of classical works clear and expressive, so that his annual concerts have become an important part of the musical season.   He has gained a wide reputation as a sight reader, which greatly enlarges the scope of his powers.

Combined with his musical gifts he possesses the traits of a true gentleman, modest in his bearing, and generous toward his professional brethren.   His library contains over 1000 volumes of music, embracing the complete works of piano and chamber music of all the masters.

EDWARD BAXTER PERRY.

E DWARD Baxter Perry was born in one of the suburbs
of Boston on February 14, 1855, and became, through
an accident to one of his eyes, totally blind at three years
of age. His education, in spite of his misfortune, was
carried on in the regular public schools, all lessons being
read aloud to him by his mother or a fellow-student, and
recited from memory in the daily classes among the other
pupils. His school course was interrupted by a few years
at the Perkins Institute for the Blind in South Boston,
and resumed later. A comparison of methods and results
thoroughly convinced Mr. Perry that it is a radical error
to shut up those deprived of sight in special schools for
the blind, where the methods in vogue, though perhaps
adapted to their peculiar needs, are by no means adapted

to that life in the world which must inevitably follow the years of schooling, but rather tend to emphasize the difference between themselves and their fellows, among whom they must work and live.

Mr. Perry began the study of the piano at six years of age, and at sixteen resolved to devote himself exclusively to that instrument for life. His special musical education was obtained partly in Boston and partly in Germany. His Boston teacher was Mr. Junius W. Hill, the present Musical Director at Wellesley College; and his European studies comprised two years with Theodore Kullak in Berlin, two with Pruckner in Stuttgart, one season with Liszt at Weimar, and one with Clara Schumann in Frankfort.

The dominant idea of Mr. Perry's life has been to rise superior to his physical infirmity, to take his place as a man among men, and to stand or fall by their standards, in a fair competition and with no favors. With this in view, he never has played by ear, as do so many blind performers, but has always had all music read aloud to him from the notes, first the right hand, then the left, memorizing it before beginning practice upon it. He has acquired such facility by long practice that he takes all compositions at a first reading, even the most elaborate and difficult concert solos. As has been stated, he procured his musical education in exactly the same manner, at the same places, and of the same teachers as his fellow-students possessed of sight; and in his professional work he has proved himself the first genuine blind musician of prominence, that is, the first who stood before the public as artist, not as prodigy, and challenged a fair comparison with the leading members of his profession.

On returning to Boston after his second sojourn in Europe, Mr. Perry was assured by many prominent musicians that it was quite impossible for any American pianist to live by concert work exclusively, as was his intention;

and he in consequence settled as teacher in Boston for several winter seasons, devoting the fall months only to concerts and recitals. At the end of the third year, however, the concert work had so grown as to demand all his time, and for the past six seasons he has done nothing else.

Mr. Perry was the originator of the now popular lecture-recital, in which he appears before his audience both as lecturer and player, giving descriptions and explanations of the compositions presented as preface to their performance. This practice met with such warm and universal favor that for some years he has adopted the lecture-recital exclusively.

Mr. Perry has appeared in concert in all the large cities, both North and South, this side of the Rocky Mountains, and at nearly all of the colleges, schools, and conservatories of any size or prominence. So far as the writer's knowledge goes, no other pianist, living or dead, American or foreign, ever gave the same number of concerts in the same length of time as the subject of this sketch. He has played from 100 to 150 dates each season since he abandoned teaching, a total of nearly 1000 concerts in six years.

Mr. Perry has always made a firm and uncompromising stand for the highest ideals in his art, condemning the trivial taste of the public, which regards music as a mere pastime, on the one hand, and the mechanical tendency in the profession, on the other, to fix attention upon its technical side. A broad, general education, wide reading, a love for the other fine arts, and a knowledge of the principles of æsthetics, are points which he has always preached and practiced as essential for the musician who would do his utmost, both as artist and as man; and to raise the standard of music, of art, and of humanity has been the object of his earnest life and labors.

CONSTANTIN STERNBERG.

THIS eminent pianist was born in St. Petersburg, Russia, in 1852, of noble parentage. Though a Russian by birth and sympathies, he is a thorough cosmopolitan in culture and a German in musical training. At the age of eleven he was taken to Weimar, where Liszt was residing, who, noticing the boy, advised that he be sent to Leipsic, where he enjoyed the instruction of Moscheles, Hauptmann, Richter, and Reinecke.

In 1867, when not quite fifteen years of age, Sternberg began his public career as a conductor of light opera. He continued this line of work for nearly seven years. When twenty-one, he attracted the attention of Theodore Kullak, who told him he must study the piano. The plea of poverty was of no avail, and, at his own expense, Kullak instructed him. He repaid this generosity by practicing thirteen to fifteen hours a day. As a natural result nervous prostration ensued. An iron constitution, however, pulled him through. After concertizing a while, he was appointed Court Pianist to the Grand Duke of Mecklenburg. Sternberg remained here two years. A concert tour over the continent of Europe followed. In 1880 he received a summons to play before Emperor William I of Germany, by whom he was treated with the utmost consideration and kindness. An offer to come to America then reached him, which he accepted. 152 engagements were filled during this tour. After his first American tour Mr. Sternberg returned to Germany to be married, after which he and his wife returned to America, having determined to make this country their home. After tours with Minnie Hauk and Wilhelmj, he received an offer from Atlanta, Georgia, where he remained in charge of the music of the Female College of that city for some time. His work there was of high order, and, together with his ability as a pianist, has won him high rank in American musical life.

He is now located in Philadelphia, where he is teaching. He is still heard in concert, however. As a pianist, while his technique is of the greatest, and he is a virtuoso where needs be, he is clear and musicianly in his playing, keeping in view that the technique is merely a means to an end. In this he is greatly helped by his wide culture and literary training. He has also written largely, about 200 compositions, mostly for piano, coming from his pen.

RICHARD HOFFMAN.

THIS sterling musician was born at Manchester, England, in May, 1831. He came to the United States when sixteen years old, in 1847. He has since resided here, and so, by virtue of long residence, can claim to be an American. In 1854 Mr. Hoffman was elected an honorary member of the Philharmonic Society of New York.

He is distinguished as a pianist, teacher, and composer, and held the unique position of being the only high-class pianist in New York for many years. He has occupied a prominent place in that city for more than forty years. His professional following is of an exceptionally fine order. While Mr. Hoffman is not now frequently heard in public, he still maintains his reputation as a finished and elegant pianist. He has contributed very fully to the

394

literature of the piano, many of his compositions being received with great favor. His style of writing is clear and elegant. In 1893 he had conferred upon him, by Hobart College, the honorary degree of Doctor of Music. Mr. Hoffman is one of those who, by their devotion to their art and their great abilities, have done much for the advancement of music.

JOHN ORTH.

JOHN Orth is a native of Boston, Mass., that home of many distinguished musicians. He was born in 1850. He began the study of music at an early age, and, as has been so often the case, the first training was given by his father. Beside the work done with his father, he studied four years in Boston under the best teachers to be found there. He then went to Germany, where he spent five years in further preparation for professional life under such masters as Kullak, Liszt, Deppe, and Lebert for the piano, and Kiel, Weitzmann and Faisst in composition. He appeared as soloist with great success on various occasions, being especially appreciated in Berlin.

On his return to Boston, in 1875, he began at once a busy life as teacher and player.

He has been one of the most successful teachers of his instrument, and his annual recitals are always an important and interesting feature of the musical season in Boston.

ARTHUR FOOTE.

THIS musician belongs to the few who can unite, with the full meaning attached to each, the terms pianist-composer. Mr. Foote is one of the favored few upon whom the Muse has fallen in a twofold sense.

He was born at Salem, Mass., March 5, 1853, and as a youngster attained considerable skill in playing the piano. At this time he also made what he afterward decided were futile attempts at composition.

His decision in this matter was emphasized by his study of harmony with Stephen A. Emery in 1869. In 1870 he went to Harvard College, and during the latter part of his time there prosecuted the study of composition with Professor Paine. A year after his graduation he received the degree of A. M. (for music) in 1875. In 1879 he began the study of organ and piano playing with B. J. Lang.

It will be perceived that Mr. Foote is an American educated musician. He claims none of the borrowed greatness which comes from foreign names, but by his own work gains his place in the ranks of musicians.

Mr. Foote's work as a pianist has been largely confined to Boston, like his eminent instructor, Mr. Lang. But his work as an interpreter of chamber music in connection with various leading string organizations entitles him to notice.

He has played in his own series of chamber concerts, and, in addition, has been heard in various places in his own compositions. Like Mr. MacDowell, he has achieved success abroad.

His compositions include trios, quartets, sonatas for violin and piano, as well as works for full orchestra.

Musicians of Mr. Foote's stamp can do much by their creative talent, united as it is to the power of practical interpretation, to form and develop musical taste.

Mr. Foote's work as a teacher has also added to his reputation.

B. J. LANG.

WE have here a musician whose versatility is remarkable. A pianist of surpassing powers, a conductor of unusual ability, a teacher whose time is fully occupied, it is readily understood what a force such an one may exert upon contemporary art life. Mr. B. J. Lang was born in Boston, December 25, 1837. He was the son of a piano maker who was also an organist. From the first his surroundings were musical. His first regular musical instruction was given by his father, later by the best teachers in Boston. When his literary education was completed he was sent abroad (in 1855) and received the best teaching possible to secure in Berlin and elsewhere. On his return Mr. Lang distinguished himself both as an organist and a pianist. He held several important positions as organist, and in 1857 became the organist of the Händel and Haydn Society.   In 1868 he became the conductor of the Apollo Club, a chorus of male voices; in 1874 the Cecelia Choir of female voices was formed under his direction, the two coöperating as a mixed chorus on occasion. With these organizations Mr. Lang introduced many new works to the public. He was also the first to introduce the innovation of repeating the same work in the same evening, in order to its better understanding.

As a musician, Mr. Lang has exerted a wide influence upon musical affairs. His abilities as a teacher and as a conductor of large musical bodies have given him a wide scope for activity. His present great reputation as a pianist was made under difficult conditions. He was compelled, in his earlier days, to combat the pro-German tendencies, which were then very pronounced. He was an American, and totally unable to push himself forward, he was compelled to gain by the slow advance of unaided merit what his unusual talents deserved. But success came to him, for between 1865 and 1880 his mastery of his public was most pronounced, and since then he is sure of any audience he may desire.

In addition to his conducting he has regularly appeared as piano soloist, bringing before the public all the great, well-known concertos, and many half-forgotten ones, as well as other important compositions.

Here, then, is a record for one man! A pianist who is sure of a crowded house filled by the most cultured of hearers, a teacher whose days are busy with lessons, a conductor who has directed two great societies for years, and presented great choral works for their first hearing, a man who has always been in demand in his own city—a city full of artists, teachers, and conductors—to the extent of being a leader in matters musical with a constantly growing influence. Such is B. J. Lang, the pianist, composer, teacher, and conductor.

LEOPOLD GODOWSKY.

L EOPOLD Godowsky was born in Wilna, Russian Poland, February 13, 1870. His father, Matthew Godowsky, was a practicing physician, who fell a victim to
the cholera during the epidemic of 1871, leaving his family
in straitened circumstances.

Young Godowsky gave evidence of his musical genius
at the age of three, when, after hearing a regimental band
on parade play a selection from "Martha," he, a year
later, played the same selection on the piano, the first he
had ever seen. This determined his future career. His
mother not being able to give him the required education,
he was placed under the guardianship of a family friend,
himself an excellent violinist, from whom Godowsky re-

ceived his first musical instruction. When seven years old he further emphasized his genius by composing small piano pieces, the melodies of which were so original and mature, that they have been embodied in recent compositions. His début was made in 1879, in his native city, with such success that a concert tour was made through Poland and a section of Prussia.

Godowsky's guardian now manifesting a desire to reap monetary benefits at the sacrifice of his ward's musical education, his intentions were frustrated through the intervention of several gentlemen prominent in literature and music, who offered to give Godowsky all the advantages of the conservatory at St. Petersburg, and pay all expenses. These offers being rejected by the guardian, a movement against him was inaugurated in the press, which forced the ac ptance of an offer of Mr. Feinburg, a banker of König o o send Godowsky to the Royal Conservatory of Berli. .le remained in Berlin until 1884, when he came to America, arriving in New York October 31, 1884.

Godowsky played in the principal cities of the United States and Canada, and everywhere met with the greatest success.

In June, 1886, he returned to Europe to continue his studies in France. His ambition was to study with Saint-Saëns. Soon after his arrival in France, Godowsky played at the "Trompette," a well-known society of artists. Saint-Saëns, who was present, was so impressed with his playing and compositions that he went upon the stage and embraced him, and made an exception by agreeing to give instruction to Godowsky, who remained in Paris till 1890, when he went to London and gave a series of recitals. In the fall of 1890 Godowsky returned to America, and on April 30, 1891, married Miss Frederica Saxe, of New York. After his marriage he again went to London, but returned in October, 1891, and has since made New York his home.

26*

Mr. Godowsky has written about 100 compositions, chiefly for the piano, only a few of which have been published. He recently arranged twelve études of Chopin for the left hand, also a concert arrangement of Chopin's Rondo, Op. 16.

Mr. Godowsky is in much demand for piano recitals, and has made for himself a reputation as a scholarly and impressive artist. With a technic which is unconscious of mechanical difficulties, he is free to give expression to the flow of musical feeling aroused by the composition he is playing.

HENRY GRANGER HANCHETT, M.D.

DR. HANCHETT is conspicuous among pianists as almost wholly the product of the United States. His family for eight generations and in all branches is American; his education, even in music, was obtained in this country, his studies in Europe under Dr. Kullak having been made after he came before the public, and the teacher to whom he owes most having been Mr. Wm. Sherwood,

also an American. Dr. Hanchett inherited decided musical talent, having been a clever child pianist at seven and
a church organist at sixteen years of age. His natural
endowment includes the gift of absolute pitch, so perfect
that from infancy he could name any sound heard by the
unaided ear.

When about nineteen years of age and preparing for his
first New York appearance as a pianist, Dr. Hanchett's
career was interrupted by sudden attacks of blindness,
resulting from latent brain congestion, and destroying sight
for periods of a few days or weeks, the attacks being quite
frequent during a number of years. Piano-playing being
considered an insuperable obstacle to recovery, Dr.
Hanchett, on this account and also in the hope of learning
to understand and manage his own rather mysterious case,
studied medicine, practiced for a time, and gained some
repute as an author of medical works. But although he
desisted entirely from piano-playing for long periods, he
never entirely divorced himself from music, having been
organist and choirmaster of two of the most prominent
churches in New York while practicing medicine, and at
the same time director of three choral societies. With
restored health musical work—always the most congenial
to him and that which he regarded as his destiny in life—
was resumed with constantly increasing activity, until at
present his teaching engagements in New York city and
the Direction of the Central School of Musical Art in
Brooklyn occupy his entire time, except what is given to
concert playing and church music direction.

As an essayist on musical topics he is favorably known
and widely read, and he is pronounced by competent critics
to be a pianist of commanding excellence. Though Dr.
Hanchett is endowed with a poetic, musical temperament,
he is also a close analyzer, and knows when and where to
apply the emotional or the mental forces in musical interpretation. His pedagogical studies have undoubtedly

accentuated the analytical tendency of his mind and contributed to his fame as a teacher and artist. His memory also is phenomenal, and while we admire his extraordinary gifts and his scholarly accomplishments, we must render due homage to the high moral character of Dr. Hanchett, the man.

RICHARD BURMEISTER.

THE subject of this sketch also belongs to that class of
pianists whose talent for composition has reinforced
their executive power. His work as a composer of the
larger forms has already won him an enviable position
among musicians.

Mr. Burmeister was born at Hamburg, in December,
1860. He received an academic education, but when ready
to go to the university he decided to change science with
art, and went to Ad. Mehrkens, Director of the Bach
Society in Hamburg, studying piano and theory. Later
he became an ardent scholar of Liszt, with whom he
studied three years, accompanying him to Rome, Buda-
pesth, and Weimar.

In 1884 Mr. Burmeister accepted a position as professor at the Conservatory in Hamburg, and in 1885 at the Peabody Conservatory in Baltimore. Here he won such a reputation as a teacher, that pupils from all parts of the country came to seek his instruction, among them some that already have successfully appeared in public.

He was compelled when very young to earn his living, and served as instructor in the Conservatory at Hamburg. This condition of life, so fatal to the ambition of many, did not quench his light. It caused him to make his way slowly, but continuing his studies with a firm determination, he persevered until he has at last won an international reputation as a pianist and composer.

He has recently made a very successful European tour, and on his return to America was received with much honor. His technic is perfect, and gifted by nature with a velvet-like touch, his playing is distinguished by versatility as well as an abundance of poetry and depth.

His piano concerto in D minor has been heard with pleasure and satisfaction by both public and critics on both sides of the water.

His symphony, "The Chase After Fortune," has also made a profound impression.

AUGUST HYLLESTED.

A UGUST Hyllested is a Scandinavian pianist, and was
born in Stockholm, Sweden, in 1858. His father held
the position of Stadtmusicus in that city. Having shown
unusual musical talent the son began his study of the art
at the early age of five years. He played in public, in
Stockholm, with much success when only eight years of
age. Three years later a concert tour was made throughout Scandinavia. In 1871 he further prosecuted his piano
study with Edmund Neupert, of Copenhagen, where he
also had for his master in composition Niels Gade. After
five years spent here a second tour of Scandinavia was
made as conductor of orchestra and solo pianist. After a
second short sojourn in Copenhagen, he went to Berlin

and placed himself under the tuition of Xaver Scharwenka and Theodore Kullak. In 1880 he played for Liszt, at Weimar, and excited the master's warm interest. In 1883 a very successful tour through Great Britain was made. In 1885 Hyllested came to this country. After four concerts in Steinway, he made a tour of the principal eastern cities of the United States and Canada. That same year he became connected with the Chicago Musical College. He has remained an active teacher, earnest and conscientious, ever since. His recitals in Chicago have been very successful and he impresses all who come in contact with him as thoroughly devoted to his art.

DR. WILLIAM MASON.*

IT is hardly necessary to enlarge upon this eminent musician and pianist, for the name of Wm. Mason is too widely known to need bringing before the musical world. Yet our work would be sadly incomplete without the face and sketch of this *Nestor* of American musicians.

Dr. Mason is the son of Dr. Lowell Mason, whose name alone arouses many memories of musical progress.

With such a parentage it was only to be expected that Wm. Mason's tendencies would be toward music. He was born in Boston, January 24, 1829. His talent was manifested at a very early age. His father did not intend him

*) The sketch of Dr. Mason, which appeared in the original edition of this work, being altogether inadequate to his present reputation, it has been thought best to rewrite and incorporate it in the American edition.

to follow the musical art as a profession, but the tendency was too strong to be resisted, so after study in Boston, he was sent to Germany. Here he was under the care of Moscheles (in 1849), Hauptmann, and Richter. Later he studied at Prague with Dreyschock, and spent a portion of the years 1853 and 1854 with Liszt, in company with Rubinstein, Von Bülow, Klindworth, and Pruckner. Such an atmosphere, of course, developed all the talent of Mason. Five years were spent abroad, during which he played with success in various important art centers. In 1854 he returned to America, and soon began a series of piano recitals, which were given without assistance and were very successful. Disliking travel, however, he soon settled in New York, where he has since been mainly occupied in teaching, appearing only occasionally in public. He has been identified with many important events in the musical world, among them the widely known "Mason and Thomas Soirees of Chamber Music," in which he was associated with the now famous conductor, Theodore Thomas.

Many of the works of Robert Schumann were given their first American hearing at these concerts. In the recently published "Letters of Franz Liszt" are to be found letters from Liszt to Mason, in which the opinion of the master is very flatteringly expressed concerning Dr. Mason's abilities. As a composer for the pianoforte, Dr. Mason's name stands high both in Europe and at home. His compositions show his power both as a melodist and harmonist, and are noted for their refinement and elegance. His pedagogic works include his famous "Touch and Technic."

As a pianist he is still one of the greatest, in quality as well as technic, in memory prodigious, recalling, as he can, pieces not played for years, and yet giving them a finished performance. As an exponent of his own theories of touch, his playing is a living illustration of their power.

FANNY BLOOMFIELD-ZEISLER.

THIS very successful pianist was born at Berlitz, Austria, in 1865, but was brought to America when two years old, her parents having removed to Chicago. Her great talent made itself felt even in infancy, and after a few years' instruction she was accustomed to play in public, mostly at the concerts of the Beethoven Society, then existing in Chicago. Her performances created so much genuine admiration that she came to be considered a musical prodigy. When thirteen she played before the famous Mme. Essipoff, who urged her to go to Vienna and undergo a course of training with Leschetizky, Essipoff's husband and teacher. Accordingly, Fanny Bloomfield studied with this master five years, and on her début at Vienna won enthusiastic praises from the critics of that city. Her first American appearance was with the Beethoven Society, January 11, 1884, under the direction of Carl Wolfsohn, when she played Henselt's concerto with orchestra. Shortly after, in Milwaukee, she played the Weber concertstück, and gave recitals in Chicago, St. Louis and Baltimore. She played for the first time in Boston with the symphony orchestra under Gericke, winning the greatest applause. The most carping critics were unanimous in sounding her praises.

In 1885 she played in New York and again achieved marked success.

At all her following engagements she continued her triumphs, winning for herself a place of unusual eminence. The seasons of 1893–94 and 1894–95 were marked by remarkable European tours. In the old centers of music she won praises of the most pronounced type.

Her playing is noted for its brilliancy and precision, joined with great musical intelligence and masculinity of power. Her finger technic and octave playing are astonishing for their beauty and power.

Mrs. Bloomfield-Zeisler is still actively engaged in concertizing, and the ripening of her marvelous powers gives promise of the fullest artistic fruition.

ADELE AUS DER OHE.

THIS young lady was born in Hanover, Germany, and when a child of only seven years she was, by the advice of the late Hans von Bülow, placed in Theodore Kullak's school of music in Berlin. One year afterward she played in public. She continued her study with Kullak, and two years later played in Berlin with orchestra, being at this time only ten years old. Shortly after she was heard at her birth-place, Hanover. For two years longer she remained under Kullak's tuition, and then went to Weimar, where she continued her study under Liszt's supervision. Liszt took a great personal interest in her talent and her enthusiasm, and used quite often to listen for hours to her playing. He warmly commended her to the Court at Berlin, saying her touch was as soft as velvet and as strong as a man's. Her playing of his " Rhapsodies" and his " Don Giovanni Fantasia" and his two concertos especially pleased Liszt. In parting with her he said: "You must show the world what Liszt has taught you."

Her American success has been very pronounced, and she has been much in demand for orchestral concerts.

She was chosen to play the new Tschaikowsky concerto under the composer's conducting, on the occasion of the opening of the Carnegie Music Hall in New York, and won the highest encomiums from both composer, critic, and public.

Her technic is great, her touch beautiful, and, as has already been intimated strong and masculine. She is constantly widening her sphere and winning new triumphs in her artistic world.

CARL FAELTEN.

C ARL Faelten was born in Thuringia, December 21, 1846. Showing early talent for music, he was fortunate in securing competent preliminary instruction. He possessed an ambition to become a pianist, but fate seemed to be against him because of the inability of his parents to provide for the necessary instruction. He showed his mettle by depending upon his own exertions and entered one of the orchestral schools in Germany, where, in return for his instruction, he performed the most laborious and unsatisfactory work of the musical profession, playing dance music, etc. He was compelled, later, to neglect his piano study, and shortly after resuming it the inflexible German military law compelled him to serve as a soldier during the Franco-Prussian war. When his term of service expired he found his fingers so stiff from handling the musket that he had to practically begin his piano study over again. Difficulties such as these did but increase his ardor, and so successfully did he carry on his musical education, that after 1874 he appeared in symphony concerts with eminent artists with success, and gave recitals of his own which soon brought him reputation among critical circles. He appeared in numerous cities in Germany, Austria, and England, devoting much time to teaching also, in which he showed much skill.

When in 1877 Raff organized the conservatory at Frankfort, he selected Faelten to be associated with Madame Clara Schumann in teaching piano. Here his time was especially devoted to the training of teachers, and he delivered many lectures on the theoretical and practical requirements of teachers in piano playing.

After Raff's sudden death he decided to come to America, and in 1882 he was engaged at the Peabody Institute in Baltimore. After a few successful years spent here he was called to the New England Conservatory by the late Dr. Tourgee. He is widely known throughout the country for his talents as a musician and pianist.

WILLIAM H. SHERWOOD.

WILLIAM H. Sherwood was born at Lyons, New York, in 1854. He studied until his seventeenth year with his father, the Rev. L. H. Sherwood, M.A., founder of the Lyons Musical Academy, which institution was established in the year 1854. Before leaving this country to continue his studies with European masters he studied with Edward Heimburger, Pychowski, and Dr. William Mason, of New York.

Going to Berlin, Sherwood studied with Theodore Kullak and, later, with Deppe, and then going to Weimar he became a pupil of Liszt. In Stuttgart he studied the organ with Scotson Clarke. His masters in theory, counterpoint, and composition were Dr. Weitzman, Carl Doppler, R. Wuerst, and E. F. Richter. He became organist at the English church in Stuttgart and the English chapel in Berlin. In 1875 he played at the Philharmonic symphony concert in Hamburg, being honored with a "fanfare" from the orchestra and a voluntary increase of one-third of the fee. At the close of the concert he was invited to play again the following year. He was also invited by Carl Reinecke to play at a Gewandhaus sym· phony concert in Leipzig; also at symphony concerts with the leading orchestral organizations in Bremen, Cassel, Braunschweig, and Gera, and at Court concerts in Berlin and Weimar. Before the dates could be arranged, however, he was compelled to return to the United States, making a first appearance at Boston in concerts with Kellogg, Carey, and Brignoli, and afterward an American début at the Centennial in Philadelphia, in 1876, with the Theodore Thomas Orchestra, before an audience of 8000 people.

Mr. Sherwood has played with nearly all the leading orchestras and societies in the United States and Canada, and has given recitals in all the principal cities. He was one of the founders of the American College of Musicians, whose first elected examiner he was. He was also one of the earliest members of the Music Teachers' National Association, and a member of music societies in Boston, New York, and Chicago. Mr. Sherwood has had charge of the Piano Department of the Chautauqua Assembly, Chautauqua, N. Y., for six years, and of the Chicago Conservatory for five years. For a number of years he has been examiner at the Toronto Conservatory of Music, Toronto, Canada. Two colleges have offered him the title of Doctor of Music, but he has declined the honor. He has many pupils who occupy important positions as pianists and teachers in large cities and schools.

Mr. Sherwood has published a number of compositions

of sterling character, some of which have been very successfully given by leading artists, and have won high
commendation from critics.   He was the first American
to be honored by the publication of his work by the house
of Breitkopf & Härtel, in Leipzig.   He has also done
most excellent work in revising and editing standard compositions.

Mr. Sherwood has given fifty different programmes of
music for the piano in Chicago.   He recently played such
selections as the Raff Concerto in C minor, the Schubert-
Liszt Wanderer-Fantasie, the Weber-Liszt Polacca, and
the Grieg Concerto in A minor, with such organizations
as the Boston Symphony Orchestra in Boston, Cambridge
(Harvard College), with the Theodore Thomas Orchestra
in the Auditorium, Chicago, and at the World's Fair; with
the Boston Philharmonic and the New York Symphony
Orchestras.   Also the Schumann Quintette and Quartette,
and the Mendelssohn Trio, with the leading string quar-
tettes in Boston, New York, Cleveland, Chicago, and at
the World's Fair.

In addition to his recitals in Chicago and Chautauqua,
Mr. Sherwood is in constant demand for recitals throughout the country.   His tours extend from ocean to ocean,
and from Canada to Texas.   He is equally sought after in
musical centres and remote places.   His repertoire is an
immense one and is played entirely from memory.

As a pianist he occupies a somewhat unique position.
Pianists have been divided into two classes: those who
play but cannot tell much about how they do so, and those
who know all the whys and wherefores, but, unfortunately,
cannot play.

Mr. Sherwood can play; in fact, he is a virtuoso of virtuosi.   He not only plays, but he plays with a certainty
and assurance, and withal an economy of means, that no
technical difficulties can daunt.

His hand is small and short, his fingers stubby and very

illy adapted to piano virtuosity. This physical condition caused him to give unusual attention to the ways and means of the acquiring of his wonderful technical powers. Consequently he has a theory concerning every difficulty, both as to its nature and the best means for its mastery. He is a pianist who can play and can tell how he does so as well. In connection with this remarkable virtuosity we meet his lack of self-consciousness and the clear, unimpeded flow of his musical feeling.

He is not merely a virtuoso, but an interpretative artist of the highest type of intellectuality and musical feeling.

His gradations of tonal power from the softest pianissimo to the strongest fortissimo, guided as they are by a musical intelligence of the highest order, the subservience of his wonderful technic to his musical feeling give Mr. Sherwood a power as a pianist which is excelled by none.

He is heard with equal interest by musician and layman. The hearer departs from his recital with a sense of satisfaction and completeness.

Mr. Sherwood's work as a teacher is also remarkable. His knowledge of the process of pianism is of especial value to his pupils. With him, theory and practical illustration are both at the service of the pupil. His work as director of the Piano Department at the Chicago Conservatory has been of exceptional value, and those whom he has prepared for the musical profession are leaving their impress upon musical life.